KT-569-267

PARIS IS OLD
BUT ♡LOVE IS NEW
Michael
♡Amelia
x

CityPack
Paris

FIONA DUNLOP

*Fiona Dunlop lives in Paris.
A journalist with a
fascination for multi-cultural
crossroads and an interest in
the worlds of fashion and art,
she writes on Paris's cultural
life for several magazines and
newspapers, and has written
or contributed to a number of
guidebooks, including the*
Paris Art Guide *and AA*
Explorer Paris. *In the same
AA* Explorer *series, she has
also written guides to*
Mexico, Singapore &
Malaysia, Indonesia *and
(forthcoming)* Costa Rica.

AA Publishing

Written by Fiona Dunlop
Edited, designed and produced by AA Publishing
Maps © The Automobile Association 1996
Fold-out map:
    © RV Reise- und Verkehrsverlag Munich · Stuttgart
    © Cartography: GeoData

Distributed in the United Kingdom by AA Publishing,
Norfolk House, Priestley Road, Basingstoke, Hampshire,
RG24 9NY.

The contents of this publication are believed correct at the
time of printing. Nevertheless, the publishers cannot be
held responsible for any errors or omissions or for changes in
the details given in this guide or for the consequences of any
reliance on the information provided by the same.
Assessments of attractions, hotels, restaurants and so forth
are based upon the author's own personal experience and,
therefore, descriptions given in this guide necessarily
contain an element of subjective opinion which may not
reflect the publishers' opinion or dictate a reader's own
experiences on another occasion.
We have tried to ensure accuracy in this guide, but things do
change and we would be grateful if readers would advise us
of any inaccuracies they may encounter.

A CIP catalogue record for this book is available from the
British Library.
ISBN 0 7495 1178 8

Published by AA Publishing (a trading name of Automobile
Association Developments Limited, whose registered office
is Norfolk House, Priestley Road, Basingstoke, Hampshire
RG24 9NY. Registered number 1878835).

Colour separation by Daylight Colour Art Pte Ltd, Singapore
Printed and bound by Dai Nippon Printing Co (Hong Kong)
Ltd.

Page 1: night skyline

*Page 2: La Grande Arche,
La Défense*

*Page 5 (a): shoppers in
Les Halles*
Page 5 (b): café scene

Page 13 (a): old poster
*Page 13 (b): Place de la
Concorde, Egyptian
obelisk*

Page 23 (a): Eiffel Tower
Page 23 (b): Le Penseur,
Rodin

Page 49 (a): posters
*Page 49 (b): detail, Pont
Alexandre III*

*Page 61 (a): stall, Marche
aux Puces*
*Page 61 (b): Fauchon
window display*

Page 87 (top): TGVs

Contents

ABOUT THIS BOOK 4

PARIS LIFE 5–12
A Personal View 6–7
Paris in Figures 8
Paris People 9
A Chronology 10–11
People & Events from
    History 12

**HOW TO ORGANISE YOUR
    TIME** 13–22
Itineraries 14–15
Walks 16–17
Evening Strolls 18
Organised Sightseeing 19
Excursions 20–21
What's On 22

**PARIS'S TOP 25
    SIGHTS** 23–48
  1 Musée Marmottan 24
  2 Palais de Chaillot 25
  3 Eiffel Tower 26
  4 Champs Elysées &
        Arc de Triomphe 27
  5 Les Invalides 28
  6 Musée Rodin 29
  7 Place de la Concorde 30
  8 Musée d'Orsay 31
  9 Opéra de Paris 32
 10 Sacré Coeur 33
 11 Musée des Arts
        Decoratifs 34
 12 Musée du Louvre 35
 13 Galeries Vivienne &
        Colbert 36
 14 Jardin du Luxembourg 37

 15 Musée de Cluny (Musée
        Nationale du Moyen-Age,
        Thermes de Cluny) 38
 16 Sainte-Chapelle 39
 17 The Conciergerie 40
 18 Centre Georges
        Pompidou 41
 19 Marché aux Puces de
        St Ouen 42
 20 Notre-Dame 43
 21 Ile Saint-Louis 44
 22 Institut de Monde Arabe 45
 23 Musée Carnavalet 46
 24 Place des Vosges 47
 25 Père Lachaise Cemetery 48

PARIS'S BEST 49–60
Museums & Galleries 50–51
Places of Worship 52
Cult Cafés 53
20th-Century Architecture 54
Bridges 55
Green Spaces 56
Views 57
Children's Activities 58
Free Attractions 59
Intriguing Streets 60

PARIS: WHERE TO...
    61–86
Stay 62–65
Eat 66–73
Shop 74–81
Be Entertained 82–86

TRAVEL FACTS 87–94

INDEX 95–96

About this book

CityPack Paris is divided into six sections to cover the six most important aspects of your visit to Paris.

1. PARIS LIFE *(pages 5–12)*

Your personal introduction to Paris by author Fiona Dunlop

An overview of the city today and yesterday
Facts and figures
Leading characters
The big events in Paris's history

2. HOW TO ORGANISE YOUR TIME *(pages 13–22)*

Make the most of your time in Paris

Three one-day itineraries
Two suggested walks
Two evening strolls
Three excursions beyond the city
Calendar of events

3. PARIS'S TOP 25 SIGHTS *(pages 23–48)*

Your concise guide to sightseeing

Fiona Dunlop's own choice, including her personal introduction to each sight
Description and history
Highlights of each attraction
Comprehensive practical information
Each sight located on the inside cover of the book

4. PARIS'S BEST *(pages 49–60)*

What Paris is renowned for

Museums & Galleries
Places of Worship
Cult Cafés
20th-Century Architecture
Bridges
Green Spaces
Views
Children's Activities
Free Attractions
Intriguing Streets
Practical details throughout

5. PARIS: WHERE TO... *(pages 61–86)*

The best places to stay, eat, shop and be entertained

Three categories of hotel
Nine categories of restaurant
Eight categories of shop
Six categories of entertainment venue
Price bands and booking details

6. PARIS TRAVEL FACTS *(pages 87–94)*

Essential information for your stay

SYMBOLS

Throughout the guide a few straightforward symbols are used to denote the following categories:

🞡 map reference on the fold-out map accompanying this book (see below)

✉ address

☎ telephone number

🕐 opening times

🍴 restaurant or café on premises or near by

Ⓜ nearest subway train station

🚆 nearest overground train station

♿ facilities for visitors with disabilities

▥ admission charge

↔ other places of interest near by

❓ tours, lectures, or special events

➤ indicates the page where you will find a fuller description

MAPS

All map references are to the separate fold-out map accompanying this book. For example, the Musée Rodin, in rue de Varenne, has the following information: 🞡 F6 – indicating the grid square of the map in which the Musée Rodin will be found. All entries within the Top 25 Sights section are also plotted by number (not page number) on the city-centre plan located on the inside front and back covers of this book.

PRICES

Where appropriate, an indication of the cost of an establishment is given by £ signs: £££ denotes higher prices, while £ denotes lower charges.

PARIS *life*

A Personal View	*6–7*
Paris in Figures	*8*
Paris People	*9*
A Chronology	*10–11*
People & Events from History	*12*

5

A PERSONAL VIEW

The French state

An unmistakable characteristic of France and consequently Paris is the State's top-heavy role. What other industrialised country allows a state bank (Crédit Lyonnais) to run up losses approaching FF60 billion (US$11 billion) in five years? And what other nation offers amnesty to all traffic-offenders when a new president is elected?

Paris remains the powerhouse of the nation, despite repeated government manoeuvres for decentralisation. This is where French socio-cultural trends are born, political battles are fielded and national pride is polished. And yet it remains compact, still bordered by the *portes* (gateways) which keep the less prestigious *banlieues* (suburbs) at bay. Stay or live in central Paris and you are propelled into a maelstrom of gastronomy, fashion, cinema, literature, art ... and monuments. History is omnipresent and no ruler – whether king or president – has failed to leave his mark on the city's urban face.

Philosophy, ideas, and culture have always been favourite Parisian pursuits but in this *fin de siècle* the momentum is slowing. The population stagnates as inhabitants choose to flee big-city life for less costly environs. Live here and you spend money: the temptations are multifarious and nothing comes cheap. New buildings proliferated with President Mitterrand's *grands projets* of the 1980s, historic mansions are renovated and state culture monopolises every corner. Some say the city is becoming an asphyxiated museum, but spend a few days here and you cannot fail to be seduced by an enduring beauty, a grandeur and a dynamism that few other capital cities combine.

Café life

Place St Sulpice, in the Latin Quarter

Paris still harbours a fascinating cosmopolitan character. Stroll from one *quartier* to the next and you make a minor global tour, taking in Africa, Asia, the Caribbean and the Arab world in Pigalle or Belleville or the 13th *arrondissement*. Plunge into the heart of the French bourgeois soul in the 7th or 16th *arrondissements* or sweep up Parisian chic on the Left Bank. Stop at a café terrace to people-watch, read or dream, wander along the *quais* or collapse in a park.

Explore the Right Bank and you feel the capital's commercial pulse. Follow the city's cultural history in any of its numerous museums, catch up on new films at the countless cinemas or dive into a hot nightspot. But above all let the city lead you and do not believe the cliché that Parisians are unfriendly. Its winding streets hold surprises that even the most informative guide-book cannot cover and it is only off the tourist beat that you encounter the true Parisian spirit.

Incomparable Paris

'Paris is complete, Paris is the ceiling of human kind ... Whoever sees Paris thinks he sees the basis of all history with a sky and constellations in between. Paris is synonymous with the cosmos ... it has no limits. Paris does more than make the law, it makes fashion. Paris can be stupid if it wants, it sometimes allows itself this luxury ... It is more than great, it is immense. Why? Because it dares.'

Victor Hugo, *Les Misérables*

7

Paris in Figures

**HISTORICAL
(city growth)**

- 1851 Paris represented 3% of the French population
- 1921 Paris population was 3 million
- 1925 Exposition des Arts Décoratifs drew 16 million visitors
- 1940 Germans occupying Paris saw only 25% of its inhabitants
- 1954 Paris represented 15% of population
- 1954 80% of Parisian homes had no bathroom
- 1990 87% of Parisian homes had a WC

**SOCIO-
POLITICAL**

- 10% of Parisians regularly attend mass
- 45% of Parisians go to the cinema at least once a week
- An estimated 200,000–300,000 are homeless
- An estimated 150,000–400,000 are drug-addicts
- Parisians, forming 4% of the French population, provide 45% of total income tax revenue
- 53% of Parisians use a car daily, 35% use public transport
- The 1980s' per capita cultural budget for Paris was 20 times that of the provinces
- 15% of Parisians are manual workers
- 30% of Parisians are executives or intellectuals
- 20 million tourists visit Paris annually
- 45% of Parisians live alone
- The Louvre had 6.3 million visitors in 1994
- 200,000 Parisian dogs produce 10 tonnes of excrement daily
- 800,000 French regularly consult a psychiatrist
- 90% of French women and 50% of French men use perfume
- 53.5% of Parisians are women

GEOGRAPHICAL

- 2.1 million inhabitants within the city walls (decreasing)
- 10.6 million inhabitants in the Ile de France (increasing)
- 20,000 inhabitants per sq km and an average of 1.92 per residence
- During July and August over 2 million cars head south
- 600km of underground sewers

PARIS PEOPLE

JEAN-PAUL GAULTIER

Now in his early 40s, Jean-Paul Gaultier is still a prime mover in the fickle French fashion world. After formative years with *haut-couturiers* Pierre Cardin and Jean Patou, in 1979 he created his own label. From his first 'James Bond' collection, through 'Dadism', 'Witches' and 'High-Tech', Gaultier aimed to shock. Costumes for films, mobile furniture, a record and TV shows in the UK have paralleled his two annual fashion collections.

JOËL ROBUCHON

The man behind innovative Parisian gastronomy may be modest but his star still rises. In 1981 Robuchon took over a restaurant in the 16th *arrondissement*, and has not looked back since, accumulating gastronomy medals, writing books, playing French food ambassador and confirming his status as France's top chef. His restaurant is consistently allocated 19.5 (out of 20) in the Gallic restaurant bible, the *Gault Millau*. Hard to beat.

ANNE SINCLAIR

The thinking man's crumpet, chic TV interviewer Anne Sinclair has become the most popular woman in France in the last decade. Steering top personalities through their analysis of the week's events in her one-hour programme, *7 sur 7*, this dark-haired, blue-eyed charmer has managed to extract declarations, confessions, hopes and fears from such key names as Mikhail Gorbachev, Prince Charles, Madonna and François Mitterrand.

PHILIPPE STARCK

Tripod orange-squeezers, chairs with pointed legs, a laughing TV ... these are the hallmarks of Starck's design success. A 'Made in France' phenomenon of the 1980s, Starck – gregarious, corpulent and bearded – has presence in the 1990s. Still going strong is his redesign of the nightclub Les Bains Douches, while his latest gimmick is a mail-order house-kit composed of plans, a videotape and a hammer.

Jean-Paul Gaultier

Jacques Chirac

For over 18 years Jacques Chirac, the ebullient Mayor of Paris and leader of the Gaullist party (RPR), surveyed the city from his palatial working residence overlooking the Seine, the Hôtel de Ville. With a taste for reading Chinese poetry (in French) , he transformed the city's infrastructure and repeatedly clashed with the ruling Socialists until in May 1995, after two previously unsuccessful shots, he was finally elected President of France.

A CHRONOLOGY

c. 200 BC	Celtic tribe of Parisii settles on Ile de la Cité
c. AD 100	Growth of Gallo-Roman city of Lutetia
451	Ste Geneviève saves Paris from Attila the Hun
1100s	Tragic love-story of Abelard and Héloise
1163	Building starts on Notre-Dame
1215	University of Paris is founded
1358	Royal family installed in Marais and Louvre
1337–1453	Hundred Years War between France and England
1430	Henry VI of England crowned King of France in Notre-Dame
1437	Charles VII regains control of Paris
1572	St Bartholomew's Massacre ignites Wars of Religion
1600s	Paris reorganised and rebuilt, Le Marais developed
1648–52	Civil uprising of La Fronde
1672	Louis XIV moves to Versailles
1700s	Development of Faubourg Saint-Germain
1789	Storming of the Bastille, declaration of Rights of Man
1792	Monarchy abolished, proclamation of the Republic
1793–4	Reign of Terror, Louis XVI beheaded, inauguration of the Musée du Louvre
1804	Napoleon Bonaparte crowned Emperor
1800–14	Building of imperial monuments. Founding of

	Grandes Ecoles, increased centralisation
1830	Bourbons overthrown, Louis-Philippe crowned
1848	Revolution topples Louis-Philippe; Second Republic headed by Napoléon III
1852–70	Baron Haussmann transforms urban Paris
1870–1	Paris besieged by Prussians, civil uprising of the Commune, Republic restored
1889	Eiffel Tower built for Exposition Universelle
1900	Grand and Petit Palais built for Exposition Universelle; first métro line opens
c. 1908	Modernism is born in Montmartre with Picasso
1914–18	Paris bombarded by German cannon, Big Bertha
1925	Exposition des Arts Décoratifs introduces Art Deco style
1940	Nazis occupy Paris
1944	Liberation of Paris led by Général de Gaulle
1954	National funeral for writer Colette
1958	De Gaulle called in to head Fifth Republic
1967	Les Halles market transferred to Rungis
1969	President Georges Pompidou elected
1974	President Valéry Giscard d'Estaing elected
1977	Jacques Chirac elected first Mayor of Paris since 1871; Centre Georges Pompidou opens
1981	Election of President Mitterrand initiates *Grands Travaux*
1989	Bi-centenary celebrations of the Revolution
1990	Death of iconoclastic singer Serge Gainsbourg
1995	Election of President Chirac

PEOPLE & EVENTS FROM HISTORY

Napoleon Bonaparte (1769–1821)

Henri IV

Authoritarian, ccomplex and charismatic, Henri IV (1553–1610) was also Paris's first urban designer. In 1594, after renouncing Protestantism and uttering the legendary words 'Paris is well worth a mass', he triumphantly entered the city as a long-needed unifying force. His reigns saw the growth of new industries, a fashion for châteaux and the downfall of the peasant classes. Meanwhile, he instigated the building of Place Royale (Place des Vosges), Place Dauphine, the Pont Neuf, the rise of Le Marais and the planting of 20,000 trees in the Tuileries before losing his life by an assassin's knife.

REVOLUTION

The Revolution of 1789 signalled the end of absolute royal power and the rise of popular democracy. The royal family was forced from Versailles to the Tuileries palace but in 1792 this in turn was attacked and Louis XVI and Marie-Antoinette were imprisoned and sent to the guillotine. The year 1792–3 marked the high point of the Terror, which was led by Robespierre, himself guillotined in 1794.

NAPOLEON

Napoleon Bonaparte's meteoric rise and fall from power (1800–14) left an indelible mark on the capital. Ambitious reforms included the construction of neo-classical buildings, while his military campaigns made Paris capital of the greatest European empire since Charlemagne. More important was the increased concentration of the nation's culture and government in Paris, something that decentralisation has still not eradicated two centuries later.

OCCUPATION

The scars left by France's Vichy régime were most apparent in Paris, occupied by the Nazis from 1940. Luxury hotels and public buildings were requisitioned, and Communists and Jews were deported in their thousands. After the Allies disembarked in Normandy in June 1944, a week-long insurrection by Parisians opened their path into the capital. General Von Cholitz capitulated after disobeying Hitler's orders to blow up the city and Paris was reborn.

'LE GENERAL'

De Gaulle's role as one of France's major 20th-century figures started during the Occupation, when he headed the Free French Forces from London, continued with the Liberation and was consolidated when he was called from retirement to solve the divisive Algerian War and head the Fifth Republic in 1958. His rule heralded increased presidential powers, a burgeoning consumer society and the prominence of France within the European Union.

PARIS
how to organise your time

ITINERARIES   *14–15*
Latin Quarter
Stately Paris
Green Paris

WALKS   *16–17*
Le Marais to the Place
des Vosges
Place des Vosges to the
Latin Quarter

EVENING STROLLS   *18*
The Seine
Bastille

ORGANISED SIGHTSEEING   *19*

EXCURSIONS   *20–21*
Versailles
Vaux-le-Vicomte
Giverny

WHAT'S ON   *22*

13

ITINERARIES

One of the pleasures of Paris is its compact scale and efficient public transport service. Visiting monuments in the central *arrondissements* is easiest and most scenic on foot and always includes obligatory café stops, but do not hesitate to dive into the métro for a short burst to more distant sights.

Moving between the monuments on Sundays and public holidays from mid-April to late-September is facilitated by Balabus, a public bus-service that starts at the Gare de Lyon and stops at Saint-Michel, Musée d'Orsay, Louvre, Concorde, Champs-Elysées, Charles-de-Gaulle-Etoile, Porte Maillot and Neuilly. Services run between 12.30PM and 8PM and the whole trip takes 50 minutes. You can get off to visit a sight near a Balabus stop, then catch the next bus onwards.

An alternative way of travelling round Paris between April and September is by a public river-boat christened 'Batobus'. Fares are paid either per stage or for the entire journey, which starts at the Port de la Bourdonnais by the Eiffel Tower and continues to the Musée d'Orsay, the Pont des Arts (Louvre), Notre-Dame, Hôtel-de-Ville (Centre Georges Pompidou), then returns along the same route.

ITINERARY ONE	LATIN QUARTER
Morning	Climb the tower of Notre-Dame for a bird's-eye-view. Walk beside the river to the Sainte-Chapelle (➤ 39). Cross to Boulevard Saint-Michel and walk up to the Musée de Cluny (➤ 38). Continue up Boulevard St-Michel to the Jardin du Luxembourg (➤ 37).
Lunch	Relax in the gardens and have lunch in a café near the Panthéon,
Afternoon	Walk over to Eglise St-Etienne-du-Mont (➤ 52). Explore the winding streets that lead to the rue Monge. Have a look at the Roman Arènes de Lutèce (➤ 59).
Tea	Walk south towards the Mosquée (➤ 52) and indulge in a mint tea. Cross over to the Jardin des Plantes and the Musée d'Histoire Naturelle (➤ 51).

ITINERARY TWO	STATELY PARIS
Breakfast	At the Samaritaine (► 57).
Morning	Cross Pont Neuf (► 55) to the island and take a boat-trip along the Seine which returns here. Wander along the *quai* at river level to the Musée d'Orsay (► 31).
Lunch	Have lunch at the Musée d'Orsay or, alternatively, walk up the rue de Bellechasse, across Boulevard St-Germain, then along to the Musée Rodin (► 29) where the rose-garden café beckons.
Afternoon	Continue to Les Invalides (► 28). Visit the Eglise du Dôme (► 28). Walk along the esplanade to cross the ornate Pont Alexandre III (► 55). Visit the Petit Palais (► 27). Explore the Champs-Elysées (► 27). Catch bus No 42 down the Avenue Montaigne to the Eiffel Tower (► 26). Try and time it for sunset.
ITINERARY THREE	GREEN PARIS
Morning	Start the day at the Musée Marmottan (► 24) then take the métro to Franklin-D-Roosevelt. Walk down the shady paths of the Champs-Elysées to the Place de la Concorde (► 30). Cross to the Orangerie (► 30). Walk through the Tuileries (► 56), stopping for a drink at a kiosk.
Lunch	Have lunch at the Café Marly (► 53) or in the Louvre's underground labyrinth.
Afternoon	Visit a section of the Louvre's immense collection (► 35) then recover in the gardens of the Palais-Royal. Take bus No 67 from the rue du Louvre to Pigalle, where you can catch the Monmartrobus which spirits you to the top of Montmartre hill. Watch sunset over Paris from Sacré Coeur (► 33)
Evening	Dine near the lively Place des Abbesses.

WALKS

THE SIGHTS

- Porte de Clisson
- Les Enfants Rouges
- Cathédrale Ste-Croix-de-Paris
- Musée Picasso (➤51)
- Hôtel de Chatillon
- Musée Carnavalet (➤46)
- Place des Vosges (➤47)

INFORMATION

Distance 3km
Time 1–2 hours
Start point Plateau Beaubourg
🚇 H5/6
🚉 Rambuteau, Hôtel-de-Ville
End point Place des Vosges
🚇 J6
🍴 Café Beaubourg, rue St Martin; Ma Bourgogne, Place des Vosges

Mére et enfant, Picasso

LE MARAIS TO THE PLACE DES VOSGES

After breakfast at the Café Beaubourg walk behind the Centre Georges Pompidou to turn right into the rue Rambuteau, a colourful food-shopping street. Turn left up the rue des Archives with the magnificent turreted Porte de Clisson (1375) rising from the Hôtel de Soubise (1709) on your right. Continue past a monumental fountain (1624) on your left and the Hôtel Guénégaud (1650, which houses the Musée de la Chasse) diametrically opposite. Keep walking straight on to the rue de Bretagne where you can rest in the leafy Square du Temple, or investigate the leather-clothes market in the Carreau du Temple. Have a coffee nearby.

Along the rue de Bretagne, enter the picturesque food and flower market of Les Enfants Rouges (dating from 1620s) then exit on to the rue Charlot. Walk down here, past the impressive Cathédrale Ste-Croix-de-Paris, a former 17th-century convent, to the rue des Quatre-Fils. Turn left, past a new building which houses the National Archives and continue to the rue Vieille-du-Temple. Circle round the garden of the Hôtel Salé, now home to the Musée Picasso, then continue to the Parc Royal, a small garden which is overlooked by a row of superbly restored 17th-century mansions. Take a look at the courtyard of the Hôtel de Chatillon at 13 rue Payenne, then continue to rue de Sévigné. Pass or be tempted by the fashion offerings of Romeo Gigli at No 46, admire the two mansions of the Musée Carnavalet, then turn left into the rue des Francs-Bourgeois. Carry straight on to the Place des Vosges and stop to have lunch at Ma Bourgogne.

WALKS

PLACE DES VOSGES TO THE LATIN QUARTER

Walk through a passageway at No 9 Place des Vosges to the courtyard of the Hôtel de Sully. Exit on the rue St-Antoine, turn right and right again into the rue de Turenne, then left to the charming Place du Marché Ste-Catherine, good for a coffee-stop on a sunny day. Return to the main road and cross to rue Saint-Paul, lined with antique shops. Further down on the right enter the Village Saint-Paul, a discreetly hidden bric-à-brac market, then emerge on the other side into the rue des Jardins Saint-Paul. Here you see the largest remaining section of Philippe-Auguste's city wall. Turn left, then right along the rue de l'Ave Maria to reach the Hôtel de Sens, an exceptional example of 15th-century Gothic architecture. Look at the courtyard and the small formal garden behind the mansion. From here cross the Pont Marie to the Ile Saint-Louis. End your day in the web of Latin Quarter streets across the Seine.

THE SIGHTS

- Place des Vosges
- Village Saint-Paul (➤77)
- Philippe-Auguste's city wall
- Hôtel de Sens
- Ile Saint-Louis (➤44)

INFORMATION

Distance 2km
Time 1–2 hours
Start point Place des Vosges
➕ J6
🚇 Bastille, Chemin-Vert, St-Paul
End point Latin Quarter, around Boulevard St-Michel, Rue St-Jacques
➕ G6/7, H6/7

Place des Vosges

Evening Strolls

INFORMATION

The Seine
Start point Place du Châtelet
✚ H6
🚇 Châtelet

Bastille
Start point Place de la Bastille
✚ JK6
🚇 Bastille

Notre-Dame

THE SEINE

Start at Châtelet and walk towards the Louvre along the embankment opposite the illuminated Conciergerie, the Monnaie (Mint) and the Institut de France. At the Louvre make a detour into the Cour Carrée, magnificently lit and often deserted at night. Return to the river, cross the lively Pont des Arts then walk back along the opposite bank, this time with views north of the stately Samaritaine and the Palais de Justice on the Ile de la Cité. Continue towards St-Michel, then cross over to Notre-Dame and make your way around the north side of the island, which offers views of the Ile Saint-Louis, the Hôtel de Ville and the Gothic Tour Saint-Jacques towering over the Place du Châtelet.

BASTILLE

From the Place de la Bastille walk up the rue de la Roquette until the road forks. Turn right

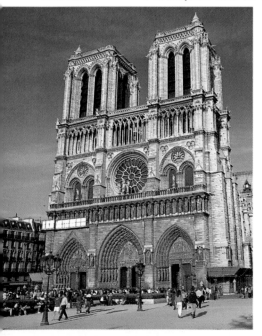

along the bustling pedestrian street of rue de Lappe, which is packed with bars, night-clubs and with restaurants, (keep a look out for No 71, a fine 18th-century house). Then turn left into the rue de Charonne. Pass art galleries and more bars before cutting back to the rue de la Roquette via the rue Keller. Notre-Dame de l'Espérance looms on your right and at No 68 there is a fountain (1839). Back at the fork turn right along rue Daval and cross two boulevards to rue du Pas de la Mule which leads to the Place des Vosges.

ORGANISED SIGHTSEEING

WALKING TOURS

CAISSE DES MONUMENTS HISTORIQUES ET DES SITES
Offers a daily programme of walking tours with qualified lecturers.
✉ 62 rue Saint-Antoine, 75004　☎ 44 61 21 69　Ⓜ Bastille, Saint-Paul　🎟 Moderate.

The **Ville de Paris** (municipality) offers guided tours to the Parc de Bagatelle, the Parc André Citroën and the Père Lachaise, Montmartre and Passy cemeteries.
☎ 40 67 97 00 (walks) 40 71 76 47 (recorded information).

BOAT TRIPS

BATEAUX PARISIENS TOUR EIFFEL
✉ Rive Gauche, port de la Bourdonnais　☎ 44 11 33 44　🕐 Mon–Thu, 10–6; Fri–Sun, 10–9　Ⓜ Trocadéro　🎟 Very expensive

BATEAUX VEDETTES DU PONT-NEUF
Classic one-hour trip along the Seine.
✉ Square du Vert Galant, 75001　☎ 47 05 71 29　🕐 Daily, 10–7　Ⓜ Pont-Neuf　🎟 Expensive

CANAUXRAMA
Three-hour canal trip (part underground) between the Bastille and the Bassin de la Villette. Booking essential.
✉ Bassin de la Villette, 13 Quai de la Loire, 75019　☎ 42 39 15 00　🕐 Departures at 9:30 and 2:45 from Bassin de la Villette, 9:45 and 2:30 from the Port de l'Arsenal, Bastille　Ⓜ Jaurès or Bastille　🎟 Very expensive

BICYCLE TOURS

PARIS BIKE
Tours of Paris and further afield on VTT bikes.
✉ 83 rue Daguerre, 75013　☎ 43 20 67 60　🕐 3-hour circuits and weekend trips　Ⓜ Denfert-Rochereau　🎟 Expensive

PARIS À VÉLO
✉ 9 rue Jacques Coeur, 75004　☎ 48 87 60 01　🕐 Short and long trips　Ⓜ Bastille　🎟 Expensive

Paris's canals
Cruising Paris's canals offers a more idiosyncratic view of Paris than the usual Seine trip. The revamped Arsenal dock at the Bastille (1806) is the kick-off for an underground vaulted passage which re-emerges at the Canal Saint-Martin. Chestnut trees, swing bridges, locks, the Hôtel du Nord (of celluloid fame) and modern apartment blocks lead to the Bassin de la Villette with its famous Rotonde (built by Ledoux in 1789). From here the Canal de l'Ourcq continues to the Parc de la Villette and then on eastwards for a further 108km.

EXCURSIONS

Versailles

- ✉ Château de Versailles
- ☎ 30 84 74 00
- 🕐 State Apartments: Tue–Sun, May–Sep 9–6, Oct–Apr 9–5; Grand and Petit Trianon: Tue–Sun, May–Sep 10–6, Oct–Apr 10–5; Park: daily 7AM–sunset.
- 🍽 Cafés, restaurants
- 🚉 RER Line C Versailles Rive-Gauche
- ♿ Few
- 💲 Château: expensive; park: free
- ❓ Fountains operate May–Sep, Sun 3:30–5; guided tours

Vaux-le-Vicomte

- ✉ Château de Vaux-le-Vicomte, 77950 Maincy
- ☎ 64 14 41 90
- 🕐 Apr–Oct, 10–6; Nov–Mar, 11–5
- 🍽 Restaurant
- 🚉 SNCF Gare de Lyon to Melun, then taxi
- ♿ Few
- 💲 Expensive
- ❓ Guided tours; fountains operate second and last Sat of month, May–Oct, 3–6; Candlelit tours May–Sep, Sat 8:30PM–11PM

Giverny

- ✉ Fondation Claude Monet, 27620 Giverny
- ☎ 32 51 28 21
- 🕐 Apr–Oct, Tue–Sun 10–6
- 🍽 Restaurant
- 🚉 SNCF Gare St-Lazare to Vernon, then bus, hire a bike or walk (6km)
- ♿ Good
- 💲 Expensive

CHÂTEAU AND PARK OF VERSAILLES

Few people miss visiting Versailles, the ultimate symbol of French grandeur and sophistication, and the backdrop to the death-throes of the monarchy. In 1661, when Louis XIV announced his intention of moving his court to this deserted swamp, it was to create a royal residence, seat of government and home to French nobility. Building continued until his death in 1715 by which time the 100-ha park had been tamed to perfection by Le Nôtre. Hundreds of statues, follies, and fountains and the royal love nests of the Grand and Petit Trianon relieve the formal symmetry while rowing-boats, bicycles and a minitrain now offer instant relief from history. Inside the château, visit the Grands Appartements (the official court and entertainment halls) which include the staggeringly ornate Hall of Mirrors with painted ceilings by Lebrun. The Petits Appartements (the royal living quarters) display France's most priceless examples of 18th-century decoration and may be visited by guided tour only.

The Latona fountain, Versailles

VAUX-LE-VICOMTE

About 50km southeast of Paris lies the inspiration for Versailles, a château erected in 1656 by Louis XIV's ambitious Regent and Minister of Finance, Nicolas Fouquet, who employed the nation's most talented artists and craftsmen. Five years later a château-warming party of

The lily pond at Giverny

extravagant proportions provoked Louis XIV's envy and Fouquet's subsequent arrest and imprisonment for embezzlement. Today the interior and magnificent grounds have been entirely restored and include the Musée des Equipages (horse-drawn carriages) in the stables. Inside the château, resplendent with Lebrun's painted ceilings, do not miss the rich Chambre du Roi. In front of the château's neo-classical façade stretch terraces and lawns, fountains and statues ending at a canal. If you have time, continue your stroll in the woods beyond.

GIVERNY

This small Normandy village is famous for one reason – Claude Monet. Monet lived in the village from 1883 until his death in 1926, inspiring a local artists' colony and producing some of Impressionism's most famous and startling canvases. His carefully tended garden with its Japanese-style lily pond gradually became his sole inspiration, and was as important to him as his painting. Only reproductions of his works are displayed here but the colourfully painted house, his personal collection of Japanese prints and the beautiful garden together offer a wonderful day out. May/June, when the borders are a riot of colour, is the best time for the flowers.

Le Petit Trianon

The Petit Trianon, the jewel in the crown of French neo-classical architecture, was built for Louis XV's mistress, Madame du Barry, and later presented by Louis XVI to his wife, Marie-Antoinette (who was to utter the inept words 'let them eat cake' from her royal chambers as the angry mob clamoured for bread below). In a pursuit of the simple life, she transformed the grounds into a 'wild' park complete with a make-believe village where she tended sheep.

21

WHAT'S ON

Information on current events is best found in *Pariscope*, an inexpensive weekly listings magazine (out on Wednesday) which covers everything from concerts to cinema, theatre, sports, nightclubs; it has a useful section in English. *Figaroscope* comes with *Le Figaro* on Wednesdays and also offers a good round-up of current events.

JANUARY	America Stakes at Vincennes racecourse
FEBRUARY	National Rugby Tournament
MARCH	International Jumping at Palais Omnisports de Paris Bercy
APRIL	International Paris fair with stands promoting gastronomy, tourism and publications from all over the world.
MAY	1 May, Labour Day, sees endless processions, thousands of bouquets of symbolic lily-of-the-valley and no newspapers.
JUNE	The end of World War II is celebrated on 8 May. Crowds spring to life on midsummer's night for the *Fête de la Musique* – a government-sponsored event which schedules major rock or world-music bands.
	The *Course des Garçons de Café* in late June: over 500 waiters and waitresses career along the streets, each armed with tray, bottle and glasses.
JULY	Number one on the French festival calendar is Bastille Day (**14 July**), which celebrates the 1789 storming of the Bastille. Fireworks and street-dances boom out on the evening of 13 July while the 14th itself is devoted to a military parade on the Champs-Elysées.
AUGUST	Annual exodus or *Fête des villages*: outdoor concerts and street theatre in each quartier.
SEPTEMBER	*Fête à Neu-Neu*, a fair in the Bois de Boulogne. From mid-September until the end of December, music, theatre and dance performances throughout the city in the *Festival d'Automne à Paris*.
OCTOBER	*Foire International d'Art Contemporain*, Paris's biggest modern art fair, at the Grand Palais.
NOVEMBER	Liberal amounts of wine descend on the third Thursday in November when the first bottles of *Beaujolais Nouveau* hit Paris.
	Antiques fair at Pelouse d'Auteuil, place de la porte de Passy.
DECEMBER	Paris International Boat Show at the Porte de Versailles.

PARIS's
top 25 sights

The sights are numbered from west to east across the city

1 *Musée Marmottan*	24	
2 *Palais de Chaillot*	25	
3 *Eiffel Tower*	26	
4 *Champs-Elysées &*		
Arc de Triomphe	27	
5 *Les Invalides*	28	
6 *Musée Rodin*	29	
7 *Place de la Concorde*	30	
8 *Musée d'Orsay*	31	
9 *Opéra de Paris*	32	
10 *Sacré-Coeur*	33	
11 *Musée des Arts Décoratifs*	34	
12 *Musée du Louvre*	35	
13 *Galeries Vivienne &*		
Colbert	36	
14 *Jardin du Luxembourg*	37	
15 *Musée de Cluny (Musée*		
Nationale du Moyen-Age,		
Thermes de Cluny)	38	
16 *Sainte-Chapelle*	39	
17 *The Conciergerie*	40	
18 *Centre Georges Pompidou*	41	
19 *Marché aux Puces de*		
St Ouen	42	

20 *Notre-Dame*	43
21 *Ile Saint-Louis*	44
22 *Institut du Monde Arabe*	45
23 *Musée Carnavalet*	46
24 *Place des Vosges*	47
25 *Père Lachaise Cemetery*	48

23

1

MUSÉE MARMOTTAN

HIGHLIGHTS

- *Impression – soleil levant,* Monet
- *Bouquet de Fleurs,* Gauguin
- Gold table-tray
- Geographical clock
- *Promenade près d'Argenteuil,* Monet
- *Charing Cross Bridge,* Monet
- *L'Allée des Rosiers,* Monet
- *Le Pont Japonais,* Monet
- Monet's water-lilies series
- Monet's spectacles

INFORMATION

- ✚ B6
- ✉ 2 rue Louis-Boilly 75016
- ☎ 42 24 07 02
- 🕐 Tue–Sun 10–5:30
- Ⓜ La Muette
- 🚌 32
- 🚆 RER Line C Boulainvilliers
- 💱 Expensive
- ↔ Bois de Boulogne (➤ 56)

"One of the few incentives to get me out into the residential 16th arrondissement is the Marmottan, where a mesmerising collection of Monet paintings makes a welcome escape from the often colourless Parisian landscape."

Rich donations This often overlooked treasure of Parisian culture offers an eclectic collection built up over the years from the original donation of Renaissance and First Empire paintings and furniture given to the nation by the art-historian Paul Marmottan in 1932. His discreetly elegant 19th-century mansion, furnished with Renaissance tapestries and sculptures and Napoleonic furniture, was later given an extra boost by an exceptional donation from Michel Monet of 65 works by his father, Claude Monet the Impressionist painter, as well as by the stunning Wildenstein collection of 230 illustrated manuscripts of the 13th to 16th centuries. Works by Monet's contemporaries Gauguin, Renoir, Pissarro, Sisley, Berthe Morisot and Gustave Caillebotte add to the Impressionist focus, but it is above all Monet's luminous canvases of dappled irises, wisteria and water-lilies, dating from his last years at Giverny, that are memorable.

Shame It happens even to the best of museums, but when nine major paintings were stolen from the Marmottan in 1985 it caused acute embarrassment, not least because the booty included Monet's seminal work, *Impression – soleil levant*, which gave the movement its name. After a police operation on a world-wide scale, the plundered paintings were discovered five years later in Corsica and are now once again on display, needless to say under greatly increased security measures.

Top: Impression – soleil levant, *Monet*

PALAIS DE CHAILLOT

"With its majestic wings curving towards the Eiffel Tower across the Seine and its monumental presence, the Palais de Chaillot impresses, but it also has a human aspect – roller-skating heroes, mime-artists and Sunday promenaders."

Attractions The 1937 Exposition Universelle instigated the Palais de Chaillot's strict colonnaded forms punctuated with bronze statues which overlook terraces and fountains. Art deco stops with the architecture, leaving four museums, a theatre and the Cinémathèque Française to take over inside. The west wing houses the Musée de l'Homme and the Musée de la Marine, the former catering for anthropological leanings and the latter for maritime and naval interest. A newly converted gallery at the Musée de l'Homme houses temporary thematic exhibitions while the main collection gathers dust upstairs. On the top floor the Salon de la Musique displays some 500 'world' musical instruments used for Sunday concerts.

Illusions In the east wing nestles an extraordinary museum, the Musée des Monuments Français, conceived by the 19th-century medievalist architect, Viollet-le-Duc. Full-scale replicas and casts of French architectural features from

An exhibit in the marine museum

pre-Roman times to the 19th century include gargoyles, frescoes, stained glass, statues and even a fountain. More replicas of reality can be found in the adjoining Musée du Cinéma, which traces the evolution of film-making through early movie cameras, sets, models and costumes.

HIGHLIGHTS

- Napoleon's imperial barge
- *Ports de France*, Vernet
- *Le Valmy*
- African frescoes
- Javanese gamelan orchestra
- King Béhanzin
- Reproduction of St-Savin-sur-Gartempe
- Baroque fountain
- Fritz Lang's robot
- Rudolf Valentino costume

INFORMATION

- ✚ D5
- ✉ Place du Trocadéro 75016
- ☎ 45 53 31 70 (Marine), 44 05 72 72 (Homme), 44 05 39 10 (Monuments), 45 53 74 39 (Cinéma)
- 🕐 Wed–Mon, Marine, 10–6; Homme, 9:45–5:15; Monuments, 10–6; Cinéma, by guided tour only, Wed–Sun 10, 11AM, 2, 3, 4, 5PM, (phone to book).
- 🍴 'Le Totem' restaurant in the west wing
- Ⓜ Trocadéro
- 🚌 22, 30, 32, 63
- ♿ Few
- 🔂 Moderate
- ↔ Musée d'Art Moderne de la Ville de Paris, Musée Guimet (▶50)
- ❓ Guided tours of Marine on request; ethnological films at Homme at 2:30 Sat, Sun

EIFFEL TOWER

"It could be a cliché but it isn't. The powerful silhouette of Eiffel's marvel of engineering is still for me a stirring sight, especially at night when its delicate, lace-like iron structure comes to the fore."

Glittering feat Built in a record two years for the 1889 Exposition Universelle, the controversial Eiffel Tower was never intended to be a permanent feature of the city. However, in 1910 it was finally saved for posterity, so preparing the way for today's 4 million annual visitors. Avoid long queues for the lift by visiting the tower at night, when it fully lives up to its romantic image and provides a glittering spectacle – whether the 292,000-watt illumination of the 'staircase to infinity' itself or the carpet of nocturnal Paris unfolding at its feet.

Violent reactions Gustave Eiffel was a master of cast-iron structures whose prolific output included hundreds of factories, churches, railway viaducts and bridges over four continents. His 320m tower attracted vociferous opposition, but his genius was vindicated by the fact that it sways no more than 12cm in high winds and for 40 years remained the world's highest structure. Eiffel kept an office there until his death in 1923; from here he may have seen the Comte de Lambert, who in 1909 circled above the tower in a flying-machine or a less fortunate Icarus who plummeted to his death from the parapet in 1912.

4

CHAMPS-ELYSÉES & ARC DE TRIOMPHE

"Like me, you may not be enamoured of fast-food outlets and airline offices, both major features of this once-glamorous avenue. But a recent facelift has upgraded the tackiness, and nothing can change the magnificent east–west perspective."

Slow start It was Marie de Médicis, wife of Henri IV, who first made this a fashionable driveway in 1616 but it was the celebrated landscape designer André Le Nôtre who contributed to its name – Elysian Fields – by planting alleys of trees and gardens. The heyday came in 1824 when new pavements and fountains made it the most fashionable promenading spot in Paris, with cafés and restaurants catering for a well-heeled clientèle. Crowning the cake was the Arc de Triomphe (►57), commissioned by Napoleon, and the 1900 Exposition Universelle added the glass and iron domes of the Grand Palais (which includes the Palais de la Découverte) and the Petit Palais at the lower end.

Parades Despite being dominated by commercial and tourist facilities, the Champs-Elysées remains the symbolic focal-point for national ceremonies, whether the traditional 14 July military parade, Armistice Day's wreath-laying at the Arc de Triomphe or the fast-pedalling *grande finale* of the Tour de France. A recent highlight was the 1989 Bicentenary procession when Jessye Norman led a spectacular host of swaying performers down to the Place de la Concorde.

Luxury These days the Champs-Elysées may be dominated by car showrooms, but there are still plush cinemas, upmarket shops and one or two fashionable watering-holes to tempt those who want to see and be seen.

HIGHLIGHTS

- Arc de Triomphe
- Rude's 'Marseillaise' sculpture on Arc de Triomphe
- L'Etoile
- Bluebell Girls at Lido
- 'Fouquets' restaurant
- Palais de l'Elysée
- 'Ledoyen' restaurant
- Grand Palais
- Petit Palais
- Philatelists' market

INFORMATION

- ✚ D4
- ✉ Champs-Elysées 75008
- ☎ Grand Palais, 44 13 17 17; Petit Palais, 42 65 12 73
- 🎟 Grand Palais, Wed–Mon 10–8; Petit Palais, Tue–Sun 10–5:40; Palais de la Découverte, Tue-Sat 9:30–6; Sun 10–7,
- 🍴 Grand Palais: average cafeteria, cafés and restaurants on Champs-Elysées
- 🚇 Charles-de-Gaulle Etoile, Georges V, Franklin-Roosevelt, Champs-Elysées-Clémenceau
- 🚌 32, 42, 73
- ♿ Good
- 💲 Moderate to expensive
- ↔ Place de la Concorde (►30)
- ❓ Photo library and scientific films in Palais de la Découverte

LES INVALIDES

HIGHLIGHTS

- 196m façade
- Sword and armour of François I
- Salle Orientale
- Napoleon's stuffed horse
- *Emperor Napoleon*, Ingres
- Galerie des Plans-Reliefs
- Napoleon's tomb
- Dome
- 17th-century organ
- A Renault light tank

INFORMATION

- ✚ E6
- ✉ Esplanade des Invalides 75007
- ☎ 44 42 37 67 (Musée de l'armée)
- 🕐 Daily Oct–Mar, 10– 5; Apr–Sep, 10–6
- 🚇 La Tour Maubourg, Invalides, Varenne
- 🚌 28, 49, 69, 82, 92
- 🚆 RER Line C Invalides
- ♿ Good
- 🎫 Expensive
- ↔ Musée Rodin (➤ 29)
- ❓ Guided tours on request ☎ 45 51 95 05; films on World Wars I and II

"The gilded dome rising above the Hôtel des Invalides reminds me of the pomp and glory of France's two greatest promoters – the Sun King, who built Les Invalides, and the power-hungry Napoleon Bonaparte, who is entombed there."

Glory The vast, imposing edifice of Les Invalides was built to house invalided soldiers, a handful of whom still live there. Its classical façade and majestic Cour d'Honneur date from the 1670s with the ornate Eglise du Dôme completed in 1706 and the long grassy esplanade established soon after. Home to military institutions, Les Invalides is also a memorial to the endless battles and campaigns that have marked French history and which are extensively illustrated in the Musée de l'Armée. Here you can trace the evolution of warfare from early days to World War II, and there are daily screenings of war films.

The Cour d'Honneur

Tombs There are more relics inside the Eglise St-Louis, where tattered enemy standards hang despondently from cornices, but it is above all the baroque cupolas, arches, columns and sculptures of the Eglise du Dôme that highlight France's military achievements and heroes. Tombs of generals fill the chapels while the circular crypt contains Napoleon's grandiose sarcophagus (which incorporates six successive layers) guarded by 12 statues, symbols of his military campaigns.

MUSÉE RODIN

❝As a complete antidote to the military might of Les Invalides, wander into this enchanting museum, often forgotten by Parisians. This surprisingly peaceful enclave lifts you out of the hurly-burly of the boulevards into another sphere.❞

Hard times This rococo mansion, built for a prosperous wig-maker in 1730, has a chequered history. One owner (Maréchal de Biron) was sent to the guillotine and the house has been used successively as a dance-hall, convent, school and as artists' studios. Rodin lived here from 1908 until his death in 1917, with neighbours such as the poet Rainer Maria Rilke and dancer Isadora Duncan. In 1919 it was transformed into a museum.

Sculpture The elegant, luminous interior houses the collection of works which Rodin left to the nation on his death in 1917. It ranges from his early academic sketches to the later watercolours and displays many of his most celebrated white marble and bronze sculptures, including *The Kiss*. There are busts of the composer Mahler, the suffragette Eva Fairfax, and Victor Hugo to name but a few, as well as a series of studies of Balzac in paunchy splendour. Alongside the Rodins are works by his contemporaries, in particular his tragic mistress and model, Camille Claudel, as well as Eugène Carrière, Munch, Renoir, Monet and Van Gogh. Rodin's furniture and antiques complete this exceptional collection.

Retreat The private gardens are Paris's third largest and contain several major sculptures, a pond, flowering shrubs, benches for a quiet read, a converted chapel used for temporary exhibitions and an open-air café.

HIGHLIGHTS

- Les Bourgeois de Calais
- Le Penseur
- La Porte de l'Enfer
- Le Baiser
- La Main de Dieu
- Saint Jean Baptiste
- Adam et Eve
- Ugolin
- Le Père Tanguy, Van Gogh
- Original staircase

INFORMATION

- F6
- 77 rue de Varenne 75007
- 47 05 01 34
- Tue–Sun, winter 9:30–4:45; summer 9:30–5:45
- Peaceful garden café
- Varenne
- 69
- Good
- Moderate
- Les Invalides (▶28)

PLACE DE LA CONCORDE

HIGHLIGHTS

- *Les Nymphéas, Monet*
- Jeu de Paume
- Hieroglyphs
- Hôtel Crillon
- *Chevaux de Marly*
- View up the Champs-Elysées

DID YOU KNOW?

- Obelisk weighs 230 tonnes
- 133 peope trampled to death here in 1770
- 1,300 heads guillotined here 1793–5

INFORMATION

- ✚ F5
- ✉ Place de la Concorde 75008
- ☎ Jeu de Paume, 47 03 12 50; Orangerie, 42 97 48 16
- ◉ Jeu de Paume, Wed–Fri 12 noon–7, except Tue 12 noon–9:30; Sat–Sun 10–7.00; Orangerie, Wed–Mon 9:45–5:15
- 🍴 Small designer café in Jeu de Paume
- Ⓜ Concorde
- 🚌 24, 42, 52, 72, 73, 84, 94
- ♿ Jeu de Paume: excellent; Orangerie: none
- 💲 Moderate to expensive
- ↔ Champs-Elysées (➤27); Jardin des Tuileries (➤56)

"*As you stand in this noisy traffic–choked square it is hard to imagine the crowds baying for the deaths of Marie-Antoinette and Louis XVI, who were both guillotined here at the height of the Terror of the French Revolution.***"**

Chop-chop This pulsating square was initially laid out in 1775 to accommodate a statue of King Louis XV, then, under the new name of the Place de la Révolution, it witnessed the mass executions of the French Revolution, and was finally renamed the Place de la Concorde in 1795 as revolutionary zeal abated. In the 19th century, Guillaume Coustou's *Chevaux de Marly* were erected at the base of the Champs-Elysées; these have been replaced by reproductions, with the originals now in the Louvre. Crowning the centre of the Concorde is a 3,000-year-old Egyptian obelisk overlooking eight symbolic statues of French cities. Dodging the traffic to have a closer look is to dice with death, but plans are currently under consideration to ease the pedestrian's lot.

Grandeur To the north, bordering the rue Royale, stand the colonnaded Hôtel Crillon (on the left) and the matching Hôtel de la Marine (right), both relics from pre-Revolutionary days. The rue Royale itself, with its luxury establishments, leads to the Madeleine. The eastern side of the Concorde is dominated by two public art galleries, the Jeu de Paume (by rue de Rivoli), which displays contemporary art exhibitions, and the Orangerie (nearer the river), famous for its impressive basement panels of Monet's *Water Lilies* and rather second-rate Impressionist paintings. Visible across the bridge to the south is the Palais Bourbon, home to the French parliament, the Assemblée Nationale.

MUSÉE D'ORSAY

❝You either love or hate this conversion of a turn-of-the-century railway station, but either way its art collections, covering the years 1848–1914, are a must for anyone interested in this crucial art-historical period.❞

Monolithic When this museum finally opened in 1986 controversy ran high: Gae Aulenti's heavy stone structures lay unhappily under Laloux's delicate iron and glass shell, built as a railway terminus in 1900. But the collections redeem this *faux pas*, offering a solid overview of the momentous period from Romanticism to Fauvism. Ignore the monolithic mezzanine blocks and, after exploring the 19th-century

paintings, sculptures and decorative arts on the ground floor, take the front escalator to the upper level. Here the Pont-Aven, Impressionist, and Nabis schools are displayed along with the giants of French art – Cézanne, Monet, Renoir, Van Gogh, Degas, Sisley and Pissaro. Don't miss

The Church at Auvers, *Van Gogh*

the views from the outside terrace and café behind the station clock at the top.

To the ball The middle level is devoted to painting (Symbolism and Naturalism) and sculpture from 1870 to 1914 and includes works by Rodin, Bourdelle and Maillol. In the spectacular ballroom hang paintings by Gérôme and Bouguereau.

HIGHLIGHTS

- *Olympia*, Manet
- *Déjeuner sur l'Herbe*, Manet
- *Orphée*, Gustave Moreau
- *La Mère*, Whistler
- *L'Angélus du soir*, Millet
- *La Cathédrale de Rouen*, Monet
- *L'Absinthe*, Degas
- *La chambre à Arles*, Van Gogh
- *Femmes de Tahiti*, Gauguin
- Chair by Charles Rennie Mackintosh

INFORMATION

- ✚ F6
- ✉ 1 rue de Bellechasse, 75007
- ☎ 40 49 48 14, 40 49 48 48
- ⏱ Tue–Sun 10–5:45, except Thu 10–9:30
- 🍴 Café des Hauteurs for good snacks, plush restaurant/tea-room in ballroom
- Ⓜ Solférino
- 🚌 24, 68, 69
- 🚉 RER Line C Musée d'Orsay
- ♿ Excellent
- 💲 Expensive
- ↔ Louvre (►35)
- ❓ Audio and guided tours; pedagogical activities, concerts and lectures

31

OPÉRA DE PARIS

HIGHLIGHTS

● Grand Escalier
● Grand Foyer
● *Apollo*, Millet
● Façade
● Lamp-bearers

DID YOU KNOW?

● Garnier's design was selected from 171 others
● Total surface of building is 11,000sq m
● Auditorium holds 2,200 spectators
● Stage accommodates over 450 performers

INFORMATION

✚ G4
✉ Place de l'Opéra 75009
☎ 40 01 17 89
◷ Daily 10–4:30
🍴 Bar open during shows
Ⓜ Opéra
🚌 20, 21, 22, 27, 29, 42, 52, 53, 66, 68, 81, 95
🚉 RER Auber
♿ Few, call for appointment
💲 Moderate
↔ Place de la Concorde (►30)
❓ Guided tours daily at 11 except Sun; exhibitions

"I find it hard to take this ornate wedding cake of a building seriously, but its sumptuous and riotous details are in fact the perfect epitaph to the frenetic architectural activities of the Second Empire."

Past glory When Charles Garnier's opera house was inaugurated in 1875 it marked the end of Haussmann's ambitious urban face-lift and announced the socio-cultural build-up to the Belle Epoque with Nijinsky and Diaghilev's Ballets Russes as later highlights. Today the Salle Garnier still stages dance and opera though many prestigious operatic performances have been switched to the Opéra Bastille. In 1994–5 it was closed for total renovation to counter the comfort of Opéra Bastille. Rudolf Nureyev was director of the Paris Ballet here between 1983 and 1989, and this was where he first danced in the West. The brilliant dancer Patrick Dupond has steered the national ballet company fairly traditionally since 1990.

Dazzle Competing with a series of provocative lamp-bearing statues, the Palais Garnier's extravagant façade of arches, winged horses, friezes and columns topped by a copper-green dome leads into a majestic foyer. This is dominated by the Grand Escalier, dripping with balconies and chandeliers, which sweeps upwards to the Grand Foyer laden with gilded mirrors, marble, murals and Murano glass. Do not miss the equally ornate auditorium, with its dazzling gold-leaf decorations and red velvet seats, or Chagall's incongruous false ceiling, painted in 1964. It is open outside rehearsals (your best bet is between 1 and 2PM). To visit enter through Riccardo Pedruzzi's library and museum, now sporting a very 1990s look, which houses operatic memorabilia.

SACRÉ-COEUR

"Few people would admit it, but the high point of a trip up here is not the basilica but the stunning views. Do not forget, however, that Sacré-Coeur was built in honour of the 58,000 dead of the Franco-Prussian War."

Weighty Although construction started in 1875 it was not until 1914 that this white neo-Romanesque-Byzantine edifice was completed, partly due to the problems of building founda-tions in the quarry-riddled hill of Montmartre. Priests still work in relays to maintain the tradi-tion of perpetual prayer for forgiveness of the horrors of war and for the massacre of some 20,000 Communards by government troops.

The square bell-tower was an afterthought and houses one of the world's heaviest bells, La Savoyarde, which weighs in at 19 tonnes. The stained-glass win-dows are replacements of those which were shattered by enemy bombs in 1944.

The Byzantine mosaic of Christ, in the chancel vault

Panoramas This unmistakable feature of the Paris skyline magnetises the crowds either by funicular or via the steep steps of the terraced garden. Dawn and dusk offer sparkling panora-mas over the city, especially from the exterior terrace of the dome, the second highest point in Paris after the Eiffel Tower. Access is from the left-hand side of the basilica. Just to the east of Sacré-Coeur is the diminutive St-Pierre, a much reworked though charming church which is all that remains of the Benedictine Abbey of Montmartre founded in 1133.

HIGHLIGHTS

- Savoyarde bell
- View from dome
- Mosaic of Christ
- Treasure of Sacré-Coeur
- Bronze doors at St-Pierre
- Stained-glass gallery
- Statue of Christ
- Statue of Virgin Mary and Child
- The funicular

INFORMATION

- ✚ H3
- ✉ 35 rue Chevalier de la Barre 75018
- ☎ 42 51 17 02
- 🕐 Basilica, daily 7–11:30PM; dome and crypt, daily 9–7; Oct–Mar, daily 9–6
- Ⓜ Abbesses
- 🚌 Montmartrobus from Pigalle or Abbesses
- ♿ Few
- 🎫 Cheap (Montmartre village)
- ↔ Montmartre Village (rue Lepic, Vineyard of Montmartre, Place des Abbesses)

MUSÉE DES ARTS DÉCORATIFS

HIGHLIGHTS

- Sculpted wood panels
- Reveillon wallpaper designs
- Bronze and wood cradle
- Dufour Leroy wallpaper
- Empress Joséphine's tea service
- Georges Hoentschell woodwork
- Jeanne Lanvin's apartment
- Glass radiator
- Martin Szekely *chaise longue*
- Toy collection

INFORMATION

- G5
- 107 rue de Rivoli 75001
- 42 60 32 14
- Wed–Sat 12:30–6; Sun 12noon–6
- Palais-Royal/Musée du Louvre
- 21, 27, 39, 48, 67, 69, 72, 81
- Excellent
- Moderate
- Louvre (➤ 35)

Top: Jeanne Lanvin's bedroom by A A Rateau (1920–22)

"This uncrowded museum is one of my favourites for its discreet, old-fashioned atmosphere and its idiosyncratic collections. These may not necessarily be valuable, but they offer a clear view of developments in interior design and decoration."

The collection Tucked away in the northwest wing of the Louvre, this rather oddly arranged museum houses five floors of predominantly French furniture, furnishings and *objets d'art* from the Middle Ages through rococo to the present. It was founded early this century by an association of designers to collect and exhibit 'beauty in function', and certainly lives up to its role. Subsequent donations have greatly enriched the collection which, more recently, acquired the contents of the former Musée de la Publicité, thus adding graphic arts to the list. It has recently been refurbished.

What to see The collection is arranged chronologically. The ground floor is devoted to a fascinating collection of 20th-century design ranging from Le Corbusier to Nikki de St Phalle and Philippe Starck, with superb rooms devoted to art nouveau and art deco as well as temporary exhibitions. Do not miss the excellent specialist bookshop and small designer giftshop at the entrance. The upper floors display medieval and Renaissance pieces with better coverage of Louis XIII, Louis XIV, Louis XV, Empire, Restoration, Louis Philippe and Second Empire furnishings, some of which are arranged in reconstructed décors. On the third floor a changing exhibition displays toys throughout the centuries beside an outstanding collection of dolls. Top-floor collections of wallpaper, glass and graphic arts can be viewed only by appointment.

MUSÉE DU LOUVRE

"Nocturnal lighting transforms the Louvre's glass pyramid into a gigantic cut diamond – just a foretaste of the treasures contained inside. It is hard to ignore the state-of-the-art renovation, but that is just the icing on the cake."

The world's largest museum Few visitors bypass this palatial museum, but definitions of personal interest need to be made beforehand, as mere wandering could become a lifetime's occupation. Since 1981 the Louvre has been undergoing a radical transformation which crowns six centuries of eventful existence and will be completed in 1997. Originally a medieval castle, it first took shape as an art gallery under François I, eager to display his Italian loot, but it was Catherine de Médicis who extended it to become a palace in 1578. After escaping the excesses of the Revolutionary mob, in 1793 it became a people's museum and was later enlarged by Napoleon I, who also greatly enriched its collection.

Mona Lisa, *Leonardo da Vinci*

Art fortress The vast collection of some 30,000 exhibits is arranged on three floors of three wings: Sully (east), Richelieu (north) and Denon (south), while beneath the elegant Cour Carrée lie the keep and dungeons of the original medieval fortress. Do not miss the two spectacular skylit halls flanking the passageway from Palais-Royal which display monumental French sculptures, nor the tasteful commercial attractions in the central marble hall.

HIGHLIGHTS

- Palace of Khorsabad
- Egyptian scribe
- Glass pyramid
- *Bataille de San Romano*, Uccello
- *Mona Lisa*, Leonardo da Vinci
- *La Dentellière*, Vermeer
- *Le Radeau de la Méduse*, Géricault
- *Vénus de Milo*
- *Gabrielle d'Estrées et une des ses soeurs*, Ecole de Fontainebleau
- Cour Carrée at night

INFORMATION

- G5
- 99, rue de Rivoli 75001
- 40 20 50 50, 40 20 53 17, recorded information 40 20 51 51
- Wed–Mon 9–6; Mon and Wed 9AM–10PM
- Wide selection of restaurants and cafés
- Palais-Royal/Musée du Louvre
- 21, 27, 39, 48,67, 68, 69, 72, 75, 76, 81, 95
- Excellent
- Very expensive till 3PM, moderate after 3PM and Sun.
- Musée des Arts Décoratifs (▶34); Musée d'Orsay (▶31)
- Audio and digital tours; regular lectures, films, concerts in Auditorium

GALERIES VIVIENNE & COLBERT

HIGHLIGHTS

- Mosaic floor
- Bronze statue
- Staircase at 13 Galerie Vivienne
- Clock
- Bookshop
- Gaultier's shop

DID YOU KNOW?

- Explorer Bougainville lived here
- Simon Bolivar lived here
- Crook-turned-cop Vidocq lived here in the 1840s

INFORMATION

- ✚ G5
- ✉ Galerie Vivienne, Galerie Colbert, 75002
- ☎ None
- 🛈 Gate at 5 rue de la Banque permanently open
- 🍴 A Priori Thé, Brasserie Le Grand Colbert
- 🚇 Bourse, Palais-Royal/Musée du Louvre
- 🚌 29
- ♿ Good
- 🎟 Free
- ⬌ Jardin du Palais Royal (➤ 59)

The mosaic floor (top) and the bronze statue (right) in the Galeries Vivienne

" *One of my favourite places for people-watching and window-gazing, these connecting 19th-century passages, with their original mosaic floors and neo-classical decoration, offer a complete contrast to the fashionable buzz of neighbouring streets.* **"**

Shopping arcades Between the late 18th and early 19th centuries the Right Bank included a network of 140 covered passageways – the fashionable shopping-malls of the time. Today there are less than 30, of which the Galeries Vivienne and Colbert are perhaps the best known, strategically squeezed in between the Bibliothèque Nationale and the Place des Victoires. Bookworms and fashion-victims cross paths in this elegant, skylit setting lined with potted palms where there is also the occasional fashion show. It is perfect for a rainy day browse.

Hive of interest The Galerie Vivienne (1823) opens on to three different streets while the parallel Galerie Colbert (1826) has its own entrances. Colbert is now an annexe of the Bibliothèque Nationale, and regular exhibitions (prints, photos, theatre accessories) and concerts are held in its galleries and auditorium. Galerie Vivienne is commercial in spirit, and this is where you can track down Jean-Paul Gaultier's eccentric shop, designer watches, antiquarian or one-off artists' books, contemporary design, fine wines, intriguing toys or simply sit sipping exotic tea beneath the skylight, watching the world go by.

JARDIN DU LUXEMBOURG

"Despite the crowds, these gardens are serene in all weathers and are perfect epitomes of French landscaping. Their occupants present an idealised image of an unhurried Parisian existence far from the daily truth of noise, traffic and congestion."

Layout Radiating from the large octagonal pond in front of the Palais du Luxembourg (now the Senate) are terraces and paths and a wide tree-lined alley that leads down to the Observatory crossroads. Natural attractions include shady chestnut trees, potted orange and palm-trees, lawns and even an experimental fruit-garden and orchard, while fountains, tennis-courts, bee hives, a puppet-theatre and children's playgrounds offer other distractions. Statues of the queens of France, artists and writers are dotted about the terraces and avenues. All year round joggers work off their *foie gras* on the circumference, and in summer sunbathers and bookworms settle into park chairs, card- and chess-playing retirees claim the shade in front of the palace, bands tune up at the bandstand near the Boulevard St-Michel entrance and children burn off energy on swings and donkeys.

History The Palais du Luxembourg and surrounding garden were originally commissioned by Marie de Médicis, wife of Henri IV, in 1615, and designed to resemble her Florentine childhood home. The allée de l'Observatoire and the English-style garden were added in the early 19th century. A petition signed by 12,000 Parisians luckily saved the garden from Haussmann's urban ambitions, and since then its formal charms have inspired countless literary and celluloid tributes.

HIGHLIGHTS

- Médicis fountain
- Cyclops, Acis and Galateus sculptures
- Bandstand
- Statue of Delacroix
- Orange-tree conservatory
- Experimental fruit-garden
- Bee-keeping school
- Statues of Queens of France

DID YOU KNOW?

- Isadora Duncan danced here
- Ernest Hemingway claimed to capture pigeons here for his supper

INFORMATION

- G7
- 15 rue de Vaugirard 75006
- Senate 42 34 20 00
- Apr–Oct, daily 7:30AM–9:30PM ; Nov–Mar, daily 8:15–5 (times may vary slightly)
- Open-air cafés, kiosk restaurant
- Luxembourg
- 21, 27, 38, 58, 82, 84, 85, 89
- RER Line B Luxembourg
- Very good
- Free
- Eglise de Saint-Sulpice (►52)

MUSÉE DE CLUNY

HIGHLIGHTS

- *La Dame à la Licorne* tapestries
- Gold altar frontal
- *Pilier des nautes*
- Heads from Notre-Dame
- Visigoth votive crown
- Italian processional cross
- Statue of Adam
- Stained glass
- Averbode altarpiece
- Abbot's Chapel

INFORMATION

- ✚ H7
- ✉ 6 Place Paul-Painlevé 75006
- ☎ 43 25 62 00
- 🕐 Wed–Mon 9:15–5:45
- Ⓜ Cluny
- 🚌 21, 27, 38, 63, 85, 86, 87, 96
- ♿ Moderate
- ↔ Sainte-Chapelle (➤39)
- ❓ Guided tours of vaults, Wed, Sat, Sun at 2PM; of collection at 3:30PM

" *Take a deep breath outside the Cluny and prepare to enter a time warp – the days of the troubadours and courtly love recreated in its panelled rooms hung with tapestries. Here you can steep yourself in France of the Middle Ages.* **"**

Baths The late 2nd-century Gallo-Roman baths adjoining the Hôtel de Cluny are composed of three stone chambers: the Caldarium (steam bath), the Tepidarium (tepid bath) and the Frigidarium (cold bath) with ruins of the former gymnasium visible on the Boulevard St-Germain side. Important Roman stonework is exhibited in the niches while Room VIII houses 21 mutilated heads from Notre-Dame. Recent excavations have also opened up a labyrinth of Roman vaults which can be toured with a guide.

Treasures The Gothic turreted mansion was built in 1500 by the abbot Jacques d'Amboise and is one of France's finest examples of domestic architecture of this period. Some 23,000 objects compose the collection, much of which was gathered by the 19th-century medievalist and collector, Alexandre du Sommerard. Perhaps the most famous piece is the beautiful *La Dame à la Licorne* tapestry woven in the late 15th century. Six enigmatic panels depict a woman, a lion and a unicorn, animals, flowers and birds, all exquisitely worked. Costumes, accessories, textiles and tapestries are of Byzantine, Coptic or European origin while the gold and metalwork room houses some outstanding pieces of Gallic, Barbarian, Merovingian and Visigoth artistry. Stained glass, table-games, ceramics, wood-carvings, illuminated manuscripts and Books of Hours, altar-pieces and religious statuary complete this exceptional and very manageable display.

Top: A mon Seul Désir, one of the La Dame à la Licorne tapestries

SAINTE-CHAPELLE

"Sainte-Chapelle's 75m spire soaring towards the heavens is in itself an extraordinary expression of faith, but inside this is surpassed by the glowing intensity of the magnificent stained-glass windows reaching up to a star-studded roof."

Masterpiece One of Paris's oldest and most significant monuments stands within the precincts of the Palais de Justice. The chapel was built by Louis IX (later canonised) to house relics he had acquired at exorbitant cost during the crusades, which included what was reputed to be the Crown of Thorns, as well as fragments of the

cross and drops of Christ's blood (now kept in Notre-Dame). Pierre de Montreuil masterminded this delicate Gothic construction, bypassing the use of flying buttresses, incorporating a lower chapel for palace servants and installing 618sq. m. of stained glass above. Completed in 1248 in record time, it served as Louis IX's private chapel with discreet access from what was then the royal palace.

Apocalypse No fewer than 1,134 biblical scenes are illustrated by the 16 windows, starting with Genesis and finishing with the Apocalypse (the central rose window). To follow the narrative chronologically read from left to right and bottom to top, row by row. The statues of apostles against the pillars are mostly copies – the damaged originals are at the Musée de Cluny.

HIGHLIGHTS

- Rose window
- Oratory
- 19th-century restoration
- Tombs of canons
- Stained-glass of Christ's Passion
- Saint Louis himself in 15th window

INFORMATION

- ✚ H6
- ✉ 4 Boulevard du Palais 75001
- ☎ 43 54 30 09
- 🕐 Oct–Mar, 10–4:30;Apr–Sep, 9:30–6 daily
- Ⓜ Cité, St Michel
- 🚌 21, 38, 85, 96
- 🚆 RER Line B, St Michel
- ♿ Moderate
- ↔ Musée National du Moyen Age, Thermes de Cluny (Musée de Cluny, ➤ 38)

Top: the stained glass windows of the upper chapel

THE CONCIERGERIE

HIGHLIGHTS

- Public clock
- Sculptures
- Barber's cell
- Tour Bonbec

DID YOU KNOW?

- 288 prisoners were massacred here in 1792
- 4,164 citizens were held during the Terror
- Comte d'Armagnac was assassinated here
- 22 left-wing Girondins were held in one room
- Robespierre spent only one night before his execution
- Three types of cell according to prisoners' means

INFORMATION

- ✚ H6
- ✉ 1 Quai de l'Horloge, 75001
- ☎ 43 54 30 06
- 🕑 Daily, Oct–Mar 10–4:30; Apr–Sep 9:30–6
- Ⓜ Cité, Châtelet
- 🚌 21, 38, 85, 96
- ♿ Moderate
- ↔ Sainte-Chapelle (➤ 39)

Top: Salle des Gens d'Armes

"*The ghosts of the victims of the guillotine must surely haunt this stark and gloomy place, a prison and torture chamber for over five centuries, full of macabre mementoes of its grisly past.***"**

Gloom Rising over the Seine in menacing splendour, the turreted Conciergerie was built in 1299–1313 originally to house Philippe-le-Bel's caretaker (concierge) and palace guards, and with Sainte-Chapelle formed part of a royal complex on the Ile de la Cité. The square corner tower displays Paris's first public clock, an ornate masterpiece constructed in 1370 although restored along with the rest of the Gothic interior in the 19th century. Access to the Conciergerie is through the Salle des Gardes, a vaulted stone chamber now plunged into shadow by the embankment outside, which in turn opens on to the vast but equally gloomy Salle des Gens d'Armes. This is thought to be Europe's oldest surviving medieval hall, and it was where the royal household ate their meals. From here a curious spiral staircase leads to the original kitchens with their four gigantic fireplaces.

Victims From 1391 until 1914 the building functioned as a prison and torture chamber, its reputation striking terror into the hearts of thousands. A network of cells, both shared and private, lines the corridor (the rue de Paris) leading to the Galerie des Prisonniers where lawyers, prisoners and visitors once mingled. A staircase goes up to rooms relating the Conciergerie's bloody history (including a list of the guillotine's 2,278 victims); back downstairs are re-creations of Marie-Antoinette's, Danton's and Robespierre's cells, and the Chapelle des Girondins.

CENTRE GEORGES POMPIDOU

"Late opening-hours make an exhibition visit possible between an apéritif and dinner in this still-controversial cultural centre. You can take your pick between the genesis of modernism, an art film or a performance."

High-tech culture More than a mere landmark in the extensive facelift that Paris has undergone in the last 20 years, the high-tech Centre Pompidou (commonly known as Beaubourg) is a hive of constantly changing cultural activity. Contemporary art, architecture, design, photography, theatre, cinema and dance are all represented while the lofty structure itself offers exceptional views over central Paris. Take the transparent escalator tubes for a bird's-eye view of the piazza below where musicians, street artists and portraitists ply their trades to the teeming crowds.

The fountain in nearby Place Igor Stravinsky

Non-stop action The Musée National d'Art Moderne, located on the third and fourth floors, has an exceptional collection which covers most of the 20th century. Above this, the Grande Galerie holds major exhibitions of artists or movements; the next-door cafeteria is great for views but not for food. Temporary shows of contemporary art and/or design are held downstairs in the mezzanine Galeries Nord and Sud which overlook the Forum. Don't miss the art bookshop or the photography gallery tucked beneath the mezzanine.

HIGHLIGHTS

- Design by Richard Rogers, Renzo Piano and Gianfranco Franchini
- Stravinsky fountain
- *The Deep*, Jackson Pollock
- *Phoque*, Brancusi
- *Le magasin*, Ben
- *Bleu II*, Miro
- *Infiltration homogène*, Joseph Beuys
- Gouache cut-outs, Matisse
- *Improvisations* Kandinsky,
- Electronic countdown to year 2000

INFORMATION

- H5/6
- Rue Rambuteau 75004
- 44 78 12 33, 42 77 11 12 (information on daily events)
- Wed–Mon 12noon–10PM, except Sat–Sun 10–10
- Mediocre cafeteria with a view
- Rambuteau, Hôtel-de-Ville
- 38, 47
- RER Line A B, Châtelet-Les Halles
- Excellent
- Very expensive, free on Sun 10–2
- Musée National des Techniques (➤ 51)
- Guided and audio tours to Musée National d'Art Moderne; frequent lectures, concerts, parallel activities, Atelier des Enfants

MARCHÉ AUX PUCES DE ST OUEN

HIGHLIGHTS

- Marché Serpette – antiques, art deco, jewellery
- Marché Paul Bert – antiques, quality bric-à-brac
- Marché Jules Vallès – bric-à-brac, furniture, prints
- Marché Biron – repro furniture, objets d'art
- Marché Vernaison – antiques
- Marché Cambo – paintings, furniture
- Marché Malik – second-hand clothes, accessories, ethnic goods

INFORMATION

- ➕ G1
- ✉ Porte de Clignancourt
- ☎ None
- 🕐 Sat–Mon 7:30–5
- 🍴 Cafés and restaurants on rue des Rosiers
- 🚇 Porte de Clignancourt, Porte de St-Ouen
- 🚌 56, 60, 81, 95
- ♿ Good
- 💰 Free
- ↔ Sacré-Coeur (▶ 33)
- ❓ Beware of pickpockets

"My classic Sunday occupations are hardly original as they often revolve around the Paris flea-markets, of which the crème de la crème is still this one. Nowhere else can you find such a fascinating cross-section of Parisian society."

Duck and banter The approach from the métro to this sprawling 30-ha market is hardly inspiring as it entails bypassing household goods, jeans and shoe-stands before ducking under the *périphérique* flyover and finally entering the fray. Persevere and you may discover an antique gem, a fake, or a second-hand pilot's jacket. Everything and anything is displayed here but all commerce is carried on in the true bantering style of the *faubourgs*, a habit which dates from the late-19th century when the first rag-and-bone men moved in to offer their wares for sale.

Bargain Registered dealers are divided into seven official markets which interconnect through passageways bustling with crowds. Along the fringes are countless hopefuls who set up temporary stands with arrays of mind-boggling diversity ranging from obsolete kitchenware to old juke boxes and cheap junk. Although unashamedly a tourist trap, there is something for everyone here but go early – trading starts at 7:30AM. Bargaining is obligatory and prices are directly related to the weather: high on sunny, crowded days and low under cold wet skies. Stop for lunch in one of the animated bistros along the rue des Rosiers – try the garden setting of Chez la Mère Marie at No 82 (☎ 40 11 90 48). At weekends as many as 150,000 bargain-hunters, tourists and dealers can cram passageways – avoid Sunday afternoons in particular, when the throng reaches claustrophobic proportions and pickpockets abound.

NOTRE-DAME

❝ *'Spectacular' is the word that springs to mind to describe Paris's most extraordinary monument, with its 90m spire and some of the world's best-known flying buttresses. One of my favourite views of it is from the* quais *to the east.* **❞**

Evolution Construction started on this labour of love and faith in 1163 but it was not finished until 1345, so making it transitional in style between Romanesque and Gothic. Since then the cathedral has suffered from pollution, politics, aesthetic trends and religious change. Louis XV declared stained glass outmoded and replaced most of the rose windows with clear glass (the stained glass was later restored), Revolutionary anti-clericalism toppled countless statues and the spire was amputated in 1787. Not least, Viollet-le-Duc, the fervent 19th-century medievalist architect, was let loose on restoration and made radical alterations.

Interior grandeur The gloomy stone interior contains numerous chapels, tombs and statues, as well as the sacristy (south side of choir) where the treasure of Notre-Dame is kept. Climb the towers – 386 steps – for fantastic views and a close-up on the gargoyles. Look closely at the three asymmetrical sculpted portals on the cathedral's façade which once served as a Bible for illiterate worshippers. Then walk round the cathedral for a view of its extravagant flying buttresses.

HIGHLIGHTS

- South rose window
- Porte Rouge
- Portail du cloître
- Sculptures of St Anne
- Treasure of Notre-Dame
- 'Emmanuel' bell
- 1730 organ
- *Pieta*, Nicolas Coustou
- Statue of Notre-Dame de Paris
- Choir stalls

INFORMATION

- ✚ H6
- ✉ Place du Parvis Notre-Dame 75004
- ☎ 42 34 56 10, 43 29 50 40 (crypt)
- ◷ Cathedral, daily 8–7; tower and crypt, Oct–Mar, daily 10–4; Apr–Sep, 10–5:30
- Ⓜ Cité, St-Michel
- 🚌 24, 47
- 🚆 RER Lines B and C, St-Michel
- ♿ Good
- 🎟 Cathedral: free; tower and crypt: moderate
- ↔ Musée National du Moyen-Age, Thermes de Cluny (Musee de Cluny, ➤38); Ile Saint-Louis (➤44)
- ❓ Organ recitals at 5:30PM on Sun.

The southern aspect of Notre-Dame, showing the South rose window (detail above)

ILE SAINT-LOUIS

HIGHLIGHTS

- Church
- Arch of Hôtel de Bretonvilliers
- Hôtel Lambert
- Camille Claudel's home and studio
- Square Barye
- Brasserie de l'Ile
- Pont Marie
- High-water mark, 1 Quai d'Anjou
- Helena Rubinstein's home

INFORMATION

- ✚ H/J 6/7
- 🍴 Sunny terrace of La Brasserie de l'Ile
- Ⓜ Pont Marie, Sully-Morland
- 🚌 67, 86, 87
- ♿ Good
- ↔ Notre-Dame (▶43)

"Floating mid-Seine is this fascinating residential island, a living museum of 17th-century architecture and also a popular tourist haunt. Join the crowds and spot an illustrious resident but above all indulge in the island's own ice-cream.**"**

History Once a marshy swamp, the Ile Saint-Louis was transformed into an elegant residential area in the 17th century, when it was joined to the

Courtyard, Quai de Bourbon

Ile de la Cité. Today, six bridges join it to the Rive Droite and the Rive Gauche but nevertheless it still maintains a spirit of its own, and residents brazenly declare that its food-shops are unsurpassable. Cutting across it lengthwise, the rue Saint-Louis-en-l'Ile is lined with up-market groceries, arts and craft shops and a plethora of restaurants and is also home to a church begun by Le Vau in 1664. Sidestreets are mainly residential.

Hashish On the northeast side, the Quai d'Anjou has a rich past. Former residents include the architect Le Vau himself (No 3), Honoré Daumier (No 9), Baudelaire, and Théophile Gautier who, at No 17, animated his Club des Haschichins. Commemorative plaques to the famous pepper the façades of the island's harmonious town houses and the river level paths offer quintessential Parisian views, romantic trysts, and summer sunbathing. Before leaving, make sure you try a Berthillon ice-cream, reputedly the best in the world!

INSTITUT DU MONDE ARABE

"It is difficult to miss this gleaming, ultra-contemporary building as you cross the Seine. Although I find it limited, the museum's collection nevertheless offers a sleekly presented introduction to the brilliance of Islamic civilisation."

Arab inspiration Clean lines, aluminium walls and glass are the hallmarks of Jean Nouvel's design for the Arab Institute, which was inaugurated in 1980 to foster cultural exchange between Islamic countries and the West. Innovative features include high-speed transparent lifts, a system of high-tech metal screens on the south elevation which filter light entering the Institute and were inspired by the *musharabia*, (carved wooden screens) on traditional Arab buildings, and an enclosed courtyard achieved by splitting the Institute in two. The Institute's facilities comprise a museum, library, exhibition halls, lecture and concert halls, and an elegant roof-top restaurant and terrace café boasting spectacular views across the Seine and pricey but delicious Lebanese hors d'oeuvres.

Museum First take the lift to the 9th floor for sweeping views across the Ile Saint-Louis and northeastern Paris, then go down to the museum on the 7th floor. Here, finely crafted metalwork, ceramics, textiles, carpets and calligraphy reflect the exceptional talents of Islamic civilisation although the collection remains small in relation to its ambitious setting. Temporary exhibitions are often of a high quality and cover both historical and contemporary themes. There is an audio-visual centre in the basement with thousands of slides, photographs, films and sound recordings. Other research facilities include current news broadcasts from all over the Arab world.

HIGHLIGHTS

- Light screens
- Astrolabes in museum
- Statue of Amma'alay
- Head of sun god
- Rope and palm-fibre sandal
- Sultan Selim III's Koran
- Miniature of Emperor Aurengzeb
- Indian glass vase
- Egyptian child's tunic
- Hors d'oeuvres at Fakhr El Dine restaurant

INFORMATION

- ✚ J7
- ✉ 1 rue des Fossés Saint-Bernard 75005
- ☎ 40 51 38 38; restaurant 46 33 47 70
- 🕐 Tue–Sun 10–6
- 🍴 Gourmet Arab restaurant/tea-room, convivial snack bar
- Ⓜ Jussieu, Cardinal Lemoine
- 🚌 24, 63, 67, 86, 87, 89
- ♿ Excellent
- Moderate
- ↔ Ile Saint-Louis (➤44); Arènes de Lutèce (➤59)
- ❓ Occasional Arab music, films, and plays

MUSÉE CARNAVALET

HIGHLIGHTS

- Statue of Louis XIV
- Façade sculptures on Hôtel Carnavalet
- Lebrun's ceiling painting,
- *Destruction of the Bastille*, Hubert Robert
- Bastille prison keys
- Le Sueur's comic-strip
- Proust's bedroom
- Ballroom from Hôtel de Wendel
- Napoleon's picnic-case

INFORMATION

- J6
- 23 rue de Sévigné 75003
- 42 72 21 13
- Tue–Sat 10–5:40
- Saint-Paul
- 29, 96
- Excellent
- Moderate
- Place des Vosges (▶47); Musée Picasso (▶51)
- Photography exhibitions

"There is no better museum than this to plunge you into the history of Paris, and its renovated mansion setting is hard to beat. Period rooms, artefacts, documents, paintings and objets d'art combine to swing you through the city's turbulent past."

Ornamental excess Two adjoining 16th- and 17th-century town houses house this captivating collection. Entrance is through the superb courtyard of the Hôtel Carnavalet (1548), once the home of the celebrated writer Madame de Sévigné. Here attention focuses on the Roman period, the Middle Ages, the Renaissance and the heights of decorative excess reached under Louis XIV, Louis XV and Louis XVI. Some of the richly painted and sculpted interiors are original to the building; others, such as the wood-panelling from the Hôtel Colbert de Villacerf and Brunetti's *trompe-l'oeil* staircase paintings, have been brought in.

Revolution to the present Next door, the smartly renovated Hôtel Le Peletier de Saint-Fargeau (1690) exhibits some remarkable objects from the Revolution – a period when anything and everything was emblazoned with slogans – and continues with Napoleon I's reign, the Restoration, the Second Empire, the Commune and finally the Belle Epoque. Illustrious figures such as Robespierre or Madame Le Récamier come to life within their chronological context. The collection ends at the early

20th century with some remarkable reconstructions of interiors, and paintings by Utrillo, Signac, Marquet and Foujita.

PLACE DES VOSGES

"Paris's best-preserved square connects the quarters of the Marais and the Bastille. I always marvel at its architectural unity, and love to stroll under its arcades now animated by outdoor restaurants and window-shoppers."

Place Royale Ever since the square was inaugurated in 1612 with a spectacular fireworks display, countless luminaries have chosen to live in the red-brick houses overlooking the central garden of plane trees. Before that, the square was the site of a royal palace, the Palais des Tournelles (1407), which was later abandoned and demolished by Catherine de Médicis in 1559 when her husband Henri II died in a tournament. The arcaded façades were commissioned by the enlightened Henri IV, who incorporated two royal pavilions at the centre of the north and south sides of the square and named it 'Place Royale'.

Celebrities After the Revolution the square was renamed Place des Vosges in honour of the first French district to pay its new taxes. The first example of planned development in the history of Paris, these 36 town houses (nine on each side and still intact after four centuries) with their steep-pitched roofs surround a formal garden laid out with gravel paths and fountains. The elegant symmetry of the houses has always attracted a string of celebrities. Princesses, official mistresses, Cardinal Richelieu, the Duc de Sully, Victor Hugo (his house is now a museum), Théophile Gautier and more recently the late painter Francis Bacon, Beaubourg's architect Richard Rogers and former Minister of Culture, Jack Lang, have all lived here. Upmarket shops and chic art galleries, with prices to match and perfect for window-gazing, line its arcades.

HIGHLIGHTS

- Pavillon du Roi
- Statue of Louis XIII
- Hôtel de Coulanges
- No 6, Maison Victor Hugo
- No 21, residence of Cardinal Richelieu
- Archaeological finds at No 18
- Door-knockers
- *Trompe-l'oeil* bricks
- Auvergne sausages at Ma Bourgogne restaurant

INFORMATION

- ✚ J6
- ✉ Place des Vosges 75004
- 🚇 Bastille, Chemin-Vert, St-Paul
- 🚌 29, 96
- ♿ Good
- 🎟 Free
- ↔ Hôtel de Sully (►17); Musée Carnavalet (►46)

47

PÈRE LACHAISE CEMETERY

HIGHLIGHTS

- Oscar Wilde's tomb
- Edith Piaf's tomb
- Chopin's tomb
- Marcel Proust's tomb
- Mur des Fédérés
- Delacroix's tomb
- Tomb of Victor Hugo's family
- Baron Haussmann's tomb
- Molière's tomb
- Jim Morrison's tomb

INFORMATION

- L/M 5/6
- Boulevard de Ménilmontant 75020
- 43 70 70 33
- Oct–Mar, 8–5:30; Apr–Sep, Mon–Fri 8–6, Sat 8:30–5:30/6, Sun 9–5:30/6
- Père-Lachaise
- 61, 69
- Free

❝*If you think cemeteries are lugubrious, then I recommend a visit to Père Lachaise to change your mind. A plethora of tomb designs, shady trees and twisting paths combine to create a peaceful setting that has become a popular park.***❞**

Pilgrimage Up in the *faubourgs* of Ménilmontant this landscaped hillside is now a favourite haunt for rock-fans, Piaf-fans, lovers of poetry, literature, music and history. Since its creation in 1803 this vast cemetery has seen hundreds of the famous and illustrious buried or cremated within its precincts and a walk around its labyrinthine expanse presents a microcosm of French socio-cultural history. Pick up a plan at the entrance or the kiosk by the metro, then set off on this Parisian path of the holy grail to track down your heroes.

Incumbents The cemetery was created in 1803 on land once owned by Louis XIV's confessor, Father La Chaise. It was the site of the Communards' tragic last stand in 1871, when the 147 survivors of a night-long fight met their bloody end in front of a government firing-squad and were thrown into a communal grave, now commemorated by the Mur des Fédérés in the eastern corner. A sombre reminder of the victims of World War II are the memorials to those who died in the Nazi concentration camps. Paths meander past striking funerary monuments and the graves of such well-known figures as the star-crossed medieval lovers Abelard and Héloïse, painters Delacroix and Modigliani, actress Sarah Bernhardt, composers Poulenc and Bizet, and writers Balzac and Colette. Crowds of rock fans throng round Doors singer Jim Morrison's tomb, whose death in Paris in 1971 is still a mystery.

PARIS's
best

Museums & Galleries	*50–51*
Places of Worship	*52*
Cult Cafés	*53*
20th-Century Architecture	*54*
Bridges	*55*
Green Spaces	*56*
Views	*57*
Children's Activities	*58*
Free Attractions	*59*
Intriguing Streets	*60*

MUSEUMS & GALLERIES

Other museums

If you are hooked on the intimate atmosphere of one-man museums, then head for the former home-studio of sculptor Antoine Bourdelle, recently renovated by top architect Christian de Portzamparc ✉ 18 rue Antoine Bourdelle, 75014 🚇 Falguière.

Other jewels include the Maison Victor Hugo (►47), the Musée Delacroix (►60), the Musée Hébert (►60), and the Maison de Balzac (47 rue Raynouard 75016 🚇 Passy).

Visit the Musée d'Art Moderne for modern and contemporary paintings and sculpture

See TOP 25 sights for
CENTRE POMPIDOU ►41
GALERIE DU JEU DE PAUME, ORANGERIE ►30
LOUVRE ►35
MUSÉE DE L'ARMÉE ►28
MUSÉE DES ARTS DÉCORATIFS ►34
MUSÉE CARNAVALET ►46
MUSÉE DE L'HOMME, MUSÉE DES MONUMENTS FRANÇAIS ►25
MUSÉE MARMOTTAN ►24
MUSÉE NATIONALE DU MOYEN-AGE, THERMES DE CLUNY (MUSÉE DE CLUNY) ►38
MUSÉE D'ORSAY ►31
MUSÉE RODIN ►29
PETIT PALAIS, GRAND PALAIS ►27

CITÉ DES SCIENCES ET DE L'INDUSTRIE

Vast, enthralling display covering the earth, universe, life, communications, natural resources, technology and industry. Temporary exhibitions, planetarium, children's section and THX cinema, La Géode.
🚼 L2 ✉ 30 Avenue Corentin Cariou 75019 ☎ 36 68 29 30 🕐 Wed–Mon 10–6, except Sun 10–7 🍴 Cafés in park 🚇 Porte de la Villette 💷 Very expensive

MUSÉE D'ART MODERNE DE LA VILLE DE PARIS

Dufy's mural *La Fée Electricité*, Matisse's *La Danse* and a solid collection of the early moderns offer a parallel to exhibitions of the contemporary avant-garde.
🚼 D5 ✉ 11 Avenue du Président Wilson 75016 ☎ 53 67 40 00 🕐 Tue–Fri 10–5:30, Wed 10–8:30, Sat–Sun 10–7 🍴 Cafeteria 🚇 Iéna, Alma-Marceau 💷 Expensive

MUSÉE DES ARTS ASIATIQUES-GUIMET

Inspiring Buddhas, Hindu gods, mandalas and Mogul miniatures. For Chinese and Japanese works see annexe at 19 Avenue d'Iéna.
🚼 D5 ✉ 6 Place d'Iéna 75116 ☎ 47 23 61 65 🕐 Wed–Mon 9:45–6 🍴 None 🚇 Iéna 💷 Moderate

MUSÉE GUSTAVE MOREAU

A rare one-man museum dedicated to the Symbolist painter (teacher of Matisse and

Rouault) in his former home-studio. Atmospheric paintings, watercolours and drawings.

✚ G4 ✉ 14 rue de la Rochefoucauld 75009 ☎ 48 74 38 50 ⏰ Wed–Mon 10–12:45/2–5:15, except Mon & Wed 11–5:15. 🍽 None 🚇 Trinité 🚹 Moderate

MUSÉE DES LUNETTES ET LORGNETTES DE JADIS

Eccentric display of 3,000 types of spectacles, binoculars and monocles, including some Eskimo designs, amassed by an optician.

✚ F5 ✉ 380 rue Saint-Honoré 75001 ☎ 40 20 06 98 ⏰ Tue–Sat 10–12/3–6. Closed Aug 🍽 None 🚇 Concorde, Tuileries 🚹 Moderate

MUSÉE NATIONAL DES ARTS AFRICAINS ET OCÉANIENS

Fascinating artefacts from the Pacific, Africa and Maghreb, extending to Australian aboriginal art. Sculptures, textiles, jewellery, and masks. Kids love the aquariums and the building (1931) is stunning.

✚ M8 ✉ 293 Ave Daumesnil 75012 ☎ 44 74 84 80 ⏰ Wed–Mon 10–5:30; Sat–Sun 10–6 🍽 None 🚇 Porte Dorée 🚹 Moderate

MUSEUM NATIONAL D'HISTOIRE NATURELLE

Spectacular displays of comparative anatomy, paleontology and mineralogy. Interesting temporary exhibitions and botanic gardens (1635).

✚ J8 ✉ 57 rue Cuvier 75005 ☎ 40 79 30 00 ⏰ Wed–Mon 10–5; Thu 10–10, and Entomology 1–5 🍽 None 🚇 Monge, Gare d'Austeritz 🚹 Expensive, reduced in morning

MUSÉE NATIONAL DES TECHNIQUES

An eccentric museum where art meets science through antique clocks, glass, vintage cars, optics and mechanical toys. Undergoing massive renovation, some parts closed until 1996.

✚ J5 ✉ 292 rue Saint-Martin 75003 ☎ 40 27 23 31 ⏰ Tue–Sun 10–5:30 🍽 None 🚇 Arts et Métiers, Réaumur-Sébastopol 🚹 Moderate

MUSÉE PICASSO

Massive collection of Picasso's paintings, sculptures, drawings and ceramics in a beautifully renovated 17th-century mansion. Fixtures by Diego Giacometti and some works by Picasso's contemporaries.

✚ J6 ✉ Hôtel Salé, 5 rue de Thorigny 75003 ☎ 42 71 25 21 ⏰ Wed–Mon 9:30–5:30 🍽 None 🚇 Chemin Vert 🚌 29 🚹 Moderate

Grand Nu au Fauteuil Rouge *(1929)*, in the Picasso Museum

Musée Picasso

The contents of the Musée Picasso – no fewer than 200 paintings, 158 sculptures and 3,000 drawings – were acquired by France in lieu of death duties. The process of evaluating his vast estate was no simple task as he had the annoying habit of moving château once the rooms were filled with his prodigious works. Eleven years of cataloguing followed by legal wrangling with his heirs finally produced this superb selection, one quarter of his collection.

51

PLACES OF WORSHIP

St-Etienne-du-Mont

St-Germain-des-Prés

The first church of St-Germain-des-Prés was erected in the 6th century in the middle of fields (*les prés*). From the 8th century the abbey was part of a Benedictine monastery but was destroyed by the Normans, after which the present church was built. The abbey was surrounded by a fortified wall and adjoined a Bishop's palace, but this eventually made way for housing in the late 17th century.

> See **TOP 25 sights** for
> **SACRÉ-COEUR** ➤33
> **SAINTE-CHAPELLE** ➤39
> **NOTRE-DAME** ➤43

EGLISE SAINT-ETIENNE-DU-MONT
Bizarre architectural combination of Gothic, Renaissance and classical dating from 15th century. Unique carved rood-screen arching over the nave.
✚ H7 ✉ Place Ste Genevieve 75005 🚇 Cardinal Lemoine

EGLISE DE SAINT-EUSTACHE
Renaissance in detail and decoration but medieval in general design. Frequent organ recitals.
✚ H5 ✉ Rue Rambuteau 75001 🚇 Les Halles

EGLISE DE SAINT-GERMAIN-DES-PRÉS
Paris's oldest abbey dates from the 10th century, preserves 12th-century flying buttresses, an original tower and choir. Regular organ recitals.
✚ G6 ✉ Place Saint-Germain-des-Prés 75006 🚇 Saint-Germain-des-Prés

EGLISE DE SAINT-MERRI
Superb example of Flamboyant Gothic though not completed until 1612. Renaissance stained glass, murals, impressive organ loft and Paris's oldest bell (1331). Concerts are held regularly.
✚ H6 ✉ 78 rue Saint-Martin 75003 🚇 Hôtel-de-Ville

EGLISE DE SAINT-SÉVERIN
Rebuilt in 13th–16th centuries on site of 12th-century oratory. Impressive double ambulatory, palm-tree vaulting and Chapelle Mansart. Some stained glass originated at Saint-Germain-des-Prés (late 14th century).
✚ H6 ✉ 1 rue des Prêtres Saint-Séverin 75005 🚇 Saint-Michel

EGLISE DE SAINT-SULPICE
Construction started in 1646 and ended 134 years later, producing asymmetrical towers and very mixed styles. Note Delacroix's murals in the first chapel on the right, France's largest organ, and statues by Bouchardon.
✚ G7 ✉ Place Saint-Sulpice 75006 🕐 7:30–7:30 🚇 Saint-Sulpice

LA MOSQUÉE
Startling Moorish construction completed in 1926. Richly decorated interior, patio and arcaded garden. Hammam and mint-tea.
✚ J8 ✉ Place du Puits-de-l'Ermite 75005 ☎ 45 35 97 33 🕐 Guided tour 9–12/2–6. Closed Fri 🍴 Tea-room 🚇 Monge 💰 Cheap

CULT CAFÉS

LES DEUX MAGOTS
Some 25 whisky brands, a good concentration of tourists and the literary shades of Mallarmé, André Breton and Hemingway. Strategic spot for street-artists.
✚ G6 ✉ 6 Place St-Germain-des-Prés 75006 ☎ 45 48 55 25 🕐 Daily 7:30AM–2AM Ⓜ St-Germain-des-Prés

CAFÉ BEAUBOURG
Opposite Beaubourg, a favourite with artists, critics and book-eating poseurs. Discreet tables in spacious setting designed by Christian de Portzamparc. A good winter retreat.
✚ H6 ✉ 100 rue Saint-Martin 75004 ☎ 48 87 89 98 🕐 Daily 8AM–2AM Ⓜ Hôtel-de-Ville

Les Deux Magots, in Place St-Germain-des-Prés

LA CLOSERIE DES LILAS
Hot spot of history's makers and shakers, including Lenin, Trotsky, Verlaine and James Joyce.
✚ G8 ✉ 171 Boulevard du Montparnasse 75006 ☎ 43 26 70 50 🕐 daily 11AM–1:30AM Ⓜ Vavin/Raspail

CAFÉ DE FLORE
Haunted by ghosts of existentialists Sartre and De Beauvoir who held court here during the Occupation. Wildly overpriced but great people-watching.
✚ G6 ✉ 172 Boulevard St-Germain ☎ 45 48 55 26 🕐 Daily 7:45AM–1:30AM Ⓜ St-Germain-des-Prés

CAFÉ MARLY
The latest in fashionable watering-holes. Elegance assured overlooking Louvre pyramid, and by Olivier Gagnère's intelligent decoration.
✚ G5 ✉ Cour Napoléon, 93 rue de Rivoli 75001 ☎ 49 26 06 60 🕐 Daily 8AM–2AM Ⓜ Palais-Royal/Musée du Louvre

CAFÉ DE LA PAIX
Excessively mid-19th century décor designed by Charles Garnier. Over-the-top setting. Touristy.
✚ G4 ✉ 12 Boulevard des Capucines 75009 ☎ 40 07 30 20 🕐 Daily 10AM–1AM Ⓜ Opéra

LA PALETTE
Firmly established Left Bank arty bar/café. Run with an iron glove by bearded Jean-François, not to be trifled with. Wonderful tree-shaded terrace in summer.
✚ G6 ✉ 43 rue de Seine 75006 ☎ 43 26 84 87 🕐 Mon–Sat 8AM–2AM. Closed Aug Ⓜ Odéon.

The croissant

As you sit over your morning *café au lait* chewing a croissant, meditate on the origins of this quintessential French product. It was invented when Vienna was besieged by the Turks in 1683. A baker heard underground noises and informed the authorities, who found the enemy tunnelling away into the city. The baker's reward was permission to produce pastries – so he created one in the form of the Islamic crescent.

20TH-CENTURY ARCHITECTURE

See TOP 25 sights for
CENTRE GEORGES POMPIDOU ➤41
INSTITUT DU MONDE ARABE ➤45

Grands projets

President Mitterrand is responsible for many of Paris's late 20th-century monuments. For over a decade cranes groaned as the State's *grands projets* emerged from their foundations. Intellectual criteria often came before functional considerations and consequently not all monuments operate successfully. The Louvre renovation, topped by I M Pei's pyramid, is a notable exception.

BIBLIOTHÈQUE DE FRANCE
Mitterrand's last pet *grand projet*. Dominique Perrault's symbolic design has been dogged by technical and functional problems so inauguration delayed until early 1997.
➕ K8 ✉ 9 Boulevard Vincent Auriol 75013 ☎ 44 23 03 70 🕐 Tours of site Sun, 10–4 every half-hour 🍴 None 🚇 Quai de la Gare

CITÉ DE LA MUSIQUE
Finally completed in 1995 after 16 years of procrastination and political *volte faces*. Monumental design in white stone by Christian de Portzamparc houses a music school, concert hall and museum of music.
➕ L2 ✉ Parc de la Villette ☎ 44 84 45 00 🕐 Wed–Sun 12noon–6 🍴 Café 🚇 Porte de Pantin

LA GRANDE ARCHE
A marble window on the world designed by Otto Von Spreckelsen and completed for the 1989 Bicentenary. Take the vertiginous outside lift to the top for views along Le Nôtre's historical axis to the Louvre.
✉ 1 Parvis de La Défense ☎ 49 07 27 27 🕐 Oct–Mar, Mon–Fri 9–6; Apr–Sep, Mon–Fri 9–7, Sat–Sun 9–8 🚇 La Défense
🎫 Expensive

The Grande Arche at La Defense

HOUSE IN RUE VAVIN
Innovative building faced in blue and white ceramic with stepped balconies. Designed by Henri Sauvage in 1925 as an early attempt at a self-contained unit.
➕ G7 ✉ 26 rue Vavin 75006 🚇 Vavin

MAISON DU VERRE
Designed in art-deco style by Pierre Chareau in 1932. Astonishing use of glass.
➕ G6 ✉ 31 rue Saint-Guillaume 75006 🚇 Rue du Bac

PORTE DAUPHINE
The best remaining example (1902) of Hector Guimard's art-nouveau métro entrances with a glass canopy and writhing sculptural structures.
➕ C4 ✉ Avenue Bugeaud 75016 🚇 Porte Dauphine

RUE MALLET-STEVENS
Tiny cul-de-sac housing major symbols of 'cubist' architecture (1927) by Robert Mallet-Stevens. Stark, purist lines and volumes continue at Le Corbusier's nearby Villa La Roche (1923), now a Foundation.
➕ B6 ✉ Rue Mallet-Stevens, off rue du Dr Blanche 75016 🚇 Jasmin

BRIDGES

PONT ALEXANDRE III
Paris's most ornate bridge, rich in gilded cupids and elaborate lamps. Built for 1900 Exposition Universelle and dedicated to new Franco-Russian alliance – foundation stone was laid by Tsar Alexander III.
⊞ E5 🚇 Invalides

PONT DE L'ALMA
Originally built in 1856 to commemorate victory over Russians in Crimean War. Replaced in 1974 but the Zouave soldier remains, one of four original statues, now acting as a high-water marker.
⊞ E5 🚇 Alma-Marceau

PONT DES ARTS
The pedestrian bridge of 1804 was replaced in 1985 by an iron structure of seven steel arches crossed by resonant wooden planks. Favourite spot for impromptu parties, buskers and commercial artists.
⊞ G6 🚇 Louvre

PONT DE BIR-HAKEIM
Paris's double-decker bridge, best experienced by rattling over it in métro. Built 1903–5 with metal columns in art-nouveau style designed by Formigé.
⊞ D6 🚇 Bir-Hakeim, Passy

PONT MARIE
Named after the Ile Saint-Louis property developer, built in 1635. Once lined with four-storey houses – some later partly destroyed by floods and others demolished in 1788.
⊞ J6 🚇 Pont-Marie

PONT NEUF
Built 1578–1604, Paris's oldest bridge ironically bears the name of 'new bridge'. The innovative, houseless design was highly controversial at the time. In 1985 it was 'wrapped' by land-artist Christo.
⊞ G/H6 🚇 Pont-Neuf

PONT ROYAL
Five classical arches join the Tuileries with the Faubourg Saint-Germain area. Built in 1689 by Gabriel to Mansart's design, once frequently used for major Parisian festivities and fireworks.
⊞ G6 🚇 Palais Royal/Musée du Louvre

36 bridges

The Paris motto *Fluctuat nec mergitur* (it floats but it never sinks) did not always hold true for its bridges. For centuries there were only two, linking the Ile de la Cité north and south. Subsequent wooden bridges sank without trace after floods, fires or river-craft collisions so the construction of the stone Pont Neuf marked a real advance. The city's 36th bridge, Pont Charles-de-Gaulle, now spans the Seine between the Bibliothèque de France and Bercy.

Pont Alexandre III

55

GREEN SPACES

Parc Monceau

Parc de bagatelle

On the west side of the Bois de Boulogne is the Parc de Bagatelle. Its mini-château, built in 1775, was sold in 1870 to Englishman Richard Wallace, who added further pavilions and terraces. About 700 varieties of roses bloom here and its open-air restaurant offers a romantic summer-evening setting.

Jardin des Serres d'Auteuil

Off the tourist beat, with striking late-19th century tropical greenhouses. Terrace wall adorned with sculpted masks from Rodin's studio.

🚻 A7

✉ 3 Avenue de la Porte
d'Auteuil 75016

☎ 40 71 74 00

🕐 Daily 10–5

🚇 Porte d'Auteuil

BOIS DE BOULOGNE

An area of 845ha, 35km of paths, 150,000 trees and 300,000 bushes and endless distractions from boating to clay-pigeon-shooting or gastronomy.

🚻 A/B 4/6 🕐 Permanently open 🍴 Cafés, restaurants 🚇 Porte Dauphine, Porte d'Auteuil

JARDIN DES TUILERIES

Laid out in 1564, later radically formalised by Le Nôtre. Now replanted to match adjoining Louvre. Maillol's statues rest in the shade of chestnut trees.

🚻 F/G5 ✉ Rue de Rivoli 75001 ☎ None 🕐 Daily dawn–dusk 🍴 Open-air cafés 🚇 Tuileries 🎫 Free

PARC ANDRÉ-CITROËN

A cool futurist park divided into specialist gardens, landscaped in 1980s on site of former Citroën factory.

🚻 C8 ✉ Rue Balard, rue Leblanc, 75015 ☎ 40 71 76 00 🕐 Daily, Oct–Mar 9–6; Apr–Sep 9AM–10PM 🚇 Balard

PARC MONCEAU

Classic park planted in 1783 by Thomas Blaikie by order of the Duc d'Orléans. Picturesque *faux* ruins, statues and Ledoux's rotunda create timeless setting.

🚻 E3 ✉ Boulevard de Courcelles 75008 ☎ 42 27 08 64 🕐 Daily, Oct–Mar 7AM–8PM; Apr–Sep 7AM–10PM 🚇 Monceau

PARC MONTSOURIS

A Haussmann creation designed on English models with copses and serpentine paths. Small lake with swans, waterfall and grotto. Summer bandstand.

🚻 G10 ✉ Avenue Reille/Boulevard Jourdan 75014 🕐 Oct–Mar, 8:30–6; Apr–Sep, 8:30AM–10PM 🍴 Restaurant 🚇 RER Line B Cité Universitaire 🎫 Free

VIEWS

Don't forget superlative panoramas from
SACRÉ-COEUR ➤ 33
EIFFEL TOWER ➤ 26
CENTRE POMPIDOU ➤ 41
NOTRE-DAME ➤ 43
INSTITUT DU MONDE ARABE ➤ 45
LA GRANDE ARCHE ➤ 54

ARC DE TRIOMPHE
At the hub of Haussmann's web of 12 avenues, the ultimate symbol of Napoleon's military pretensions and might. Video projections.
🔶 D4 ✉ Place de l'Etoile, 75008 ☎ 43 80 31 31 🕐 Daily, Oct–Mar 10–5; Apr–Sep 9:30–6, Fri until 9:30PM 🚇 Charles-de-Gaulle-Etoile 💲 Expensive

LA GRANDE ROUE
Dizzy, whirling views of the Tuileries and Louvre from the Big Wheel at the heart of the fun-fair.
🔶 G5 ✉ Rue de Rivoli 75001 🕐 Late Jun–late Aug, Sun–Fri 12noon–11:45, Sat 12noon–12:45PM 🚇 Tuileries 💲 Moderate

LA SAMARITAINE
From 10th floor at Magasin 2, a spectacular close-up on the city's Left Bank monuments. Lunch in open air on 9th floor or alternatively dine in newly designed splendour at 5th-floor restaurant, Toupary.
(☎ 40 41 29 29 🕐 Mon–Sat 8PM–1AM) 🔶 H6 ✉ Rue de la Monnaie 75001 ☎ 40 41 20 20 🕐 Easter–Oct, Mon–Sat 9.30–7, except Thu 9:30AM–10PM 🍴 Cafeteria, restaurant 🚇 Pont-Neuf 💲 Free

SQUARE DU VERT GALANT
Quintessential river-level view of bridges and Louvre, shaded by willows and stunning at sunset.
🔶 G6 ✉ Place du Pont-Neuf 75001 ☎ None 🕐 Daily, Oct–Mar 9–5:30; Apr–Sep 9AM–10PM 🍴 None 🚇 Pont-Neuf

TOUR MONTPARNASSE
The 59th floor of this 209m modern tower looming over Montparnasse offers sweeping vistas. Films on Paris are screened on the 56th floor.
🔶 F8 ✉ 33 Avenue du Maine 75015 ☎ 45 38 52 56 🕐 Daily 9:30AM–10:30PM, Apr–Sep until 11:30PM 🍴 Bar, restaurant 🚇 Montparnasse-Bienvenue 💲 Expensive

Pollution over Paris

The promised views over Paris do not always materialise as the capital is often hidden in haze trapped by the saucer-like shape of the Ile de France. Measures taken since the mid-1970s have helped: in one decade industrial pollution was reduced by 50% and the replacement of coal by nuclear energy and gas further cleared the air. However carbon-monoxide levels (from traffic exhaust) often exceed EU norms.

The view from Tour Montparnasse

CHILDREN'S ACTIVITIES

Le guignol

A juvenile crowd-puller going back to the early 19th century is the *guignol*, an open-air puppet show held in several Parisian parks. Shows are staged on Wednesday, weekends and during school holidays. Find them in parks such as the Luxembourg, Montsouris, Buttes Chaumont, Champ-de-Mars or the Jardin d'Acclimatation. Winter months see most of them moving under cover.

La Géode, Parc de la Villette

DISNEYLAND PARIS
Disney's mega-resort struggles with financial problems but survives. Kids' paradise.
✉ 77777 Marne-la-Vallée ☎ 64 74 30 00, 60 30 60 30 (recorded information) ⏰ 10–6 🍴 Cafés, restaurants 🚇 RER Line A Marne-la-Vallée-Chessy ⚡ Very expensive

CIRQUE ALEXIS GRÜSS
Perennial favourite with a new high-tech circus show.
➕ F10 ✉ 21 Avenue de la porte de Châtillon 75014 ☎ 40 36 08 00 ⏰ Shows on Wed, Sat, Sun and public holidays 🚇 Porte d'Orléans ⚡ Very expensive

LA GÉODE
The cinema's hemispherical screen is designed to plunge the spectators into the action with frequent nature and science films. Nearby is Le Cinaxe, a mobile cinema, and the children's activities at the Cité des Sciences (►50).
➕ L2 ✉ 26 Avenue Corentin Cariou 75019 ☎ 36 68 29 30 ⏰ Sessions Tue–Sun 🍴 Cafés in park 🚇 Porte de la Villette ⚡ Very expensive

JARDIN D'ACCLIMATATION
Specially designed part of Bois de Boulogne with minitrain (which leaves from Porte Maillot Wed, Sat, Sun and public holidays), playground, fairground, educational museum, 'enchanted river', circus, zoo and puppet theatre.
➕ B4 ✉ Bois de Boulogne 75016 ☎ 40 67 90 82 ⏰ Daily 10–6 🍴 Café 🚇 Sablons ⚡ Cheap

PARC ASTÉRIX
Some 35km north of Paris, a theme-park dedicated to comic-strip hero, Astérix. Plenty of animation, rides, games and food.
✉ 60128 Plailly ☎ (16)44 62 34 34, (16)36 68 30 10 ⏰ Apr–mid-Oct, Mon–Fri 10–6; Sat–Sun 10–10 🍴 Cafés, restaurants 🚇 RER Line B, Roissy Charles-de-Gaulle ⚡ Very expensive

FREE ATTRACTIONS

ARÈNES DE LUTÈCE
A partly ruined Gallo-Roman amphitheatre now favoured by *boules*-playing retirees. Destroyed in AD 280 but restored early this century.
✚ H7 ✉ Rue des Arènes 75005 🕐 Daily, Oct–Mar 8–5:30; Apr–Mar 8AM–10PM 🍴 None 🚇 Jussieu

DROUOT RICHELIEU
Let yourself be tempted at Paris's main auction rooms. A Persian carpet, a Louis XV commode or a bunch of cutlery may come under the hammer. Auctions start at 2PM.
✚ G4 ✉ 9 rue Drouot 75009 ☎ 48 00 20 20 🕐 Tue–Sun, 11–6. Closed Jul–Aug 🚇 Richelieu-Drouot

JARDIN DU PALAIS-ROYAL
Elegant 18th-century arcades surround this peaceful formal garden and palace (now the Conseil d'Etat and the Ministère de la Culture), redolent of Revolutionary history. Daniel Buren's conceptual striped columns occupy the Cour d'Honneur.
✚ G5 ✉ Place du Palais-Royal 75001 🕐 Daily, Oct–Mar 7:30AM–8:30PM; Apr–Sep 7AM–11pm 🍴 Restaurants, tea-room 🚇 Palais-Royal

MÉMORIAL DE LA DÉPORTATION
In the Ile de la Cité's eastern tip is a starkly designed crypt lined with 200,000 quartz pebbles to commemorate French citizens deported by the Nazis.
✚ H6 ✉ Square de l'Ile de France 75004 🕐 Mon–Fri 8:30–5:30; Sat–Sun 9–5.30 🍴 None 🚇 Cité

PALAIS DE JUSTICE
Follow in the footsteps of lawyers, judges and crooks down echoing corridors, staircases and courtyards and, if your French is up to it, sit in on a court case. This former royal palace took on its present function during the Revolution.
✚ H6 ✉ Boulevard du Palais 75001 ☎ 44 32 50 00 🕐 Mon–Fri 9–6 🍴 None 🚇 Cité

PAVILLON DE L'ARSENAL
Well-conceived exhibitions of urban Paris and a permanent display of its architectural evolution in a strikingly designed space.
✚ J7 ✉ 21 Boulevard Morland 75004 ☎ 42 76 33 97 🕐 Tue–Sat 10:30–6:30; Sun 11–7 🍴 None 🚇 Sully-Morland

Bargain Paris
Nothing comes cheap in this city of light and the *franc fort*. Gastronomy, official culture and history cost money, but browsing at the *bouquinistes* along the Seine, picnicking on the riverbanks, reading in a park, exploring backstreets or spinning hours away for the cost of a coffee on a *terrasse* are some of Paris's bargains.

The Palais Royal

59

INTRIGUING STREETS

Cour de Rohan

This narrow cobbled passage tucked away on the Left Bank, the Cour de Rohan connects rue St-André-des-Arts with Boulevard St-Germain and dates from 1776, though it incorporates a medieval tower. It became a hive of revolutionary activity with Marat printing pamphlets at No 8, Danton installed at No 20 and the anatomy professor Dr Guillotin (conceptor of that 'philanthropic beheading machine') at No 9.

BOULEVARD DE ROCHECHOUART

Teeming with struggling immigrants. Impromptu markets, Tati (the palace of cheap clothes), or seedy sex-shops and an all-pervading aroma of *merguez* and chips.

✚ H3 🚇 Barbès-Rochechouart

FAUBOURG SAINT-HONORÉ

Price-tags and politics cohabit in this street of luxury. See Hermès's imaginative window-dressing or salute the gendarmes in front of the Elysée Palace.

✚ F 4/5 🚇 Madeleine

RUE DU CHERCHE-MIDI

César's sculpture on the rue de Sèvres crossroads marks out this typical Left Bank street, home to the famous Poîlane bakery (No 8) and the Musée Hébert (No 85). Main interest ends at the Boulevard Raspail.

✚ G7 🚇 Saint-Sulpice

RUE JACOB

Antique and interior-decoration shops monopolise this picturesque stretch. Make a 20m detour to the Musée Delacroix on the delightful Place Furstenberg.

✚ G6 🚇 St-Germain-des-Prés

RUE MONSIEUR-LE-PRINCE

An uphill stretch lined with university bookshops, antique and ethnic shops, and a sprinkling of student restaurants. Sections of the medieval city wall are embedded in Nos 41 and 47.

✚ G7 🚇 Odéon

RUE DES ROSIERS

Effervescent street at heart of Paris's Jewish quarter. Kosher butchers and restaurants, the old hammam and Hebrew bookshops rub shoulders with designer boutiques. Quietens considerably on Saturdays.

✚ J6 🚇 St-Paul

RUE VIEILLE-DU-TEMPLE

The pulse of the hip Marais, dense in bars, cafés, boutiques and, further north, the historic Hôtel Amelot-de-Bisseuil (No 47), the Maison J Hérouët, the Hôtel de Rohan (No 87) and the garden of the Musée Picasso.

✚ J6 🚇 St-Paul

PARIS
where to...

STAY   62–65
  Luxury Hotels   62
  Mid-Range Hotels   63
  Budget Accommodation   64–65

EAT   66–73
  Haute Cuisine   66
  Regional French
      Restaurants   67
  Asian Restaurants   68–69
  Italian Restaurants   69
  Arab Restaurants   70
  Brasseries & Bistros   71
  Salons de Thé   72
  Miscellaneous Restaurants   73

SHOP   74–81
  Department Stores   74
  Designer Boutiques   74–75

  Markets   76
  Art & Antiques   77
  Books & Records   78
  Design & Interior   78–79
  Food & Wine   79
  Miscellaneous
      & Offbeat   80–81

BE ENTERTAINED   82–86
  Concert Venues   82
  Jazz Clubs   82–83
  Nightclubs   83
  Bars   84–85
  Special Cinemas   85
  Sporting Venues   86

LUXURY HOTELS

Expect to pay over FFr1000 for a single room in the luxury category.

Le Crillon

Whether you stay at the Ritz, the Crillon, the Meurice, the Bristol or Georges V, all will have their tales to tell, but that of the Crillon is perhaps the most momentous as this family mansion (still 100 per cent French-owned by the Taittingers of champagne fame) managed to survive the Revolution despite having the guillotine on its doorstep. Mary Pickford and Douglas Fairbanks spent their honeymoon here.

LE CRILLON
An old Parisian classic which reeks glamour, history and major investments. Suites are almost the norm here.
➕ F5 ✉ 10 Place de la Concorde 75008 ☎ 44 71 15 00 fax 44 71 15 02 🚇 Concorde

L'HÔTEL
A Parisian legend redolent of Oscar Wilde's last days.Kitsch piano-bar/restaurant and some superbly furnished rooms.
➕ G6 ✉ 13 rue des Beaux Arts 75006 ☎ 43 25 27 22 fax 43 25 64 81 🚇 St Germain

HÔTEL DU JEU DE PAUME
Delightful, refined small hotel carved out of a 17th-century royal tennis court. Tasteful rooms with beams and marble bathrooms, some duplex suites. No restaurant.
➕ J7 ✉ 54 rue Saint-Louis-en-l'Ile 75004 ☎ 43 26 14 18 fax 40 46 02 76 🚇 Pont Marie

HÔTEL LUTETIA
Completely refurbished in art-deco style by Sonia Rykiel in 1989. Avoid the cheaper back rooms. Well-located between St Germain and Montparnasse.
➕ F7 ✉ 45 Boulevard Raspail 75006 ☎ 49 54 46 46 fax 49 54 46 00 🚇 Sèvres-Babylone

HÔTEL MEURICE
Classically ornate luxury, once home to Salvador Dali and before that the Nazi HQ during the Occupation. Now efficiently run by the CIGA group.
➕ G5 ✉ 228 rue de Rivoli 75001 ☎ 44 58 10 10 fax 44 58 10 15/16 🚇 Tuileries

HOTEL MONTALEMBERT
Fashionable Left-Bank hotel with garden-patio, bar and restaurant. Chic contemporary design details, well-appointed rooms. Popular with Americans.
➕ F6 ✉ 3 rue de Montalembert 75007 ☎ 45 48 68 11 fax 42 22 58 19 🚇 Rue du Bac

HÔTEL SAINTE BEUVE
Exclusive establishment between the heart of Montparnasse and the Luxembourg gardens. Period antiques mix happily with modern furnishings. Tasteful and imaginative extras.
➕ G7 ✉ 9 rue Ste-Beuve 75006 ☎ 45 48 20 07 fax 45 48 67 52 🚇 Vavin

HÔTEL SAN RÉGIS
Convenient for the couturiers in Avenue Montaigne. Elaborately decorated but modestly scaled hotel, popular with American show-bizz. Restaurant for hotel residents only.
➕ E5 ✉ 12 rue Jean Goujon 75008 ☎ 44 95 16 16 fax 45 61 05 48 🚇 Alma-Marceau

PAVILLON DE LA REINE
Set back from historic Place des Vosges. Flowery courtyard, tasteful period decoration and chintzy rooms.
➕ J6 ✉ 28 Place des Vosges 75004 ☎ 42 77 96 40 fax 42 77 63 06 🚇 Chemin Vert

MID-RANGE HOTELS

HÔTEL DE L'ABBAYE SAINT GERMAIN

Quaint, historic establishment, a former monastery. Flowery, cobbled courtyard, elegant salons, terraced duplex rooms and friendly staff.

⊞ G7 ✉ 10 rue Cassette 75006 ☎ 45 44 38 11 fax 45 48 07 86 🚇 Saint-Sulpice

HÔTEL D'ANGLETERRE

Former British Embassy. Pretty garden-patio, spacious rooms where Hemingway once stayed. Bar, and piano lounge. Book well ahead.

⊞ G6 ✉ 44 rue Jacob 75006 ☎ 42 60 34 72 fax 42 60 16 93 🚇 St-Germain

HÔTEL BERGÈRE

131-room hotel run by Best Western close to the Grands Boulevards. Reliable though anonymous service.

⊞ H4 ✉ 34 rue Bergère 75009 ☎ 47 70 34 34 fax 47 70 36 36 🚇 Rue Montmartre

HÔTEL DUC DE SAINT-SIMON

Rather pricey but the antique furnishings and picturesque setting just off Boulevard St-Germain justify it. Popular with diplomats. Comfortable rooms, intimate atmosphere. Needs advance booking.

⊞ F6 ✉ 14 rue Saint-Simon 75007 ☎ 45 48 35 66 fax 45 48 68 25 🚇 Rue du Bac

HÔTEL LENOX

Popular with design and fashion world. Chase T S Eliot's ghost and enjoy the restored, stylish 1930s bar. Book well ahead.

⊞ G6 ✉ 9 rue de l'Université 75007 ☎ 42 96 10 95 fax 42 61 52 83 🚇 Rue du Bac

RÉSIDENCE LORD BYRON

Comfortable, classy 31-room hotel just off the Champs-Elysées. Small garden and well-appointed, reasonably priced rooms.

⊞ E4 ✉ 5 rue Châteaubriand 75008 ☎ 43 59 89 98 fax 42 89 46 04 🚇 Georges V

HÔTEL DES MARRONIERS

Named after the chestnut trees that dominate the garden. Obsessively vegetal/floral-based decoration. Oak-beamed rooms, vaulted cellars converted to lounges. Book well ahead

⊞ G6 ✉ 21 rue Jacob 75006 ☎ 43 25 30 60 fax 40 46 83 56 🚇 St-Germain

HÔTEL MOLIÈRE

On quiet street near the Louvre and Opéra. Well-appointed, reasonably priced rooms, and helpful staff.

⊞ G5 ✉ 21 rue Molière 75001 ☎ 42 96 22 01 fax 42 60 48 68 🚇 Pyramides

HÔTEL LA PERLE

Renovated 17th-century building on a quiet street near St Germain. Charming breakfast patio, bar, well-appointed rooms – some with fax and jacuzzi.

⊞ G6 ✉ 14 rue des Canettes, 75006 ☎ 43 29 10 10 fax 46 34 51 04 🚇 Mabillon

A moderately priced hotel will charge FFr500–1000 for a single room.

3-Star rating

All these three-star establishments are obvious favourites with business travellers so it is virtually impossible to find rooms during trade-fair seasons such as May/early June and mid-September/October. In summer many offer discounts as their clientèle shrinks. All rooms are equipped with colour TV, direct-dial phone, private bath or shower-rooms, mini-bar and most with hair-dryer. Air-conditioning is not general but lifts are.

63

BUDGET ACCOMMODATION

You should be able to find a single room in a budget hotel for under FFr500.

Budget hotels

Gone are the heady days when Paris was peppered with atmospheric one-star hotels with their inimitable signs *Eau à tous les étages* (water on every floor). Now there are bath or shower-rooms in every bedroom, and correspondingly higher prices, and smaller rooms. So don't expect to swing cats in budget hotel rooms, but do expect breakfast and receptionists who speak a second language in every hotel with two or more stars.

GRAND HÔTEL MALHER
Recently renovated family hotel with 31 well-equipped rooms and an excellent location in the Marais.

➕ J6 ✉ 5 rue Malher 75004 ☎ 42 72 60 92 fax 42 72 25 37 Ⓜ St-Paul

GRAND HÔTEL DE SUEZ
50-room hotel in central location on busy boulevard. Good value but lacks atmosphere.

➕ H6 ✉ 31 Boulevard St-Michel 75005 ☎ 46 34 08 02 fax 40 51 79 44 Ⓜ Cluny la Sorbonne

HÔTEL ANDRÉ GILL
Charming courtyard setting on quiet side-street close to Pigalle. Renovated rooms, reasonably priced.

➕ G3 ✉ 4 rue André Gill 75018 ☎ 42 62 48 48 fax 42 62 77 92 Ⓜ Pigalle

HÔTEL DU COLLÈGE DE FRANCE
Tranquil 29-roomed establishment near the Sorbonne. Some 6th-floor rooms offer glimpse of Notre Dame.

➕ H7 ✉ 7 rue Thénard 75005 ☎ 43 26 78 36 fax 46 34 58 29 Ⓜ Maubert-Mutualité

HÔTEL ESMERALDA
Very popular doll's-house hotel near Notre Dame. Reasonably priced, book well ahead.

➕ H6 ✉ 4 rue St-Julien-le-Pauvre 75005 ☎ 43 54 19 20 fax 40 51 00 68 Ⓜ St Michel

HÔTEL ISTRIA
Legendary Montparnasse hotel once frequented by Rilke, Duchamp and Man Ray. Twenty-six atmospheric rooms and friendly staff.

➕ G8 ✉ 29 rue Campagne Première 75014 ☎ 43 20 91 82 fax 43 22 48 45 Ⓜ Raspail

HÔTEL JARDIN DES PLANTES
Pretty hotel with good facilities overlooking botanical gardens.

➕ H7 ✉ 5 rue Linné 75005 ☎ 47 07 06 20 fax 47 07 62 74 Ⓜ Jussieu

HÔTEL KENSINGTON
Convenient for the Eiffel Tower and Champ de Mars. An up-market address for a pleasant little hotel with fully renovated rooms.

➕ E6 ✉ 79 Avenue de la Bourdonnais 75007 ☎ 47 05 74 00 fax 47 05 25 81 Ⓜ Ecole-Militaire

HÔTEL LINDBERGH
Modernised hotel on tranquil side-street near busy crossroads and shops of St-Germain. Well-equipped rooms and polyglot staff.

➕ F7 ✉ 5 rue Chomel 75007 ☎ 45 48 35 53 fax 45 49 31 48 Ⓜ Sèvres-Babylone

HÔTEL LION D'OR
Small family hotel with adequately modernised rooms and very helpful staff. Good value for its central location.

➕ G5 ✉ 5 rue de la Sourdière 75001 ☎ 42 60 79 04 fax 42 60 09 14 Ⓜ Tuileries

HÔTEL MICHELET-ODÉON
Reasonable rates and quiet location next to

Théâtre de l'Odéon. No frills, but helpful service.
✚ G7 ✉ 6 Place de l'Odéon 75006 ☎ 46 34 27 80 fax 46 34 55 35 Ⓜ Odéon

HÔTEL DE LA PLACE DES VOSGES

Charming 17th-century townhouse in quiet street close to Place des Vosges. Basic comforts, excellent location.
✚ J6 ✉ 12 rue Birague 75004 ☎ 42 72 60 46 fax 42 72 02 64 Ⓜ Bastille

HÔTEL PRIMA-LEPIC

In cleaner air up the hill of Montmartre, a bright hotel with well-decorated if smallish rooms and a courtyard-style reception area.
✚ G3 ✉ 29 rue Lepic 75018 ☎ 46 06 44 64 fax 46 06 66 11 Ⓜ Abbesses

HÔTEL RÉCAMIER

Flowery wallpaper in this tranquil, friendly little hotel close to St-Germain and Luxembourg gardens.
✚ G7 ✉ 3 bis Place St-Sulpice 75006 ☎ 43 26 04 89 Ⓜ St-Sulpice

HÔTEL DE ROUEN

Very cheap 22-room hotel with surprisingly well-equipped rooms. Central location near Louvre and Palais Royal.
✚ G5 ✉ 42 rue Croix-des-Petits-Champs 75001 ☎ 42 61 38 21 Ⓜ Louvre

HÔTEL DU 7E ART

Cinephile's hotel decorated with movie photos and memorabilia. Great location in the Marais and reasonably priced rooms.

✚ J6 ✉ 20 rue Saint-Paul 75004 ☎ 42 77 04 03 fax 42 77 69 10 Ⓜ St-Paul

HÔTEL SOLFÉRINO

A rare budget hotel in the chic 7th. Antique furniture. Opposite Musée d'Orsay on quiet street. Excellent value.
✚ F6 ✉ 91 rue de Lille 75007 ☎ 47 05 85 54 fax 45 55 51 16 Ⓜ Solférino

HÔTEL DE LA SORBONNE

On quiet side-street near the Sorbonne. Small but comfortable rooms. Well-established and unpretentious.
✚ H7 ✉ 6 rue Victor-Cousin 75005 ☎ 43 54 58 08 fax 40 51 05 18 Ⓜ Cluny

HÔTEL DU VIEUX SAULE

In a quiet street in north of Marais. Modernised, with reasonable facilities.
✚ J5 ✉ 6 rue de Picardie 75003 ☎ 42 72 01 14 fax 40 27 88 21 Ⓜ Filles du Calvaire

SUPER HÔTEL

Near Père Lachaise cemetery. Excellent value, easy transport, comfortable rooms.
✚ M5 ✉ 208 rue des Pyrénées 75020 ☎ 46 36 97 48 fax 46 36 26 10 Ⓜ Gambetta

TIMHÔTEL LE LOUVRE

One of small chain with reliable amenities and reasonably priced rooms. Well-situated for Louvre and Les Halles on quiet street.
✚ G5 ✉ 4 rue Croix des Petits-Champs 75001 ☎ 42 60 34 86 fax 42 60 10 39 Ⓜ Louvre

Bed and breakfast

Bed-and-breakfast systems now exist which fix up visitors with host families. Try Bed and Breakfast 1 ☎ 43 35 11 26 fax 40 47 69 20; France Lodge ☎ 42 46 68 19 fax 42 46 65 61; International Café Couette ☎ 42 94 92 00 fax 42 94 93 12; Accueil France Famille ☎ 45 54 22 39 fax 45 58 43 25. For those who want to stay longer and rent furnished accommodation the best source is the free classified ads magazine 'France-USA Contacts' (FUSAC). It is available at English bookshops and student travel agencies.

HAUTE CUISINE

The restaurants on the following pages are in three price categories:

£££   over FFr300 per person

££   up to FFr300 per person

£   up to FFr120 per person

French mean cuisine

'The only cooks in the civilised world are French. Other races have different interpretations of food. Only the French mean *cuisine* because their qualities – rapidity, decision-making, tact – are used. Who has ever seen a foreigner succeed in making a white sauce?'

– Nestor Roqueplan (1804–70), Editor of *Le Figaro*

Rose-tinted dining

Le Pré Catalan (£££) has an outdoor setting near the rose-gardens of the Parc Bagatelle. Excellent seasonal dishes and exquisite desserts. (Bois de Boulogne, Route de Suresnes 75016, ☎ 45 24 55 58).

LE BRISTOL (£££)

Uniquely elegant 18th-century oval-shaped restaurant, renowned for exquisite seafood and impeccable service.

🔟 E4 ✉ 112 Faubourg St-Honoré 75008 ☎ 42 66 91 45 🕐 Daily 🚇 Miromesnil

LE GRAND VEFOUR (£££)

Superb late 18th-century setting under arcades of Palais Royal, with ghosts of Napoleon, Colette and Sartre. Classic French cuisine. Relatively reasonably-priced lunch menu.

🔟 G5 ✉ 17 rue du Beaujolais 75001 ☎ 42 96 56 27 🕐 Closed Sat–Sun and August 🚇 Palais-Royal/Musée du Louvre

GUY SAVOY (£££)

One of Paris's top young chefs continues to surprise with contrasting flavours and textures. Efficient service and contemporary décor.

🔟 D4 ✉ 18 rue Troyon 75017 ☎ 43 80 40 61 🕐 Closed Sat–Sun 🚇 Charles-de-Gaulle-Etoile

JOËL ROBUCHON (£££)

Temple of Parisian *nouvelle cuisine* in pastel-coloured setting. Book and save well ahead.

🔟 C5 ✉ 59 Ave Raymond Poincaré 75116 ☎ 47 27 12 27 🕐 Closed Sat–Sun, Jul 🚇 Trocadéro

LASSERRE (£££)

A favourite with foreign visitors for impeccable service and cuisine. An extra is the sliding roof.

🔟 E5 ✉ 17 Avenue Franklin-D-Roosevelt 75008 ☎ 43 59 53 43 🕐 Closed all Sun and Mon lunch, Aug 🚇 Franklin-D-Roosevelt

LUCAS-CARTON (£££)

Majorelle's art-nouveau décor is the haunt of the dressy rich and famous. Try the roast pigeon with coriander.

🔟 F5 ✉ 9 Place de la Madeleine 75008 ☎ 42 65 22 90 🕐 Closed Sat–Sun, Aug, 24 Dec–3 Jan 🚇 Madeleine

MICHEL ROSTANG (£££)

Rostang still holds his own in the Parisian gastronomy stakes with interesting combinations, superb cheeses and desserts. Elegant table-settings.

🔟 D3 ✉ 20 rue Rennequin 75017 ☎ 47 63 40 77 🕐 Closed Sun 🚇 Pereire

TAILLEVENT (£££)

Intimate restaurant with a confirmed reputation – advance booking essential. Inventive cuisine – try the curried ravioli snails. Superlative wine-list.

🔟 E4 ✉ 15 rue Lamennais 75008 ☎ 44 95 15 01 🕐 Closed Sat–Sun, Aug, public holidays 🚇 Georges V

LA TOUR D'ARGENT (£££)

Legendary sanctuary of *canard au sang* but lighter dishes do exist. Fabulous view over the Ile Saint-Louis, warm atmosphere and great wine-cellar.

🔟 H7 ✉ 15–17 Quai de la Tournelle 75005 ☎ 43 54 23 31 🕐 Closed Mon 🚇 Maubert-Mutualité

REGIONAL FRENCH RESTAURANTS

AUBERGE BRESSANE (£/££)

Delectable dishes from eastern France in a mock medieval décor. Impressive wine-list of Bordeaux and Burgundies. Excellent-value lunch menus.

E6 ⊠ 16 Avenue de la Motte Picquet 75007 ☎ 47 05 98 37 Closed Sat lunch Latour-Maubourg

LA BARACANE (££)

Tiny, tastefully decorated restaurant whose menu homes in on Gascony and ducks. Reasonably priced though limited choice in set lunch/dinner.

J6 ⊠ 38 rue des Tournelles 75004 ☎ 42 71 43 33 Closed Sat lunch, Sun Bastille

BRASSERIE FLO (££)

Spectacular Alsatian brasserie which dishes up mountains of delicious *choucroute spéciale*. Noisy, popular, chaotic.

H4 ⊠ 7 rue des Petites Ecuries 75010 ☎ 47 70 13 59 Open daily until 1 AM Château d'Eau

LE CAVEAU DU PALAIS (££)

A wonderful old classic, long-time favourite with Yves Montand and Simone Signoret. Homely regional cooking.

G6 ⊠ 17/19 Place Dauphine 75001 ☎ 43 26 04 28 Closed Sat, Sun Pont Neuf

CHEZ BENOIT (£££)

Longstanding favourite, classic regional dishes. Booking advisable.

H5 ⊠ 20 rue St-Martin 75004 ☎ 42 72 25 76 Open daily Rambuteau

LE CLODENIS (££)

Intimate, discreet restaurant which serves aromatic Provençal dishes.

G2 ⊠ 57 rue Caulaincourt 75018 ☎ 46 06 20 26 Closed Sun–Mon Lamarck-Caulaincourt

LE CROQUANT (££)

Reworked landmarks of southwest cuisine. Sublime *confit de canard*.

C8 ⊠ 28 rue Jean-Maridor 75015 ☎ 45 58 50 83 Closed Sun eve, Mon Lourmel

AUX FINS GOURMETS (££)

Somewhat faded 1920s splendour serving copious portions of Basque and Béarnais cuisine.

F6 ⊠ 213 Boulevard St-Germain 75007 ☎ 42 22 06 57 Closed Mon lunch, Sun Rue du Bac

LOUIS LANDES (££)

Warm atmosphere, traditional dishes from the southwest. Monthly dinners round a theme, wine-tastings.

F9 ⊠ 157 Avenue du Maine 75014 ☎ 45 43 08 04 Sat lunch, Sun Mouton-Duvernet

LE SUD (££)

Vibrant colours, plenty of foliage and Provençal specialities such as *boeuf en daube*

C3 ⊠ 91 Boulevard Gouvion-St-Cyr 75017 ☎ 45 74 02 77 Closed Sun Porte Maillot

Alsace and the southwest

Gastronomically speaking, Alsace and the southwest are probably the best represented regions in Paris. Numerous brasseries churn out *choucroute* (sauerkraut), but it is the southwest which carries off the prizes with its variations on goose and duck. Recent research has found that inhabitants of this region have unexpectedly low rates of cardiac disease – despite daily consumption of cholesterol-high *foie gras*.

ASIAN & ITALIAN RESTAURANTS

13th Arrondissement

The Parisian Chinese community is concentrated in Belleville, where it coexists with Arabs and Africans, in the 3rd *arrondissement*, where invisible sweat-shops churn out cheap leather goods, and above all in the 13th *arrondissement* (métros Tolbiac and Porte d'Ivry). Here Chinese New Year is celebrated with dragon parades in late-January to early February. Gastronomically speaking it offers a fantastic array of Indochinese and Chinese restaurants and soup kitchens – all at budget prices.

ASIAN

BHAI BHAI SWEETS(£)
In a dilapidated covered passageway, the hub of Paris's Little India. Not as spicy-hot as it could be, but tasty curries.
✚ H4 ✉ 77 Passage Brady 75010 ☎ 42 46 77 29
◷ Open daily Ⓜ Strasbourg St Denis

CHEZ ROSINE (££)
Orchestrated by charismatic Rosine Ek from Cambodia. Succulent, imaginative dishes. Sophisticated.
✚ G5 ✉ 12 rue du Mont Thabor 75001 ☎ 49 27 09 23
◷ Closed Mon lunch, Sun

CHIENG-MAI (££)
Elegant Thai restaurant. Subtle flavours (fish steamed in banana-leaf, grilled spicy mussels) and charming service.
✚ H7 ✉ 12 rue Frédéric-Sauton 75005 ☎ 43 25 45 45
◷ Closed Sun, part of Aug
Ⓜ Maubert-Mutualité

CHINE ELYSÉES (£)
Off Champs-Elysées, useful for pre- or post-cinema. A rare budget restaurant for the area, with Peking specialities.
✚ E4 ✉ 6 rue du Colisée 75008 ☎ 43 59 83 46
◷ Open daily Ⓜ Franklin-Roosevelt

HAWAÏ (£)
Huge, animated canteen-style restaurant, popular with local Chinese. Generous soups, Southeast Asian specialities.
✚ J10 ✉ 87 Avenue d'Ivry 75013 ☎ 45 86 91 90
◷ Open daily Ⓜ Porte d'Ivry

KAPPA (££)
Family-style Japanese sushi restaurant. Animated, warm atmosphere.
✚ G6 ✉ 6 rue des Ciseaux 75006 ☎ 43 26 33 31
◷ Closed Sun Ⓜ St-Germain-des-Prés

LAO SIAM (£)
Wide selection of Southeast Asian cuisines: giant prawns sautéed in ginger and chives or a whole crab cooked in coconut milk and chilli pepper.
✚ K4 ✉ 49 rue de Belleville 75011 ☎ 40 40 09 68
◷ Open daily Ⓜ Belleville

LE NIOULLAVILLE (£)
Vast, kitsch Hong-Kong-style restaurant with long menu of Chinese, Laotian, Thai and Vietnamese specialities.
✚ K4 ✉ 32-4 rue de l'Orillon 75011 ☎ 43 38 95 23
◷ Closed Sun evening
Ⓜ Belleville

PATTAYA (£)
Unpretentious, with outside tables in summer. Delicious prawn and lemon-grass soup and other Thai dishes.
✚ H5 ✉ 29 rue Etienne-Marcel 75001 ☎ 42 33 98 09
◷ Open daily Ⓜ Les Halles

PHÖ DONG-HUONG (£)
Popular Vietnamese family 'canteen' which serves generous soups, seafood and meat dishes. Bustling atmosphere, distinct smoking and no-smoking sections.
✚ K4 ✉ 14 rue Louis Bonnet 75011 ☎ 43 57 42 81
◷ Closed Tue Ⓜ Belleville

TAN DINH (££)
Up-market Vietnamese cuisine, in an elegantly designed restaurant just behind the Musée d'Orsay. Impressive wine-list and polished service.
✚ F6 ✉ 60 rue de Verneuil 75007 ☎ 45 44 04 84
ⓒ Closed Sun Ⓜ Rue du Bac

YAMAMOTO (£)
Super-fresh sushi bar with excellent-value set lunches. Popular so crowded until 2PM. Less animated in the evening.
✚ G5 ✉ 6 rue Chabanais 75002 ☎ 49 27 96 26
ⓒ Closed Sun Ⓜ Bourse

YUGARAJ (££)
One of Paris's best Indian restaurants. Discreet, elegant atmosphere, charming Sri Lankan waiters, excellent-value 'Delhi-Express' lunch menu.
✚ G6 ✉ 14 rue Dauphine 75006 ☎ 43 26 44 91
ⓒ Closed Mon lunch Ⓜ Pont Neuf

ITALIAN

CASA BINI (££)
Chic but relaxed, a favourite with Catherine Deneuve. Carpaccio and Tuscan dishes are specialities.
✚ G6 ✉ 36 rue Grégoire de Tours 75006 ☎ 46 34 05 60
ⓒ Closed Sat, Sun lunch
Ⓜ Odéon

L'ENOTECA (££)
Colourfully designed up-market Italian restaurant/wine-bar in the Marais. The buffet of *antipasti* is delicious

and the pasta dishes are refined.
✚ J6 ✉ 25 rue Charles V 75004 ☎ 42 78 91 44
ⓒ Open daily Ⓜ St Paul

PASTAVINO (£)
Bresaola and choice of three freshly prepared pasta dishes every day. Clean contemporary design, cheerful service.
✚ G6 ✉ 55 rue Dauphine 75006 ☎ 46 33 93 83
ⓒ Open daily Ⓜ Odéon

SIPARIO (££)
Theatrically styled restaurant convenient for Bastille Opera house. Wide and inventive choice of pasta, seafood and meat dishes.
✚ K7 ✉ 69 rue de Charenton 75011 ☎ 43 45 70 26
ⓒ Closed Sun Ⓜ Bastille

STRESA (££)
Fashionable isn't the word. Local couturiers drop in here for a quick pasta, risotto or plate of divine *antipasti*. Run with gusto by Neapolitan identical twins. Book ahead.
✚ E5 ✉ 7 rue de Chambiges 75008 ☎ 47 23 51 62
ⓒ Closed Sat, Sun Ⓜ Alma-Marceau

AUX TROIS CANETTES (££)
A friendly and old-fashioned establishment plastered with nostalgic views of Naples. Extensive menu of authentic Italian classics – polenta, ossobucco, sardines.
✚ G6 ✉ 18 rue des Canettes 75006 ☎ 44 07 03 02 ⓒ Sat lunch, Sun Ⓜ Mabillon

Panini reigns

It is said that Cathérine de Médicis, the Italian wife of Henri II, invented French cuisine in the 16th century – though Gallic opinions may differ. Italian cuisine in 20th-century Paris is, not surprisingly, very much a pizza-pasta affair, and authentic dishes are rare. However the latest in snack fashions is the toasted *panini*, oozing mozarella and tomatoes, especially popular with businessmen near the Bourse (Stock Exchange).

ARAB RESTAURANTS

Couscous and tajine

Couscous is a mound of steamed semolina which is accompanied by a tureen of freshly cooked vegetables (onion, tomato, carrot, potato, courgette) and the meat (or not) of your choice, from grilled lamb kebabs (*brochettes*) to chicken or *merguez* (spicy sausages). *Tajine* is a delicious all-in-one stew, traditionally cooked in a covered terracotta dish, which may combine lamb and prunes or chicken, pickled lemon and olives.

AL DAR (££)

Luxurious but over air-conditioned restaurant, highly regarded by Lebanese community. Take-away section.
➕ H7 ✉ 8/10 rue Frédéric Sauton 75005 ☎ 43 25 17 15
🍽 Open daily 🚇 Maubert-Mutualité

L'ATLAS (££)

Fabulous kitsch juxtaposition of Louis XIII chairs, Moroccan mosaics and genuine smiles. The diverse menu includes 12 types of *couscous*, pigeon and other specialities.
➕ H7 ✉ 12 Boulevard St-Germain 75005 ☎ 46 33 86 98 🍽 Open daily
🚇 Maubert-Mutualité

CAFÉ MODERNE (£)

Generous *couscous* and *tajines* as well as basic steaks and fish. 1930s décor. North African or French wines.
➕ K6 ✉ 19 rue Keller 75011
☎ 47 00 53 62 🍽 Closed Sun 🚇 Bastille

LES CÈDRES DU LIBAN (£)

A Lebanese institution with reasonable prices. Friendly service, and excellent *taboulé*, houmous and spicy meat dishes.
➕ F7 ✉ 5 Avenue du Maine 75014 ☎ 42 22 35 18
🍽 Open daily
🚇 Montparnasse-Bienvenue

DARKOUM (££)

Refined Moroccan cuisine – seafood, *pastilla*, *couscous* and *tajines* – in a spacious

Arabian Nights interior.
➕ G5 ✉ 44 rue Sainte Anne 75002 ☎ 42 96 83 76
🍽 closed Sat lunch 🚇 Bourse

DÎLAN (£)

Simple, unpretentious restaurant which serves wholesome Kurdish and Turkish dishes.
➕ H5 ✉ 11 rue Mandar 75002 ☎ 42 21 46 38
🍽 Closed Sat & Sun lunch
🚇 Les Halles

LE MANSOURIA (££)

Elegant décor, aromatic *tajines* though over-crowded on Saturdays.
➕ L7 ✉ 11 rue Faidherbe 75011 ☎ 43 71 00 16
🍽 Closed Mon lunch, Sun
🚇 Faidherbe-Chaligny

NOURA (££)

Up-market busy Lebanese snack-bar with take-away service, brother of the plush Pavillon Noura down the road (☎ 47 20 33 33).
➕ D4 ✉ 27 Avenue Marceau 75116 ☎ 47 23 02 20
🍽 Open daily 🚇 Charles-de-Gaulle-Etoile

TIMGAD (£££)

Spectacular Moorish décor. Delicate *pastilla*, perfect *couscous*, attentive service. Booking recommended.
➕ D4 ✉ 21 rue Brunel 75017 ☎ 45 74 23 70
🍽 Open daily 🚇 Argentine

BRASSERIES & BISTROS

LE BALZAR (££)
Fashionable brasserie near the Sorbonne. Seafood, pigs' trotters, *cassoulet*. Camus and Sartre had their last argument here.
✚ H7 ✉ 49 rue des Ecoles 75005 ☎ 43 54 13 67
⏰ Closed Aug 🚇 Cluny

BOFINGER (££)
Claims to be Paris's oldest brasserie (1864). Soaring glass dome, mirrored interior, chandeliers and seafood, *choucroute* and steaks.
✚ J6 ✉ 5 rue de la Bastille 75004 ☎ 42 72 87 82
⏰ Open daily 🚇 Bastille

BRASSERIE STELLA (££)
Original 1950s décor in heart of chic 16th *arrondissement*. Seafood, oysters, and wines from Sancerre and Beaujolais vineyards.
✚ C5 ✉ 133 Avenue Victor-Hugo 75016 ☎ 47 27 60 54
⏰ Open daily 🚇 Victor Hugo

CHEZ PAUL (££)
A mecca for Bastille art-dealers and artists, essential to book. Delicious stuffed rabbit, *steak tartare*. Mediocre service
✚ K6 ✉ 13 rue de Charonne 75011 ☎ 47 00 34 57
⏰ Open daily 🚇 Ledru-Rollin

LA COUPOLE (££)
A Montparnassian institution since the 1920s. Wide choice of brasserie food, reasonable late-night menu (after 11PM).
✚ F7 ✉ 102 Boulevard du Montparnasse 75014 ☎ 43 20 14 20 ⏰ Open daily 🚇 Vavin

LE DROUOT (£)
Art-deco canteen belonging to famous Chartier (along the road). Far easier to find a table here and food is equally good value.
✚ G5 ✉ 103 rue de Richelieu 75002 ☎ 42 96 68 23
⏰ Open daily 🚇 Richelieu-Drouot

LE GRAND COLBERT (££)
Restored 19th-century brasserie opening on to the Galerie Colbert. Good seafood and cheerful atmosphere.
✚ G5 ✉ 2 rue Vivienne 75002 ☎ 42 86 87 88
⏰ Open daily 🚇 Bourse

AU PETIT RICHE (££)
Wonderful old 1880s bistro. Reliable traditional cuisine and good Loire wines.
✚ G4 ✉ 25 rue Le Peletier 75009 ☎ 47 70 68 68
⏰ Closed Sun 🚇 Richelieu-Drouot

LE PETIT SAINT-BENOÎT (£)
Popular old St-Germain classic with décor barely changed since the 1930s. Outside tables in summer.
✚ G6 ✉ 4 rue Saint-Benoît 75006 ☎ 42 60 27 92
⏰ Closed Sat, Sun 🚇 St-Germain-des-Prés

AU VIEUX CHÊNE (£)
Pleasantly aged bistro east of the Bastille. Excellent value traditional dishes, friendly service.
✚ L7 ✉ 7 rue du Dahomey 75011 ☎ 43 71 67 69
⏰ Closed Sun 🚇 Faidherbe-Chaligny

La Coupole

Horror struck Parisian hearts in the mid-1980s when it was announced that La Coupole had been bought by property developers and several floors were to be added on top. This happened, but the famous old murals (by Juan Gris, Soutine, Chagall, Delaunay and many more) have been reinstated, the red velvet seats preserved and the art-deco lights duly restored. The 1920's décor is now classified as a historic monument.

SALONS DE THÉ

Mariage-Frères

It's hard to escape from Mariage-Frères without a minor investment in their tastefully presented products — whether a decorative tin of obscure Japanese green tea, a Chinese teapot, a tea-brick or a delicately tea-scented candle. The Mariage brothers started importing tea to France back in 1854 and the choice now extends to over 400 varieties. Reading the menu is an exotic excursion through India to the Far East.

ANGÉLINA (££)

Over-priced and overrated lunches but exquisite cakes and hot chocolate make it a favourite for tea. Proustian Belle-Epoque décor.

✚ G5 ✉ 226 rue de Rivoli 75001 ☎ 42 60 82 00 ⏰ Closed evenings, Aug 🚇 Tuileries

LES ENFANTS GÂTÉS (£)

Deep arm-chairs, plants and pictures. Good choice of teas, juices, salads, tarts, cakes. Fills up fast for weekend brunches.

✚ J6 ✉ 43 rue des Francs-Bourgeois 75004 ☎ 42 77 07 63 ⏰ Open daily until 7:30PM 🚇 Rambuteau

LE FLORE EN L'ILE (£)

Good teas, cakes and above all Berthillon sorbets and ice-creams. Doubles as a café, open late, and throws in a free view of Notre Dame.

✚ H6 ✉ 42 Quai d'Orléans 75004 ☎ 43 29 88 27 ⏰ Open daily 🚇 Pont-Marie

LADURÉE (££)

Rides on the back of an illustrious past and local luxury shoppers. Avoid over-priced lunches. Tea and cakes under a ceiling fresco of a cherubic pastry chef.

✚ F5 ✉ 18 rue Royale 75008 ☎ 42 60 21 79 ⏰ Closed Sun, Aug 🚇 Concorde

LE LOIR DANS LA THÉIÈRE (£)

Established local favourite, salads, vegetable tarts, cakes and plenty of tea and fruit-juices.

✚ J6 ✉ 3 rue des Rosiers 75004 ☎ 42 72 90 61 ⏰ Open daily until 7PM 🚇 St Paul

MARIAGES-FRÈRES (££)

Chic, discreet tea-shop with elegant upstairs tea-room perfect for non-smoking tête-à-têtes over divine cakes or Sunday brunch. Sibling in the Marais at 30/32 rue du Bourg Tibourg, 75004 ☎ 42 72 28 11

✚ G6 ✉ 13 rue des Grands Augustins 75006 ☎ 40 51 82 50 ⏰ Open daily until 7:30PM 🚇 Odéon

LA PAGODE (£)

Exotic tea-room attached to extraordinary cinema housed in an ornate Chinese pagoda. Overlooks small Japanese garden.

✚ F6 ✉ 57bis rue de Babylone 75007 ☎ 47 05 12 15 ⏰ Afternoons daily 🚇 St-François-Xavier

A PRIORI THÉ (££)

A favourite with fashion crowd, essential to book at lunch. Light lunches, teas, American cakes.

✚ G5 ✉ 36 Galerie Vivienne 75002 ☎ 42 97 48 75 ⏰ Open daily until 7PM 🚇 Bourse

TCH'A (£)

Sells 40 varieties of Chinese tea and serves delicious light lunches. Traditional service, aesthetic décor.

✚ G6 ✉ 6 rue du Pont de Lodi 75006 ☎ 43 29 61 31 ⏰ Closed Mon 🚇 Pont-Neuf

MISCELLANEOUS RESTAURANTS

MA BOURGOGNE (££)
Perfect for a summer lunch or dinner. Hearty, unpretentious food or just stop for a drink.
⊞ J6 ⊠ 19 Place des Vosges 75004 ☎ 42 78 44 64
Ⓒ Open daily, closed in Feb
Ⓜ Chemin Vert

CAFÉ DE L'INDUSTRIE (£)
Spacious, relaxed café-restaurant-tea-room open until 1:30AM. Whiffs of 1930s, rock music, and reasonable though basic food.
⊞ K6 ⊠ 16 rue St-Sabin 75011 ☎ 47 00 13 53
Ⓒ Closed Sat Ⓜ Bastille

AUX CHARPENTIERS (££)
Solid French cuisine in a popular neighbourhood restaurant dedicated to the carpenters' guild. Daily specialities.
⊞ G6 ⊠ 10 rue Mabillon 75006 ☎ 43 26 30 05
Ⓒ Open daily Ⓜ Mabillon

LA GALERIE (£)
Pleasant relief from the tourist haunts of Montmartre. Very good value set lunch and dinner menus which may include salmon ravioli or duck with cherries. Cheerful and friendly.
⊞ G3 ⊠ 16 rue Tholozé 75018 ☎ 42 59 25 76
Ⓒ Closed Sun Ⓜ Abbesses

JOE ALLEN (£)
Reliable hamburger-based fare served with humour and background music in a still fashionable late-night haunt of Les Halles.
⊞ H5 ⊠ 30 rue Pierre Lescot

75001 ☎ 42 36 70 13
Ⓒ Open daily Ⓜ Etienne-Marcel

ORESTIAS (£)
Pushy, lively Greek restaurant. Good value, above all the giant shoulder of lamb. Highlight is the chandelier.
⊞ G6 ⊠ 4 rue Grégoire de Tours 75006 ☎ 43 54 62 01
Ⓒ Closed Sun Ⓜ Odéon

LA POTÉE DES HALLES (£/££)
Famed for its delicious *potée* (a steaming pot of stewed meat and vegetables) and other regional dishes. Exceptional Belle-Epoque interior.
⊞ H5 ⊠ 3 rue Etienne-Marcel 75001 ☎ 42 36 18 68
Ⓒ Closed Sat lunch, Sun
Ⓜ Etienne-Marcel

PRUNIER (£££)
Recently refurbished to return to former art-deco splendour. Glamorous clientèle indulges in excellent fresh seafood specialities under the accomplished eye of a former Taillevent director.
⊞ D4 ⊠ 16 Avenue Victor Hugo 75016 ☎ 44 17 35 85
Ⓒ Closed Sun eve, Mon
Ⓜ Charles-de-Gaulle-Etoile

WILLI'S WINE BAR (££)
Cheerful, British-owned restaurant/wine-bar with extensive international wine-list. Fresh French cuisine plus the inimitable Cambridge dessert.
⊞ G5 ⊠ 13 rue des Petits Champs 75001 ☎ 42 61 05 09
Ⓒ Closed Sun Ⓜ Palais-Royal

Pharamond

Alexandre Pharamond served his first plate of *tripes à la mode de Caen* in 1870, two doors from the site of the present restaurant. After he moved to No 24 the restaurant was entirely redecorated for the 1900 Exposition Universelle and most of this structure and decoration has been preserved. The pretty floral and vegetal friezes which cover the walls of the rooms once adorned the entire four-floor façade. A sanctuary for lovers of tripe, pigs' trotters, *andouillette* ... Prices are high and booking essential.

⊞ H5 ⊠ 24 rue de la Grande Truanderie 75001 ☎ 42 33 06 72 Ⓒ Closed Mon lunch, Sun, Jul Ⓜ Les Halles

DEPARTMENT STORES & DESIGNER BOUTIQUES

DEPARTMENT STORES

BHV (Bazar de l'Hôtel de Ville)

The do-it-yourself mecca. Browse among the basement nuts and bolts, choose paint or have wood cut on the 5th floor.

H6 ✉ 52/64 rue de Rivoli, 75004 ☎ 42 74 90 00 Mon–Sat 9:30–7, except Wed 9:30AM–10PM Hôtel-de-Ville

LE BON MARCHÉ RIVE GAUCHE

Very BCBG (*bon chic bon genre*). Gourmet food department, designer clothes, household linens, haberdashery and excellent basement bookshop.

F7 ✉ 22 rue de Sèvres 75007 ☎ 44 39 80 00 Mon–Sat 9:30–7 Sèvres-Babylone

GALERIES LAFAYETTE

Under a giant glass dome, an enticing display of everything a home and its inhabitants need. Marginally better quality and pricier than Printemps. Top fashion designers are all represented and accessories are endless. Smaller branch by the Tour Montparnasse.

G4 ✉ 40 Boulevard Haussmann 75009 ☎ 42 82 34 56 Mon–Sat 9:30–6:45, except Thu 9:30–9 Chaussée d'Antin

PRINTEMPS

A classic for men's and women's fashion, accessories, household goods, furniture, designer gadgets and more. Budget-conscious fashion victims should look for the store's own collection under the label Sélection Printemps.

G4 ✉ 64 Boulevard Haussmann 75009 ☎ 42 82 50 00 Mon–Sat 9:35–7, except Thu 9.35AM–10PM Havre-Caumartin

SAMARITAINE

Labyrinthine department with main store in Magasin II, a superb 1904 construction. Good basement hardware section. Fashion is so-so, but toy department is a paradise for kids. Useful separate store for sports equipment and clothes.

H6 ✉ 19 rue de la Monnaie 75001 ☎ 40 41 20 20 Mon–Sat 9:30–7, except Thu 9:30AM–10PM Pont-Neuf

LES TROIS QUARTIERS

Mainly fashion, perfumes, accessories and household goods aimed at a more mature clientèle.

F5 ✉ 23 Boulevard de la Madeleine 75001 ☎ 42 97 80 12 Mon–Sat 10–7 Madeleine

DESIGNER BOUTIQUES

AGNÈS B

Pioneering designer who now rests on her comfortable reputation. Her shops monopolise most of this street. Still a favourite for her unchanging classics but fabrics and cut are no longer what they were.

Opening hours

Parisian opening hours follow a Monday–Saturday pattern. Smaller shops generally open by 10AM, sometimes closing for lunch, and shut at 7PM. Avoid shopping on Saturdays, when every citizen seems to hit the streets, and take advantage of department store late-opening nights. Chain-stores such as Prisunic and Monoprix are useful for picking up inexpensive household goods and even fashion accessories.

Children's and men's clothes too.

✚ H5 ✉ 1-6 rue du Jour 75001 ☎ 45 08 56 56 ⓜ Les Halles

AMELIA MENDES

Interesting fabrics and cuts, young and chic label by KYO who also designs for Dior and Scherrer at much less affordable prices.

✚ G5 ✉ 8 rue de la Vrillière 75001 ☎ 42 61 07 30 ⓜ Bourse

BARBARA BUI

Silky flowing fabrics in subtle colours, well-cut suits and a superbly designed boutique by Pucci de Rossi. One of Paris's most talented young designers.

✚ H5 ✉ 23 rue Etienne Marcel 75001 ☎ 40 26 43 65 ⓜ Etienne-Marcel

CHANTAL THOMASS

Paris's sexiest clothes shop, suspiciously reminiscent of an up-market brothel. Frills and thrills, stockings, lacey lingerie and some equally seductive clothes.

✚ G5 ✉ 1 rue Vivienne 75001 ☎ 40 15 01 36 ⓜ Bourse

DOROTHÉE BIS

Classically imaginative knitwear in colourful, supple styles, popular for more mature avant-garde clientèle.

✚ H5 ✉ 46 rue Etienne-Marcel 75002 ☎ 42 21 04 00 ⓜ Les Halles

IRIÉ

Former assistant of Kenzo who creates superbly cut and accessibly priced separates. A pioneer in this discreet street.

✚ G6 ✉ 8 rue du Pré-aux-Clercs 75007 ☎ 42 61 18 28 ⓜ St-Germain-des-Prés

KASHIYAMA

Look out for the label of Martin Margiela, a rising star from Antwerp who worked for Gaultier and now designs his own version of the avant garde.

✚ G6 ✉ 147 Boulevard St-Germain 75006 ☎ 46 34 11 50 ⓜ St-Germain-des-Prés

LOLITA LEMPICKA

Established inventive chic, very Parisienne. Ultra-feminine details and shop design.

✚ J6 ✉ 3bis rue des Rosiers 75004 ☎ 42 74 42 94 ⓜ St Paul

MICHEL KLEIN

Reliably chic from season to season. Search out the Klein d'Oeil label which offers very feminine designs for smaller budgets – but not as small as that.

✚ G6 ✉ 6 rue du Pré aux Clercs 75007 ☎ 47 03 93 76 ⓜ St-Germain-des-Prés

ROMEO GIGLI

Venetian carnival invades an old printers' workshop. Gigli's rich velvet, taffeta, silk and jersey designs are presented like works of art, which they are. Men's creations on mezzanine.

✚ J6 ✉ 46 rue de Sévigné 75004 ☎ 48 04 57 08 ⓜ St Paul

Fashion hubs

Three epicentres of women's high fashion make clothes shopping, or mere window-gazing easy. The hub of Place des Victoires (home to Kenzo, Stephane Kélian, Plein Sud, Victoire) continues along the rue Etienne-Marcel and towards Les Halles. The Marais' enticing offerings run between the rue de Sévigné, rue des Rosiers, Place des Vosges and side-streets. Saint-Germain burgeons along and off the boulevard, rue de Grenelle and continues up the Boulevard Raspail.

Zen cuts

Issey Miyake reigns OK! His sculptural, finely pleated creations in imaginative synthetics are sold at 3 Place des Vosges 75004 (☎ 48 87 01 86) but Plantation/Issey Miyake at 17 Boulevard Raspail 75007 (☎ 45 48 12 32) is where more accessible designs are available. And if black and white is your style, head for Yohji Yamamoto at 25 rue du Louvre 75001 (☎ 42 21 42 93) for sober geometric cuts for men and women, just a few doors apart.

MARKETS

Food markets

Parisians shop daily for ultra-fresh produce and perfectly oozing cheeses. Circulating food markets spring up on boulevards throughout the city (the Bastille Sunday market being particularly enormous) but permanent food markets exist from the rue Poncelet (75017) to the rue Daguerre (75014) or the Left-Bank intellectuals' classic in the rue de Buci (75006). All keep provincial lunch hours, so avoid 1–4PM.

CARREAU DU TEMPLE

Covered market specialising in leather goods. Bargain hard and you may pay half the price you would in a shop.

✚ J5 ✉ Rue E. Spuller 75003
🕐 Tue–Sun 9–noon 🚇 Temple

MARCHÉ D'ALIGRE

Second-hand clothes, crockery and bric-à-brac huddle in the middle of a large, low-priced food-market.

✚ K7 ✉ Place d'Aligre 75012
🕐 Tue–Sun 8–1 🚇 Ledru-Rollin

MARCHÉ DE MONTREUIL

Jeans and jackets start at the métro, but persevere across the bridge for domestic appliances, carpets, bric-à-brac and some great second-hand. Morning choice is best.

✚ N6 ✉ Avenue de la Porte de Montreuil 75020
🕐 Sat–Mon 7–6 🚇 Porte de Monreuil

MARCHÉ AUX OISEAUX

Caged birds whistle and chirp for new owners every Sunday. During the week (except Mon) feathered friends make way for a flower market.

✚ H6 ✉ Place Louis Lépine 75004 ☎ None 🕐 Sun 9–7
🚇 Cité

MARCHÉ AUX PUCES DE SAINT-OUEN (►44) MARCHÉ DE LA RUE LEPIC

Another uphill struggle, but worth it. Keep going down the other side of the hill to the rue du Poteau (🚇 Jules-Joffrin)

for African foods.

✚ G3 ✉ Rue Lepic 75018
🕐 Tue–Sat 9–1, 4–7; Sun 9–1
🚇 Abbesses

MARCHÉ DE LA RUE MONTORGUEIL

The leftovers of Les Halles food market, now a marble-paved pedestrian street with atmosphere and plenty of trendy little bars and lunch places.

✚ H5 ✉ Rue Montorgueil 75001 🕐 Tue–Sat 9–1, 4–7; Sun 9–1 🚇 Les Halles

MARCHÉ DE LA RUE MOUFFETARD

A tourist classic straggling down a winding, hilly street. Wonderful array of fruit and vegetables and plenty of aromatic cheeses and charcuterie. Good café stops *en route*.

✚ H8 ✉ Rue Mouffetard 75005 🕐 Tue, Thu, Sat 9–1, 4–7 🚇 Monge

MARCHÉ AUX TIMBRES

Philatelists zoom in here to buy and sell their miniature treasures.

✚ E5 ✉ Rond-Point des Champs-Elysées 75008 🕐 Thu, Sat, Sun and holidays 9–7
🚇 Franklin-D-Roosevelt

MARCHÉ DE VANVES

A favourite with young yuppies and hot on 1950s and deco styles. Second-hand furniture, bric-a-brac, paintings, prints and some ethnic stands.

✚ E9 ✉ Avenue Georges Lafenestre, Avenue Marc Saugnier 75014 ☎ None 🕐 Sat–Sun 7–7:30 🚇 Porte de Vanves

ART & ANTIQUES

ARTCURIAL
Large store of contemporary art (prints, jewellery, sculpture, carpets) and an excellent art bookshop.

➕ E4 ✉ 9 Avenue Matignon 75008 ☎ 42 99 16 16 ⏰ Tue–Sat 10:30–7:15 Ⓜ Franklin-D-Roosevelt

CARRÉ RIVE GAUCHE
This grid of streets is home to some of Paris's top antique dealers. Archaeological pieces, Louis XIV, XV, Empire, Japanese scrolls, 19th-century bronzes, astrolabes, prints ... it's all there.

➕ G6 ✉ Rue du Bac, Quai Voltaire, rue des Saints-Pères, rue de l'Université 75007 ⏰ Tue–Sat 10:30–7 Ⓜ Rue du Bac

LA COUR AUX ANTIQUAIRES
Tiny group of antique shops which sell anything from icons to porcelain, candelabra to *chaise-longues*.

➕ F5 ✉ 54 rue Faubourg St-Honoré 75008 ☎ 42 66 96 63 ⏰ Tue–Sat Ⓜ Concorde

GALERIE DOCUMENTS
Original posters and etchings from period 1890–1940 by such masters as Toulouse-Lautrec and Mucha. Mail-order service.

➕ G6 ✉ 53 rue de Seine 75006 ☎ 43 54 50 68 ⏰ Tue–Sat 10:30–12:30, 2:30–7 Ⓜ Odéon

GALERIE DURAND-DESSERT
Spectacular conversion of an old Bastille mattress factory into a conceptual art mecca.

➕ K6 ✉ 28 rue de Lappe 75011 ☎ 48 06 92 23 ⏰ Tue–Sat 11–7 Ⓜ Bastille

GALERIE MONTENAY
A long-standing contemporary art gallery where young French and foreign artists are regularly exhibited.

➕ G6 ✉ 31 rue Mazarine 75006 ☎ 43 54 85 30 ⏰ Tue–Sat 11–1, 2:30–7 Ⓜ Odéon

LOUVRE DES ANTIQUAIRES
Huge, modernised complex of antique shops which sell everything from Eastern carpets to Lalique glass, jewellery, furniture, silver, porcelain or paintings. High prices.

➕ G5 ✉ 2 Place du Palais Royal 75001 ☎ 42 97 27 00 ⏰ Tue–Sun 11–7 Ⓜ Palais-Royal

VILLAGE SAINT-PAUL
A cluster of antique and bric-à-brac shops opening onto an enclosed square. Shops continue down the streets on either side with everything from Asian textiles to glass, old furniture or clothes.

➕ J6 ✉ Rue Saint-Paul, rue Charlemagne 75004 ⏰ Thu–Mon 11–7 Ⓜ St-Paul

VILLAGE SUISSE
Network of up-market furniture and antique shops in this chic residential area.

➕ D7 ✉ 54 Avenue de la Motte-Piquet & 78 Avenue de Suffren 75015 ☎ 43 06 69 90 ⏰ Thu–Sun 10:30–7 Ⓜ Motte-Piquet

Galleries
Even if you cannot afford to invest in contemporary art, Paris offers a good window on the latest movements. Art traditionally centred on the Left Bank around the rue de Seine but today the more avant-garde galleries spread from around the Centre Georges Pompidou east through the Marais to the Bastille. Pick up a free gallery map at one of the galleries and follow the creative route.

BOOKS & RECORDS, DESIGN & INTERIOR, FOOD & WINE

Sunday openings

Sundays now have a strong consumer itch to them with the new marble-clad Carrousel du Louvre, perfect for a rainy day. Offerings include a Virgin record/book-store, a newsagent with a wide international selection, Bodum kitchenware, Nature et Découvertes (a fashionably 'ecological' toy and gadget shop), a stylish optician and various boutiques. Entrance is from 99 rue de Rivoli or by the Carrousel arch in the Louvre.

BOOKS & RECORDS

BRENTANO'S
Well-stocked American bookshop with good travel and art sections at back. Bilingual staff.
✚ G5 ✉ 37 Avenue de l'Opéra 75001 ☎ 42 61 52 50 🚇 Opéra

LA CHAMBRE CLAIRE
Excellent photography bookshop with wide range of international publications. Occasional exhibitions.
✚ G7 ✉ 14 rue St-Sulpice 75006 ☎ 46 34 04 31 🕐 Mon–Sat 🚇 Odéon

FNAC
The main branch of this firmly established cultural chain. Books, records, cameras, hi-fi, computer accessories. Fair-price policy reigns and staff are helpful.
✚ G7 ✉ 136 rue de Rennes 75006 ☎ 49 54 30 00 🚇 St Sulpice

GALIGNANI
Pleasantly traditional, spacious bookshop brimming with laden tables and shelves. Large stock of English, German and French literature and artbooks. Helpful staff.
✚ G5 ✉ 224 rue de Rivoli 75001 ☎ 42 60 76 07 🚇 Tuileries

LA HUNE
Great for late-night browsing with week-day doors open till midnight. Excellent literary bookshop with extensive art and architecture section. French and imported books.
✚ G6 ✉ 170 Boulevard St-Germain 75006 ☎ 45 48 35 85 🚇 St-Germain-des-Prés

LIBRAIRIE DES FEMMES
Next to the St-Germain market, a feminist bookstore with vast choice of international women writers. ✚ G7 ✉ 74 rue de Seine 75006 ☎ 43 29 50 75 🚇 Odéon

VIRGIN MEGASTORE
Enormous palace of records with generous opening-hours. Chic café. New branch in the Carrousel du Louvre, 99 rue de Rivoli.
✚ E4 ✉ 52/60 Champs-Elysées 75008 ☎ 49 53 50 00 🕐 Mon–Thu 10AM–12PM, Fri–Sat 10AM–1AM, Sun 12PM–12AM 🚇 Franklin-D-Roosevelt

DESIGN & INTERIOR

DEHILLERIN
A foodie's paradise, brimming with copper pans, knives, *bains maries*, sieves and more, in true traditional style. Mail-order service.
✚ H5 ✉ 18 rue de la Coquillière 75001 ☎ 42 36 53 13 🚇 Les Halles

EN ATTENDANT LES BARBARES
Colourful hive of primitive-baroque designer objects, from resin candlesticks to funky furniture by young French designers.
✚ H5 ✉ 50 rue Etienne-Marcel 75001 ☎ 42 33 37 87 🚇 Sentier

ETAMINE

Vast home-interior shop with superb objects and fabrics imported from all over the world but firmly stamped with Parisian taste.

➕ F6 ✉ 63 rue du Bac 75007 ☎ 42 22 03 16 🚇 Rue du Bac

SOULEIADO

Cheerful range of fabrics, table-linen and cushions in bright, sunny Provençal prints.

➕ G6 ✉ 78 rue de Seine 75006 ☎ 43 54 62 25 🚇 Mabillon

FOOD & WINE

ANDROUET

Encyclopaedic range of pungent French cheeses in perfectly ripened states. Cheese restaurant attached, delivery service in Paris.

➕ F3 ✉ 41 rue d'Amsterdam 75008 ☎ 48 74 26 90 🚇 Liège

FAUCHON

THE gourmet's paradise – at a price. Established luxury delicatessen offering only the best in spices, exotic fruit, tea, coffee, charcuterie, pâtisseries ... and more. Snacks available on spot.

➕ F5 ✉ 26 Place de la Madeleine 75008 ☎ 47 42 60 11 🚇 Madeleine

IZRAËL

Colourful souk spilling North African and Middle-Eastern goodies onto pavement. Sacks of grains, bottles of spices, piles of African baskets.

➕ J6 ✉ 30 rue François Miron 75004 ☎ 42 72 66 23 🚇 St-Paul

LEGRAND FILLES ET FILS

Fine wines and selected groceries in a shop dating from 1890. Helpful advice, wide price range but reliable quality. Occasional wine-tastings.

➕ G5 ✉ 1 rue de la Banque 75002 ☎ 42 60 07 12 🚇 Bourse

LA MAISON DU MIEL

Countless types of honey – chestnut, lavender, pine-tree, acacia – presented in a pretty, tiled interior dating from 1908.

➕ F4 ✉ 24 rue Vignon 75009 ☎ 47 42 26 70 🚇 Madeleine

A LA MÈRE DE FAMILLE

Original 18th-century grocery shop with shelves laden with imaginatively created chocolates, sweets, jams and unusual groceries. Friendly service.

➕ H4 ✉ 35 rue du Faubourg Montmartre 75009 ☎ 47 70 83 69 🚇 Le Peletier

ROBERT LABEYRIE

Celebrated shop which specialises in products from the Landes. Goose and duck livers, *foie gras*, truffles, dried mushrooms of all types.

➕ H5 ✉ 6 rue Montmartre 75001 ☎ 45 08 95 26 🚇 Les Halles

TACHON

Unpretentious old-fashioned cheese-shop, renowned for its goat, sheep and cow products.

➕ G5 ✉ 38 rue de Richelieu 75001 ☎ 42 96 08 66 🚇 Palais-Royal

Ethnic attractions

Foodies suffering from a surfeit of delectable but outrageously priced French groceries should head for Paris's ethnic areas. For Indian products the Passage Brady (75010) is unbeatable, while the nearby rue d'Enghien harbours several Turkish grocery-shops. Belleville offers both Arab and Chinese specialities but for a real taste of the Far East go to the 13th *arrondissement* and the Chinese supermarket, Tang Frères, at 47 Avenue d'Ivry.

MISCELLANEOUS & OFFBEAT

Window-shopping

Some Parisian streets do not fit any convenient slot and so make for intriguing window-shopping. Try rue Jean-Jacques Rousseau and Passage Véro-Dodat (75001), rue Saint Roch (75001), rue Monsieur-le-Prince and parallel rue de l'Odéon (75006), rue Saint-Sulpice, rue des Francs-Bourgeois (75004), rue du Pont Louis-Philippe (75004) or rue de la Roquette (75011). And for luxury goods take a stroll along the Faubourg Saint-Honoré (75008).

ANTHONY PETO
The male answer to Marie Mercié. Inventive and wearable men's quality headgear from top-hats to berets, aimed at the young and hip.
✚ G5 ✉ 12 rue Jean-Jacques Rousseau 75001 ☎ 42 21 47 15 🚇 Louvre

LES ARCHIVES DE LA PRESSE
Treasure-trove of old magazines, newspapers and catalogues.
✚ J6 ✉ 51 rue des Archives 75003 ☎ 42 72 63 93 🚇 Rambuteau

L'ART DU BUREAU
High-tech and designer accessories for the desk-top, tasteful stationery.
✚ J6 ✉ 47 rue des Francs Bourgeois 75004 ☎ 48 87 57 97 🚇 St-Paul

AXIS
Witty contemporary objects, plates, tea-pots, jewellery, clocks. Another shop at the Bastille, 13 rue de Charonne.
✚ G6 ✉ 18 rue Guénégaud 75006 ☎ 43 29 66 23 🚇 Odéon

CHÉRI-BIBI
Amusing and inventive women's hats at very affordable prices. Bit of a trek but worth it.
✚ K6 ✉ 82 rue de Charonne 75011 ☎ 43 70 51 72 🚇 Charonne

CHRISTIAN TORTU
Anemones, amaryllis and apple-blossom ... the ultimate bouquet from Christian Tortu's florist shops. Wrapping is in understated brown paper bound with raffia.
✚ G6 ✉ 6 Carrefour de l'Odéon 75006 ☎ 43 26 02 56 🚇 Odéon

CUISINOPHILE
Tiny little shop packed with decorative old kitchen utensils, mostly in working order.
✚ J6 ✉ 28 rue du Bourg Tibourg 75004 ☎ 40 29 07 32 🚇 Hôtel-de-Ville

DEBAUVE & GALLAIS
Original wood-panelled 18th-century pharmacy which developed into a chocolate shop when medicinal properties of cocoa were discovered.
✚ G6 ✉ 30 rue des Saints-Pères 75007 ☎ 45 48 54 67 🚇 St-Germain-des-Prés

DIPTYQUE
For over 30 years this boutique has sold its own exquisite label of perfumed candles and *eaux de toilette*. Also men's ties, scarves and superb glasses.
✚ H7 ✉ 34 Boulevard St-Germain 75005 ☎ 43 26 45 27 🚇 Maubert-Mutualité

L'HABILLEUR
End of designer lines at huge discounts. Plenty of choice, with helpful sales staff.
✚ J5 ✉ 44 rue de Poitou 75003 ☎ 42 72 07 13 🚇 St-Sébastien-Froissart

IKUO
Tiny little shop, a treasure chest of interesting jewellery mainly by Japanese creators. Good value.
✚ G6 ✉ 11 rue des Grands Augustins 75006 ☎ 43 29 56 39 🚇 Pont-Neuf

JEAN LAPORTE

An aromatic universe of pot-pourris, essences, candles and perfumes based on floral, fruity and spicy themes.

F6 ⊠ 84bis rue de Grenelle 75007 ☎ 45 44 61 57 🚇 Rue du Bac

JOUETS & CIE

Vast emporium of toys, games, costumes, party gear, computer games, trains etc. An early Philippe Starck design.

H6 ⊠ 11 Boulevard de Sébastopol 75001 ☎ 42 33 67 67 🚇 Châtelet

MARIE MERCIÉ

Compulsive creator of extravagant hats. Choose your headgear here or in her original shop near Les Halles at 56 rue Tiquetonne.

G7 ⊠ 23 rue St-Sulpice 75006 ☎ 43 26 45 83 🚇 Mabillon

MI-PRIX

Designer numbers at a fraction of the price, including shoes by Michel Perry.

C8 ⊠ 27 Boulevard Victor 75015 ☎ 48 28 42 48 🚇 Porte de Versailles

MOUTON À CINQ PATTES

Cut-price designer clothes packed into a crowded shop. Another shop in the Marais at 15 rue Vieille du Temple.

G6 ⊠ 19 rue Grégoire des Tours 75006 ☎ 43 29 73 56 🚇 Odéon

NAÏLA DE MONBRISON

Gallery showing some of the most sought-after contemporary jewellery designers' work, including Marcial Berro, Tina Chow, Mattia Bonetti.

F6 ⊠ 6 rue de Bourgogne 75007 ☎ 47 05 11 15 🚇 Varenne

PAPIER +

Wonderful emporium of quality paper in endless subtle hues. Superbly bound books, files, and bouquets of coloured pencils.

J6 ⊠ 9 rue du Pont Louis-Philippe 75004 ☎ 42 77 70 49 🚇 Pont-Marie

SCOOTER

To get that real Les Halles look, drop in here for latest accessories: ethnic, 1960s/70s revival transformed into jewellery, bags, clothes.

H5 ⊠ 10 rue de Turbigo 75001 ☎ 45 08 89 31 🚇 Les Halles

SI TU VEUX

Charming and affordable toy shop with interesting toys, games and dressing-up gear. Separate section devoted to teddy-bear related items.

G5 ⊠ 68 Galerie Vivienne 75002 ☎ 42 60 59 97 🚇 Bourse

TATI

Originally aimed at the emptiest purses in Paris, Tati now attracts the rich and famous but is still cheap. Women's men's, and kids' clothes, as well as household goods.

H3 ⊠ 2-30 Boulevard Rochechouart 75018 ☎ 42 55 13 09 🚇 Barbès-Rochechouart

Chocaholics

Chocolate came to Europe via Spain from South America. Under Louis XIV it became a fashionable drink and was served three times a week at Versailles. Paris's first chocolate shop opened in 1659, Voltaire drank up to 12 cups a day and Napoleon apparently had a *penchant* for it first thing in the morning. But the French with their consumption of a mere 5.5kg per person still lag behind the Swiss, who consume an annual 10kg, and the Belgians (7kg).

81

CONCERT VENUES, JAZZ CLUBS & NIGHTCLUBS

Church concerts

Numerous classical music concerts are held in churches — try St-Eustache, St-Germain des Prés, St-Julien le Pauvre, St-Louis en l'Ile, St Roch and St Séverin. Seats are reasonably priced and the quality of music is sometimes very high. In May–September free concerts are held in parks all over the city. Programmes are available at the Office du Tourisme or the Hôtel de Ville, or ☎ 40 71 76 47.

Recitals

The most prestigious venue on the classical-buff's circuit, now home to the Orchestre de Paris, is the Salle Pleyel (252 rue du Faubourg Saint-Honoré, ☎ 45 61 53 00). Chopin gave his last recital here and it is the venue for many of Paris's major concerts, often with world-famous soloists, and for radio and record recordings. Another established concert-hall, the Salle Gaveau, still attracts top international opera singers or pianists in spite of its shabby appearance (45 rue de la Boétie 75008, ☎ 49 53 05 07).

CONCERT VENUES

AUDITORIUM DES HALLES

Lunch-time and early evening concerts and recitals: classical, world-music, jazz.

🔢 H5 ✉ Forum des Halles, Porte Ste-Eustache 75001 ☎ 42 36 13 90 🚇 Les Halles

CITÉ DE LA MUSIQUE

Accessible classical, jazz, world-music at this new concert hall in a rather out-of-the-way location.

🔢 L2 ✉ 209 Avenue Jean-Jaurès 75019 ☎ 44 84 44 84 🚇 Porte de Pantin

OPÉRA BASTILLE

Long-term teething problems continue at Paris's 'people's' opera house. Opera, recitals, dance and even theatre .

🔢 K6 ✉ 120 rue de Lyon 75012 ☎ 44 73 13 99 🚇 Bastille

OPÉRA COMIQUE

Sumptuously decorated opera house which stages light opera, dance and sometimes theatre.

🔢 G4 ✉ 5 rue Favart 75002 ☎ 42 60 04 99 🚇 Richelieu-Drouot

THÉÂTRE DU CHÂTELET

Varied programme of opera, symphonic music and dance. Cheap seats for lunchtime.

🔢 H6 ✉ Place du Châtelet 75001 ☎ 40 28 28 40 🚇 Châtelet

THÉÂTRE DES CHAMPS-ELYSÉES

Top international orchestras play in a high-priced, stately setting.

🔢 E5 ✉ 15 Avenue Montaigne 75008 ☎ 49 52 50 50 🚇 Alma-Marceau

THÉÂTRE DE LA VILLE

Modern theatre with adventurous programme of contemporary dance, avant-garde music, theatre and early evening recitals of world-music.

🔢 H6 ✉ Place du Châtelet 75004 ☎ 42 74 22 77 🚇 Châtelet

JAZZ CLUBS

BILBOQUET

Strait-laced crowd with good sprinkling of tourists. Traditional jazz, pricey cocktails. Restaurant.

🔢 G6 ✉ 13 rue St-Benoît 75006 ☎ 45 48 81 84 🚇 St Germain-des-Prés

CAVEAU DE LA HUCHETTE

Still going strong, a smoky basement bar with dancing and live jazz from 9:30PM.

🔢 H6 ✉ 5 rue de la Huchette 75005 ☎ 43 26 65 05 🚇 St Michel

CHAPELLE DES LOMBARDS

Funky Bastille haunt with hot atmosphere and live raï (Algerian rock), rap, open until dawn.

🔢 K6 ✉ 19 rue de Lappe 75011 ☎ 43 57 24 24 🚇 Closed Sun 🚇 Bastille

NEW MORNING

One of Paris's top jazz/blues/soul bars. Good atmosphere, dedicated crowd, quality assured. Top names

require booking.
🔤 H4 ✉ 7/9 rue des Petites Ecuries 75010 ☎ 45 23 56 39 Ⓜ Château d'Eau

PASSAGE DU NORD-OUEST

Interesting experimental venue which combines jazz/rock/world music concerts with offbeat cinema programme. Live music Thu–Sun.
🔤 H4 ✉ 13 rue du Faubourg Montmartre 75010 ☎ 36 68 03 32 Ⓜ Rue Montmartre

LE SUNSET

Part of the Les Halles cluster, a restaurant-bar with good jazz concerts from 10PM until the small hours. Reasonably priced food.
🔤 H6 ✉ 60 rue des Lombards 75001 ☎ 40 26 46 60 Ⓜ Châtelet

LA VILLA

Top jazz names. Sleekly designed cocktail-bar setting in stylish post-modern hotel basement, open late. Book.
🔤 G6 ✉ 29 rue Jacon 75006 ☎ 43 26 60 00 🕐 Closed Sun Ⓜ St-Germain-des-Prés

NIGHTCLUBS

L'ARC

Fairly up-market club with selective door-policy. Piano-bar restaurant and interior garden.
🔤 D4 ✉ 12 rue de Presbourg, 75016 ☎ 45 00 45 00 🕐 From 11:30PM nightly Ⓜ Charles-de-Gaulle-Etoile

LES BAINS

Still number one for fashion and showbiz set. Heavy door-policing,

restaurant. Go very late.
🔤 H5 ✉ 7 rue du Bourg-l'Abbé 75003 ☎ 48 87 01 80 🕐 Nightly Ⓜ Etienne-Marcel

LE BALAJO

Over 60 years old, ritzy 1930s décor, music mainly disco, techno, funk.
🔤 K6 ✉ 9 rue de Lappe 75011 ☎ 47 00 07 87 🕐 Thu–Sat Ⓜ Bastille

LE BATACLAN

An old favourite now rejuvenated. Fashion-media set with fancy dress on Fridays, mainly house music on Saturday.
🔤 K5 ✉ 50 Boulevard Voltaire 75011 ☎ 47 00 30 12, 47 00 55 22 🕐 Thu–Sat from 11PM Ⓜ Oberkampf

PIGALL'S

Latest Pigalle haunt which thunders soul, acid-jazz. Transvestites add to the funkiness.
🔤 G3 ✉ 77 rue Pigalle 75009 ☎ 46 27 82 82 🕐 Fri–Sat from 12PM Ⓜ Pigalle

RÉGINE

Flashy mature crowd, rich in media stars. Careful grooming at door so look smart – you may be lucky.
🔤 E4 ✉ 49–51 rue de Ponthieu, 75008 ☎ 43 59 21 13 Ⓜ Franklin-D-Roosevelt

LE TANGO

Unpretentious club with hot-blooded Afro-Latino rhythms, tango, salsa, reggae, and soul.
🔤 J5 ✉ 13 rue au Maire 75003 ☎ 42 72 17 78 🕐 Fri–Sat from 11PM Ⓜ Arts et-Métiers

Clubs and raves

Paris clubbing is both serious and fickle – serious because no truly cool Parisian turns up before midnight, and fickle because mass loyalties change rapidly. Most clubs keep going through the night till dawn and nearly all charge an entry on Friday and Saturday nights which usually includes a drink. For one-off raves, theme nights and house parties outside Paris with shuttles laid on, check Pariscope's English section or key in to Minitel 3615 Party News.

BARS & SPECIAL CINEMAS

Cinephile's paradise

Though French film production dropped below the 100 mark in 1994 the capital is still a cinephile's paradise. With some 350 films on offer each day, the choice can be tantalising. Foreign films shown in their original languages have 'VO' (*version originale*) after the title. New films come out on Wednesdays, which is also the day for all-round reductions. Gaumont and UGC offer multiple-entry cards which can be used for up to three people and save extra precious francs.

BARS

BAR DU MARCHÉ
Hip watering-hole with good sounds and cheerful service. Nice terrace in summer.
G6 ✉ 75 rue de Seine 75006 ☎ 43 26 55 15
🕐 Daily 8AM–1AM 🚇 Odéon

BAR ROMAIN
Original 1905 décor brightens this bar-restaurant. Choice of over 200 cocktails, popular with more mature showbiz crowd.
G4 ✉ 6 rue Caumartin 75009 ☎ 47 42 98 04
🕐 Mon–Sat 12PM–2AM
🚇 Havre-Caumartin

BIRDLAND
An old St-Germain favourite. Relaxed, with great jazz records.
G6 ✉ 8 rue Princesse 75006 ☎ 43 26 97 59
🕐 Nightly 7PM–6AM
🚇 Mabillon

LES BOUCHONS
Late-night basement bar with occasional live jazz. Cheerful restaurant upstairs.
H6 ✉ 19 rue des Halles 75001 ☎ 42 33 28 73
🕐 Nightly 11:30PM until dawn
🚇 Châtelet

CAFÉ NOIR
Popular late-night haunt on fringe of Les Halles. High-decibel rock and unmistakable technicolour exterior.
H5 ✉ 65 rue Montmartre 75002 ☎ 40 39 07 36
🕐 Daily 7:30AM–2AM, closed Sun 🚇 Sentier

CAFÉ DE LA PLAGE
Bastille bohemia homes in to this small bar to tank up. Mixed crowd, regular soul/jazz concerts downstairs.
K6 ✉ 59 rue de Charonne 75011 ☎ 47 00 91 60
🕐 6PM–2AM; Sun, Mon 10PM–2AM 🚇 Ledru-Rollin

LA CASBAH
Moorish-styled bar with dancing, fancily dressed bar staff, great cocktails and décor but supremely unfriendly bouncers.
K7 ✉ 18 rue de la Forge-Royale 75011 ☎ 43 71 71 89
🕐 Tue–Sat 11:30PM onwards
🚇 Faidherbe-Chaligny

CHINA CLUB
Shady red-lacquered bar/restaurant peopled by Mao-style waiters. Hip and crowded, avoid the food, go for a drink. Another bar upstairs.
K7 ✉ 50 rue de Charenton 75012 ☎ 43 43 82 02
🕐 Nightly 7PM–2AM 🚇 Ledru-Rollin

HARRY'S BAR
Old pub atmosphere. Rowdy, mature, well-tanked up crowd.
G5 ✉ 5 rue Daunou 75002 ☎ 42 61 71 14 🕐 Nightly 10:30PM–4AM 🚇 Opéra

JACQUES MÉLAC
Inexpensive French wines by the glass or bottled for you from the barrel.
L6 ✉ 42 rue Léon Frot 75011 ☎ 43 70 59 27
🕐 Closed Sat–Sun, mid-Jul–mid-Aug 🚇 Charonne

LILI LA TIGRESSE
Weekend cover charge at this hip hot spot in Pigalle. Over-the-top decor, dancing and

occasional theme nights.
🔲 G3 ✉ 98 rue Blanche
75009 ☎ 48 74 08 25
🕐 Nightly 10PM–2AM
Ⓜ Blanche

MAYFLOWER

Lively, reasonably
priced bar-pub that has
attracted student
nighthawks for years.
🔲 H7 ✉ 49 rue Descartes,
75005 ☎ 43 54 56 47
🕐 Daily 7AM–2AM Ⓜ Cardinal-
Lemoine

LE MOLOKO

Cavernous popular bar
on two floors. Loud rock
still lets you talk.
🔲 G3 ✉ 26 rue Fontaine,
75009 ☎ 48 74 50 26
🕐 Daily 9:30PM–6AM
Ⓜ Blanche

LA TARTINE

An old daytime classic.
French wines by the
glass, cold platters of
charcuterie and cheese.
🔲 J6 ✉ 24 rue de Rivoli
75004 ☎ 42 72 76 85
🕐 8:30AM–10PM, closed Tue and
Aug Ⓜ Hôtel-de-Ville

LE TRAIN BLEU

Striking Belle-Epoque
setting which functions
as restaurant-bar. Food
pricey; stick to drinks.
🔲 K7 ✉ 1st floor, Gare de
Lyon, 75012 ☎ 43 43 09 06
🕐 Daily 9AM–11PM Ⓜ Gare de
Lyon

SPECIAL CINEMAS

VIDÉOTHÈQUE DE PARIS

Movies or
documentaries shot in or
connected with Paris, or
a changing daily
programme of wide-

ranging film classics.
Cheap day pass covers
four different films.
🔲 H5 ✉ Forum des Halles,
Porte Ste-Eustache 75001
☎ 40 26 34 30 Ⓜ Les Halles

LA CINÉMATHÈQUE FRANÇAISE

Cinema classics with
foreign films always in
original language.
🔲 D5 ✉ 7 Avenue Albert de
Mun 75016 ☎ 47 04 24 24
Ⓜ Trocadéro

LE DOME IMAX

The world's largest
hemispherical screen –
all 1,144sq m of it
Digital sound system.
🔲 Off A2 ✉ 1 Place du Dôme
92905 Paris La Défense ☎ 46
92 45 45 Ⓜ La Défense

L'ENTREPOT

Stimulating programme
of French and foreign
films and festivals
devoted to one director.
Bookshop, pleasant café.
🔲 F8 ✉ 7–9 rue Francis de
Pressensé 75014 ☎ 45 43 41 63
Ⓜ Pernety

LA PAGODE

A unique cinema hall
housed inside an exotic
Japanese pagoda.
Adjoining tea-room
(►72) and garden.
🔲 F6 ✉ 57 bis, rue de
Babylone 75007 ☎ 45 55 48
48 Ⓜ St-François Xavier

SALLE GARANCE

Films arranged by
theme or by country.
Comfortable, cheap
seats. Art films
connected with major
exhibitions on 5th floor.
🔲 H5 ✉ Centre Georges
Pompidou, rue Beaubourg 75004
☎ 42 78 37 29 Ⓜ Rambuteau

Steam baths

If nocturnal bar-crawling has
been too much, why not sweat it
out at a steam-bath? The
hammam at the Mosquée
(►52) offers a lovely tiled
interior *à la* Marrakesh and is
open for men on Friday and
Sunday, for women Monday,
Wednesday, Thursday, Saturday.
A new though pricier alternative
is Les Bains du Marais, 31 rue
des Blancs-Manteaux, 75004
(☎ 44 61 02 02): women,
Monday–Wednesday; men
Thursday, Saturday.

SPORTING VENUES

Pools and horses

Paris's municipal swimming-pools have complicated opening hours which are almost entirely geared to schoolchildren. Phone beforehand to check for public hours and avoid Wednesdays and Saturdays, both favourites with children off school. Gymnase Clubs are generally open till 9PM but close on Sundays. If horse-racing is your passion, don't miss the sulky-racing at Vincennes with its brilliant flashes of colour-coordinated horses and jockeys. Check *Paris-Turf* for race programmes.

AQUABOULEVARD

Huge family complex with water-shoots, palm-trees, jacuzzis. Gym, putting-greens, tennis and squash courts too – at a price.

✚ C8 ✉ 4-6 rue Louis Armand 75015 ☎ 40 60 10 00 Ⓜ Porte de Versailles

GYMNASE CLUB

Best-equipped gymnasium in this chain. Call for details on other gyms throughout Paris. Day passes, book of 10 passes or annual subscription.

✚ D3 ✉ 17 rue du Débarcadère 75017 ☎ 45 74 14 04 Ⓜ Porte-Maillot

HIPPODROME D'AUTEUIL

Flat-racing and hurdles. Hosts the prestigious Prix du Président de la République hurdle race.

✚ A6 ✉ Bois de Boulogne, 75016 ☎ 42 24 47 04 Ⓒ Closed Jul–Aug Ⓜ Porte d'Auteuil

HIPPODROME DE LONGCHAMP

Longchamp is where the hats and champagne come out for the annual Prix de l'Arc de Triomphe. Regular flat-races.

✚ A6 ✉ Bois de Boulogne 75016 ☎ 42 24 13 29 Ⓒ Closed Jul–Aug Ⓜ Porte d'Auteuil, then shuttle.

HIPPODROME DE VINCENNES

Colourful sulky-racing pulls in the crowds. Watch out for the Prix d'Amérique, the top sulky race of the season.

Vincennes 75012 ☎ 49 77 17 17 Ⓒ Closed Jul–Aug Ⓜ Château de Vincennes, then shuttle.

PARC DES PRINCES

Huge municipal stadium takes 50,000 spectators for major football and rugby matches.

✚ A8 ✉ 24 rue du Commandant-Guilbaud 75016 ☎ 42 88 02 76 Ⓜ Porte de Saint-Cloud

PISCINE DES HALLES (SUZANNE BERLIOUX)

Underground 50m pool overlooked by lush tropical garden.

✚ H5 ✉ 10 Place de la Rotonde 75001 ☎ 42 36 98 44 Ⓜ Les Halles

PISCINE JEAN TARIS

Two 25m pools with view of Panthéon. Electronically-cleaned water, so no chlorine.

✚ H7 ✉ 16 rue Thouin 75005 ☎ 43 25 54 03 Ⓜ Cardinal-Lemoine

PISCINE QUARTIER LATIN

A 33m pool with a distinct 1930 s air. Solarium, squash-courts, gym and sauna.

✚ H7 ✉ 19 rue de Pontoise 75005 ☎ 43 25 31 99 Ⓜ Maubert-Mutualité

ROLAND-GARROS

Hard-court home to the French Tennis Open. Tickets are sold months ahead but plenty of racketeers sell seats on the day at the main entrance.

✚ A7 ✉ 2 Avenue Gordon-Bennett 75016 ☎ 47 43 00 47 Ⓜ Porte d'Auteuil then walk or bus 32, 52, 123.

PARIS
travel facts

Arriving & Departing   *88–89*

Essential Facts   *89–90*

Public Transport   *90 91*

Media & Communications   *91–2*

Emergencies   *92–93*

Language   *93–94*

ARRIVING & DEPARTING

Before you go

- Visas are not required for EU nationals, US or Canadian citizens but are obligatory for Australians and New Zealanders.
- Anyone entering France must have a valid passport (or official identity card for EU nationals).
- There are no vaccination requirements.

When to go

- 'Paris in the spring' rarely starts before mid-May; June is always a glorious month.
- July and August see the Great Parisian Exodus. Cultural activities move into bottom gear, but accommodation is easier.
- Avoid mid-September to mid-October, the peak trade-fair period, when hotels are full.
- Winter temperatures rarely drop below freezing but rain is common in January and March.

Arriving by train

- The Eurostar train service from London arrives at Gare du Nord.
- Trains arrive at the Gare de l'Est from Germany, Austria, and Eastern Europe.
- The Gare de Lyon serves southeast France and Italy, the Gare d'Austerlitz southwest France, Spain and Portugal.
- The central TGV stations are Gare Montparnasse and Gare de Lyon.
- All stations have métro, bus and taxi services.
- Ticket reservations and information for SNCF stations ☎ 45 82 50 50 (7AM–9PM daily).

Arriving by air

- Air passengers arrive either at Roissy-Charles de Gaulle airport (23km north of Paris) or at Orly (14km to the south).
- Taxis charge a surcharge at airports and at stations and also for each item of luggage carried.

Roissy

- Connections to the city centre are: via a direct RER train into Châtelet-Les Halles; the Air France bus which stops at Etoile (Arc de Triomphe) and Porte Maillot; the cheaper Roissybus which terminates at rue Scribe, Opéra.
- Air France bus and Roissybus run every 15/20 minutes, 5.40AM–11PM.
- Taxis are expensive.
- Passenger information ☎ 48 62 22 80.

Orly

- Connections to the centre are via the Air France bus, which goes to Invalides every 12 minutes and stops at Porte d'Orléans, or the more economical Orlybus, which goes to Denfert-Rochereau every 15 minutes.
- Avoid Orlyrail as this involves a shuttle bus.
- Passenger information ☎ 49 75 15 15.

Customs regulations

- There are no restrictions on goods brought into France by EU citizens.
- For non-EU nationals the limits are: 200 cigarettes or 100 cigarillos or 50 cigars or 250g of tobacco, 2 litres of wine, 1 litre of spirits, 50g of perfume, 500g of coffee and 100g of tea.
- Prescribed medicines and up to 50,000FF of currency may be imported.

Departing

- Airport tax for departing passengers is included in the price of your ticket.
- There are numerous duty-free shops at Orly and Roissy airports but not on Eurostar or other international trains.
- Allow one hour to reach Roissy airport, by any transport means, and 45 minutes for Orly.

ESSENTIAL FACTS

Travel insurance

- Insurance to cover theft, illness and repatriation is strongly advised.

Opening hours

- Banks: 9–4:30, Mon–Fri. Closed on public holidays and often the afternoon before.
- Post-offices; 8–7, Mon–Fri; 8–12noon, Sat. The Central Post Office ✉ 52 rue du Louvre, 75001 ☎ 40 28 20 00 provides a 24-hour service for post, telegrams, phone.
- Shops: 9–7 or 9:30–6:30, Mon–Sat with minor variations (lunch closures in smaller shops). Arab-owned groceries stay open until 9 or 10PM, including Sun.
- Museums: National museums close on Tuesday, municipal museums on Monday. Individual opening hours vary considerably; always phone to check closure over national holidays.

National holidays

- 1 January, 1 May, 8 May, Ascension (last Thursday in May), Whit Monday (early June), 14 July, 15 August, 1 November, 11 November, 25 December.
- Sunday services for public transport operate; many restaurants, large shops and local groceries disregard national holidays.

Money matters

- The French currency is the franc (FF): 1FF = 100 centimes.

Foreign exchange

- Only banks with *change* signs change foreign currency/travellers' cheques: a passport is necessary. *Bureaux de change* are open longer hours but rates can be poorer.
- Airport and station exchange desks are open 6:30AM–11PM.
- For late-night exchange in central Paris use the Exchange Corporation ✉ 63 Ave des Champs Elysées 75008 ☎ 42 56 11 35 ⓜ Franklin-D-Roosevelt ⊙ 8–12 daily.

Credit cards

- Credit cards are widely accepted.
- VISA cards (including MasterCard and Diners Club) can be used in cash dispensers. Most machines flash up instructions in the language you choose.
- American Express is less common so Amex cardholders needing cash should use American Express, ✉ 11 rue Scribe 75009 ☎ 47 14 50 00 ⓜ Opéra.

Etiquette

- Shake hands on introduction and on leaving; once you know people better replace this with a peck on both cheeks.
- Always use *vous* unless the other person breaks into *tu*.
- It is polite to add Monsieur, Madame or Mademoiselle when addressing strangers or salespeople.

- Always say hello and goodbye in shops.
- When calling waiters, use *Monsieur* or *Madame* (NOT *garçon*!)
- More emphasis is put on grooming than in other countries, so avoid looking scruffy.

Women travellers
- Women are safe to travel alone or together in Paris. Any unwanted attention should be dealt with firmly and politely.

Places of worship
- The International Centre for Religious Information ✉ 6 Place du Parvis Notre-Dame, 75004 ☎ 46 33 01 01 Ⓜ St-Michel, an English-speaking service, supplies information on services and churches for Catholic, Protestant and Orthodox worshippers.
- Protestant churches: American Church ✉ 65 Quai d'Orsay 75007 ☎ 47 05 07 99 Ⓜ Invalides. St George's English Church ✉ 7 rue Auguste Vacquerie ☎ 75016 47 20 22 51 Ⓜ Etoile.
- Jewish: Synagogue ✉ 10 rue Pavée 75004 ☎ 42 77 81 51 Ⓜ St-Paul.
- Russian Orthodox: Saint Alexandre de la Néva ✉ 12 rue Daru 75008 ☎ 42 27 37 34 Ⓜ Courcelles.

Student travellers
- An International Student Identity Card reduces cinema charges, entrance to museums, and air and rail travel.
- AJF (Accueil des Jeunes en France) ✉ 119 rue St-Martin 75004 ☎ 42 77 87 80 Ⓜ Châtelet Ⓒ 9–6.30, Mon–Sat. Advice on hostel accommodation, discounts

on train tickets.
- CIDJ (Centre d'Information et de Documentation Jeunesse) ✉ 101 Quai Branly 75015 ☎ 44 49 12 00 Ⓜ Bir-Hakeim Ⓒ 10–6, Mon–Fri. Youth information centre for jobs, courses, sports etc.

Time differences
- France runs on GMT + 1 hour. Clocks change at the autumn and spring solstice.

Toilets
- Cream-coloured public toilet booths, generally well maintained, are common.
- Every café has a toilet, although standards vary (you should not use a cafe's toilet without ordering at least a drink). Museum and restaurant WCs are generally better.

Electricity
- Voltage is 220V and sockets take two round pins.

Tourist Information Office
- Office de Tourisme de Paris ✉ 129 Avenue des Champs Elysees, 75008 ☎ 49 52 53 54 Charles-de-Gaulle Etoile. Masses of tourist information and helpful polyglot staff.

PUBLIC TRANSPORT

Métro
- Métro lines are identified by their terminus (*direction*) and a number; connections are indicated with orange panels marked *correspondances* on the platform.
- Blue *sortie* signs show the exits.
- First métros run at 5:30AM, last around 12:30AM.

- Keep your ticket until you exit – it has to be re-slotted on the RER and ticket inspectors prowl the métro.
- Avoid rush-hours 8–9:30AM and 4:30–7PM.

Bus

- Buses should be hailed from bus stops.
- Enter, and punch your ticket into the machine beside the driver or flash your pass.
- Night buses run hourly 1:30AM–5:30PM from Place du Châtelet out to the portes and suburbs.

Maps

- Free métro/bus/RER maps are available at every station and on some buses.
- RATP information (in French) ☎43 46 14 14 ⏰6AM–9PM.
- RATP tourist office ✉53bis Quai des Grands Augustins 75006 ☎40 46 42 17.

Ticket types

- Tickets and passes function for métro, bus and RER.
- Pass prices and the number of tickets required for a journey depend on how many of five travel zones you intend to pass through.
- A *carnet* of ten tickets is considerably cheaper than individual tickets.
- *Formule 1* is a one-day pass, valid on métro, buses and RER.
- A *Paris Visite* card gives unlimited travel for three or five days plus discounts at certain monuments.
- The *carte hebdomadaire* pass (photo required), is valid Mon–Sun.
- Monthly passes (*carte orange*), also needing a photo, are valid for one calendar month.

Taxis

- Taxis can be hailed in the street if the roof sign is illuminated or found at a rank.
- Sunday and night rates (7PM–7AM) rise considerably and extra charges are made at stations, Air France terminals, for luggage and for animals.
- Taxi drivers expect tips of 10 per cent.
  Radio-taxi firms: Taxis Bleus (☎49 36 10 10); Alpha (☎45 85 85 85); G7 (☎47 39 47 39); Artaxi (☎42 41 50 50).

MEDIA & COMMUNICATIONS

Telephones

- Most Parisian phone booths use France Telecom phone cards (*télécarte* for 50 or 120 units), available from post offices, *tabacs*, stations or at main métro stations. A few phone booths still use coins, particularly those in cafés.
- Cheap periods for international calls vary: for Europe, Australia and New Zealand 9:30PM–8AM daily, and all day Sun; for the US and Canada 2AM–12PM daily, with lesser reductions 8PM–2AM.
- Repairs: 13
- Directory enquiries: 12
- International directory enquiries: 00 33 12 + country prefix
- In spring 1996 French telephone numbers change to 10 digits. 19+ for international calls becomes 00+ 16+ formerly used for calling the French provinces is replaced by: 02 Northwest, 03 Northeast, 04 Southeast, 05 Southwest. All numbers in the Ile-de-France, including Paris, start with 01.

Post offices

- Stamps can be bought at *tabacs* and mail posted in any yellow postbox.
- All post offices have free access to the Minitel directory service, express courier post (Chronopost), phone boxes and photocopying machines.

Press

- The main dailies are *Le Monde* (out at 2PM), *Libération* and *Le Figaro*.
- Weekly news magazines range from the left-wing *Le Nouvel Observateur*, *L'Express* (centre) and *Le Point* (centre-right) to *Paris Match* and *Canard Enchaîné*. For weekly listings of cultural events, buy a copy of *Pariscope* (with an English section) or *L'Officiel des Spectacles*.
- Central newspaper kiosks and newsagents stock European dailies.
- The NMPP's central bookshop (✉ 93 rue Montmartre 75002) has a comprehensive range of French and foreign press and the newsagent in the Carrousel beneath the Louvre carries American press and international fashion publications.

Radio and television

- FM stations run the gamut from current affairs on France Inter (87.8 MHz) to unadulterated rap/rock/house music on Radio Nova (101.5 MHz).
- France 2 and France 3, the state TV channels, occasionally have good documentaries and current events programmes. TF1 has lightweight entertainment, and M6 is still evolving. Arte (on Channel 5), a serious Franco-German cultural channel, offers good European coverage.

EMERGENCIES

Precautions

- Watch wallets and handbags as pickpockets are active, particularly in crowded bars, flea-markets and cinemas.
- Keep traveller's cheque numbers separate from the cheques themselves.
- Make a declaration at a local *commissariat* (police-station) to claim any losses from your insurance.

Lost property

- The police lost-property office is ✉ 36 rue des Morillons 75015 ⏰ 8:30AM–5PM Ⓜ Convention. No phone enquiries.

Medicines and medical treatment

- Minor ailments can often be treated at pharmacies (identified by a green cross) where staff will also advise on local doctors.
- All public hospitals have a 24-hour emergency service (*urgences*) as well as specialist doctors. Payment is made on the spot but if you are hospitalised ask to see the *assistante sociale* to arrange payment directly through your insurance.
- House calls are made with SOS Médecins ☎ 47 07 77 77 or for dental problems SOS Dentistes ☎ 43 37 51 00.
- 24-hour pharmacy: Dhéry ✉ 84 Ave des Champs Elysées 75008 ☎ 45 62 02 41.
- The Drug-store chain at St-Germain, Opéra and Champs-Elysées offers pharmacies, newsagents, cafés and tobacconists open until 2AM.

Emergency phone numbers

- Crisis-line in English SOS Help

☎ 47 23 80 80 🕐 3–11PM.
- Fire (*sapeurs pompiers*) 18.
- 24-hour ambulance service (SAMU) 15.
- Police 17.
- Anti-poison ☎ 40 37 04 04.

Embassies and consulates

- US Embassy ✉ 2 Avenue Gabriel 75008 ☎ 42 96 12 02.
- US Consulate ✉ 2 rue St-Florentin 75001 ☎ 42 96 14 88.
- Canadian Embassy ✉ 35 Avenue Montaigne 75008 ☎ 44 33 29 00.
- Candadian Consulate ✉ 37 Avenue Montaigne 75008 ☎ 44 43 29 16.
- British Embassy ✉ 35 rue du Faubourg St-Honoré 75008 ☎ 42 66 91 42.
- British Consulate ✉ 9 Avenue Hoche 75008 ☎ 42 66 38 10.
- Australian Embassy ✉ 4 rue Jean Rey 75015 ☎ 40 59 33 00.
- New Zealand Embassy ✉ 7ter rue Léonard de Vinci 75016 ☎ 45 00 24 11.

LANGUAGE

1	un	16	seize
2	deux	17	dix-sept
3	trois	18	dix-huit
4	quatre	19	dix-neuf
5	cinq	20	vingt
6	six	21	vingt-et-un
7	sept	30	trente
8	huit	40	quarante
9	neuf	50	cinquante
10	dix	60	soixante
11	onze	70	soixante-dix
12	douze	80	quatre-vingt
13	treize	90	quatre-vingt-dix
14	quatorze	100	cent
15	quinze	1000	mille

Preliminaries
yes/no oui/ non
please s'il vous plaît

thank you merci
excuse-me excusez-moi
hello bonjour
good evening bonsoir
goodbye au revoir
how are you? comment allez-vous? ça va?
very well thanks trés bien merci
how much? combien?
do you speak English? parlez-vous anglais?
I don't understand je ne comprends pas
there are 2/3 of us nous sommes deux/trois

Directions
where is/are ...? où est/sont ...?
the nearest metro le métro le plus proche
the telephone le téléphone
the bank la banque
the toilet les toilettes
the ticket-office le guichet
the entrance l'entrée
the exit la sortie
here/there ici/là
turn left/right tournez à gauche/droite
straight on tout droit
behind/in front derrière/devant
in the basement au sous-sol
on the first floor au premier étage

Time
when? quand?
today aujourd'hui
yesterday hier
tomorrow demain
next week la semaine prochaine
this morning ce matin
this afternoon cet après-midi
this evening ce soir
how long? combien de temps?
three days trois jours
at what time? à quelle heure?
at 9:30AM à neuf heures et demie
at 8PM à vingt heures
at midnight à minuit
what time do you open/close?

à quelle heure ouvrez/
fermez-vous?

Hotel

reduced rate for children tarif
réduit pour enfants

a single room une chambre simple

a double room une chambre double

double bed un lit matrimonial

an extra bed un lit supplementaire

with/without bathroom avec/sans
salle de bains

shower douche

with phone avec téléphone

do you have ...? avez-vous ...?

a cheaper room une chambre moins
chère

a bigger/quieter room une chambre
plus grande/plus tranquille

pillow un oreiller

towel une serviette

soap du savon

iron un fer à repasser

hairdryer un seche cheveux

razor un rasoir

Restaurant

breakfast le petit déjeuner

lunch le déjeuner

dinner le dîner

a table for two une table pour deux

(no-)smoking area la salle
(non-)fumeur

fixed-price menu le menu

the menu please la carte s'il vous
plaît

salt/pepper sel/poivre

ashtray un cendrier

a carafe of water une carafe d'eau

black coffee un café

white coffee un café crème/café
au lait

tea (with milk/lemon) un thé (au
lait/citron)

some ice des glaçons

mineral water (fizzy) (de l'eau
minerale (gazeuse)

a fresh orange juice une orange
pressée

a whisky un scotch

draught beer une pression/un demi

a glass of white/red wine un verre
de vin blanc/rouge

the bill please l'addition s'il vous
plaît

Shopping

how much is this? c'est combien?

do you take credit cards? acceptez-
vous des cartes de credit?

where is there a cash-dispenser? ou
se trouve un distributeur de
billets?

do you hav e... ? avez-vous ...

a larger size? une taille plus grande?

a smaller size? une taille plus
petite?

another colour? une couleur
différente?

English newspapers? des journaux
anglais?

it's cheap/expensive c'est pas
cher/cher

a loaf of bread please une baguette
s'il vous plait

a (half) kilo of... un (demi) kilo
de ...

that's enough, thanks ça suffit,
merci

Emergencies

I need a doctor/dentist j'ai besoin
d'un médecin/dentiste

can you help me? pouvez-vous
m'aider?

where is the hospital? où est
l'hôpital?

where is the police station? où est
le commissariat?

my passport/money has been stolen
on a volé mon passeport/mon
argent

I need to declare a theft j'ai besoin
de faire une déclaration de vol

I've missed my flight j'ai raté mon
vol

I've lost my ticket j'ai perdu mon
billet

we must leave immediately nous
devons partir immédiatement

INDEX

A

Acclimatation, Jardin d' 58
accommodation 62–5
airport tax 89
airports 88, 89
Alexandre III, Pont 55
Alma, Pont de l' 55
André-Citroën, Parc 56
Arab Institute 45
Arc de Triomphe 27, 57
architecture, twentieth-century 54
Arènes de Lutèce 59
Armée, Musée de l' 28
art and antique shops 77
Art Moderne de la Ville de Paris, Musée d' 50
Art Moderne, Musée National d' 41
Arts, Pont des 55
Arts Africains et Océaniens, Musée National des 51
Arts Asiatiques-Guimet, Musée des 50
Arts Décoratifs, Musée des 34
Astérix, Parc 58
auction rooms 59

B

Bagatelle, Parc de 56
Balabus 14
Balzac, Maison de 50
banks 89
bars 84–5
Bastille 18
Batobus 14
bed and breakfast 65
Bibliothèque de France 54
Bir-Hakeim, Pont de 55
boat trips 19
Bois de Boulogne 56
Boulevard de Rochechouart 60
Bourdelle, Antoine 50
brasseries and bistros 71
bridges 55
buses 91

C

Café Beaubourg 53
Café de Flore 53
Café Marly 53
Café de la Paix 53
cafés 53
canal trips 19
Carnavalet, Musée 46
Centre Georges Pompidou 41
Champs-Elysées 27

Charles-de-Gaulle, Pont 55
Chasse, Musée de la 16
children's activities 58
Chirac, Jacques 9
church concerts 82
churches 52
Cinéma, Musée du 25
cinemas 84, 85
Cirque Alexis Grüss 58
Cité de la Musique 54
Cité des Sciences et de l'Industrie 50
La Closerie des Lilas 53
Cluny, Musée de 38
concert venues 82
Conciergerie 40
Cour Carrée 18
Cour de Rohan 60
credit cards 89
crime 92
currency exchange 89
customs regulations 88
cycling 19

D

De Gaulle, Charles 12
Delacroix, Musée 60
Les Deux Magots 53
Disneyland Paris 58
Dôme, Eglise du 28
Drouot Richelieu 59

E

Egyptian obelisk 30
Eiffel Tower 26
electricity 90
embassies and consulates 93
emergencies 92–3
Equipages, Musée des 21
etiquette 89–90
events 22
excursions 20–1

F

fashion shops 74–5
Faubourg Saint-Honoré 60
flea-markets 42
food and drink 53, 66–73, 84–5
free attractions 59

G

Galerie Colbert 36
Galerie Vivienne 36
galleries, commercial 77
Gaultier, Jean-Paul 9
La Géode 58
Giverny 20, 21
Grand Palais 27
La Grande Arche 54
La Grande Roue 57

Gustave Moreau, Musée 50–1

H

Hébert, Musée 60
Histoire Naturelle, Museum National d' 51
history 10–12
Homme, Musée de l' 25
hotels 62–5
Hugo, Victor 7, 47

I

Ile Saint-Louis 44
Institut du Monde Arabe 45
Les Invalides 28
itineraries 14–15

J

jazz clubs 82–3
Jeu de Paume 30

L

language (basic vocabulary) 93–4
Latin Quarter 17
lost property 92
Louvre, Musée du 35
Lunettes et Lorgnettes de Jadis, Musée des 51
Luxembourg, Jardin du 37

M

Maison du Verre 54
Maison Victor Hugo 47
maps 91
Marché aux Puces de St Ouen 42
Marie, Pont 55
Marine, Musée de la 25
markets 42, 76
Marmottan, Musée 24
medical treatment 92
Mémorial de la Déportation 59
métro 90–1
Monceau, Parc 56
Monet, Claude 21
money 89
Montmartre, Parc 56
Monuments Français, Musée des 25
Moreau, Gustave 50–1
La Mosquée 52
museums and galleries 50–1, 89

N

Napoleon Bonaparte 12, 28

National Archives 16
national holidays 89
Neuf, Pont 55
newspapers 92
nightclubs 83
Notre-Dame 43

O

opening hours 89
opera 82
Opéra de Paris 32
Orangerie 30
Orsay, Musée d' 31

P

Palais Bourbon 30
Palais de Chaillot 25
Palais de la Découverte 27
Palais de Justice 59
Palais-Royal, Jardin du 59
La Palette 53
Parisians 8
parks and gardens 56
passports and visas 88
Pavillon de l'Arsenal 59
Père Lachaise Cemetery 48
Petit Palais 27
Petit Trianon 21
pharmacies 92
Picasso, Musée 51
Place de la Concorde 30
Place des Vosges 47
places of worship 90
pollution 57
Porte Dauphine 54
post offices 89, 92
public transport 14, 90–1
puppet shows 58

Q

Quai d'Anjou 44

R

radio and television 92
rail services 88
rented accommodation 65
restaurants 66–70, 73
river buses 14
Robuchon, Joël 9
Rodin, Musée 29
Royal, Parc 16
Royal, Pont 55
Rue du Cherche-Midi 60
Rue Jacob 60
Rue Mallet-Stevens 54
Rue Monsieur-le-Prince 60
Rue des Rosiers 60
Rue Vavin 54
Rue Vieille-du-Temple 60

S

Sacré-Coeur 33
Sainte-Chapelle 39
Ste-Croix-de-Paris, Cathédrale 16
Saint-Etienne du Mont, Eglise 52
Saint-Eustache, Eglise de 52
Saint-Germain-des-Prés, Eglise de 52
St-Louis, Eglise 28
Saint-Merri, Eglise de 52
St-Pierre 33
Saint-Séverin, Eglise de 52
Saint-Sulpice, Eglise de 52
salons de thé 72
La Samaritaine 57
seasons 88
Seine 18
Sens, Hôtel de 17

Serres d'Auteuil, Jardin des 56
shopping 74–81
Sinclair, Anne 9
sport 86
Square du Vert Galant 57
Starck, Philippe 9
statistics 8
steam-baths 85
student travellers 90
swimming-pools 86

T

taxis 91
Techniques, Musée National des 51
telephone numbers, emergency 92–3
telephones 91
theme-parks 58
time differences 90
toilets 90
Tour Montparnasse 57
tourist information office 90
tours, guided 19
travel insurance 89
travel passes 91
travelling to Paris 88–9
Tuileries, Jardin des 56

V

Vaux-le-Vicomte 20–1
Versailles 20
views of Paris 57
Village Saint-Paul 17

W

walks 16–18, 19
women travellers 90

ACKNOWLEDGEMENTS

The Automobile Association would like to thank the following photographers, picture libraries and associations for their assistance in the preparation of this book: F DUNLOP 44b, 45; THE LOUVRE 35b; MUSÉE CARNAVALET 46a; MUSÉE DES ARTS DÉCORATIFS 34; MUSÉE MARMOTTAN 24; REX FEATURES LTD 9

All remaining pictures are held in the Association's own library (AA PHOTO LIBRARY), with contributions from: M ADLEMAN 87a; P ENTICKNAP 18, 26b; R MOORE 21; D NOBLE 20; K PATERSON 2, 5a, 5b, 6, 25a, 25b, 28a, 28b, 30, 39a, 40, 43a, 52, 53, 56, 60; B RIEGER 1, 17, 23a, 32, 44a, 55, 57, 58, 61b; A SOUTER 7, 13a, 16, 26a, 27, 29, 31a, 31b, 41b, 43b, 48, 49a, 50, 51, 54; W VOYSEY 13b, 23b, 33a, 35a, 36a, 36b, 41a, 42, 46b, 47, 49b, 59, 61a, 87b.

Copy-editor: *Susie Whimster*
Verifier: *Giselle Thain*
Indexer: *Marie Lorimer*
Original design: *Design FX*
The author would like to thank Dominique Benedittini, Christophe Boicos and Andrew Hartley for their help during the preparation of this book.

AAT

Bookkeeping
Transactions

Level 2
Foundation Certificate in
Accounting
Question Bank

Third edition 2019

ISBN 9781 5097 8118 8

British Library Cataloguing-in-Publication Data

A catalogue record for this book is available
from the British Library

Published by

BPP Learning Media Ltd
BPP House, Aldine Place
142-144 Uxbridge Road
London W12 8AA

www.bpp.com/learningmedia

Printed in the United Kingdom

Your learning materials, published by BPP Learning
Media Ltd, are printed on paper obtained from
traceable sustainable sources.

BPP
LEARNING MEDIA

Contents

		Page
Introduction		iv

Question and answer bank

Chapter tasks		Questions	Answers
Chapter 1	Business documentation	3	149
Chapter 2	The books of prime entry	11	152
Chapter 3	VAT and discounts	21	156
Chapter 4	Recording credit sales	28	161
Chapter 5	Recording credit purchases	39	168
Chapter 6	Double entry bookkeeping (part 1)	54	175
Chapter 7	Double entry bookkeeping (part 2)	66	181
Chapter 8	Maintaining the cash book	74	185
Chapter 9	Double entry for sales and trade receivables	86	191
Chapter 10	Double entry for purchases and trade payables	111	201
Chapter 11	Accounting for petty cash	130	209
Chapter 12	Initial trial balance	141	215
AAT AQ2016 practice assessment 1		221	241
AAT AQ2016 practice assessment 2		253	
BPP practice assessment 1		257	277
BPP practice assessment 2		287	311
BPP practice assessment 3		323	347
BPP practice assessment 4		359	385

Introduction

This is BPP Learning Media's AAT Question Bank for *Bookkeeping Transactions*. It is part of a suite of ground-breaking resources produced by BPP Learning Media for AAT assessments.

This Question Bank has been written in conjunction with the BPP Course Book, and has been carefully designed to enable students to practise all of the learning outcomes and assessment criteria for the units that make up *Bookkeeping Transactions*. It is fully up to date as at May 2019 and reflects both AAT's qualification specification and the practice assessments provided by AAT.

This Question Bank contains these key features:

- Tasks corresponding to each chapter of the Course Book. Some tasks are designed for learning purposes, others are of assessment standard

- AAT's AQ2016 practice assessment 1 and answers for *Bookkeeping Transactions* and further BPP practice assessments

The emphasis in all tasks and assessments is on the practical application of the skills acquired.

VAT

You may find tasks throughout this Question Bank that need you to calculate or be aware of a rate of VAT. This is stated at 20% in these examples and questions.

Approaching the assessment

When you sit the assessment it is very important that you follow the on screen instructions. This means you need to carefully read the instructions, both on the introduction screens and during specific tasks.

When you access the assessment you should be presented with an introductory screen with information similar to that shown below (taken from the introductory screen from AAT's AQ2016 practice assessment 1 for *Bookkeeping Transactions*).

> We have provided this **practice assessment** to help you familiarise yourself with our e-assessment environment. It is designed to demonstrate as many of the possible question types you may find in a live assessment. It is not designed to be used on its own to determine whether you are ready for a live assessment.
>
> At the end of this practice assessment you will receive an immediate assessment result.

Assessment information:

You have **1 hour 30 minutes** to complete this practice assessment.

This assessment contains **10 tasks** and you should attempt to complete **every** task.
Each task is independent. You will not need to refer to your answers to previous tasks.
Read every task carefully to make sure you understand what is required.

Where the date is relevant, it is given in the task data.

Both minus signs and brackets can be used to indicate negative numbers **unless** task instructions state otherwise.

You must use a full stop to indicate a decimal point. For example, write 100.57 NOT 100,57 or 100 57

You may use a comma to indicate a number in the thousands, but you don't have to. For example, 10000 and 10,000 are both acceptable.

The tasks in this assessment are set in different business situations where the following apply:

- All businesses use a manual bookkeeping system.
- Double entry takes place in the general ledger. Individual accounts of trade receivables and trade payables are kept in the sales and purchases ledgers as subsidiary accounts.
- The cash book and petty cash book should be treated as part of the double entry system unless the task instructions state otherwise.
- The VAT rate is 20%.

The actual instructions will vary depending on the subject you are studying for. It is very important you read the instructions on the introductory screen and apply them in the assessment. You don't want to lose marks when you know the correct answer just because you have not entered it in the right format.

In general, the rules set out in the AAT practice assessments for the subject you are studying for will apply in the real assessment, but you should carefully read the information on this screen again in the real assessment, just to make sure. This screen may also confirm the VAT rate used if applicable.

A full stop is needed to indicate a decimal point. We would recommend using minus signs to indicate negative numbers and leaving out the comma signs to indicate thousands, as this results in a lower number of key strokes and less margin for error when working under time pressure. Having said that, you can use whatever is easiest for you as long as you operate within the rules set out for your particular assessment.

You have to show competence throughout the assessment and you should therefore complete all of the tasks. Don't leave questions unanswered.

When asked to fill in tables, or gaps, never leave any blank even if you are unsure of the answer. Fill in your best estimate.

Note. that for some assessments where there is a lot of scenario information or tables of data provided, you may need to access these via 'pop-ups'. Instructions will be provided on how you can bring up the necessary data during the assessment.

Finally, take note of any task specific instructions once you are in the assessment. For example you may be asked to enter a date in a certain format or to enter a number to a certain number of decimal places.

Grading

To achieve the qualification and to be awarded a grade, you must pass all the mandatory unit assessments, all optional unit assessments (where applicable) and the synoptic assessment.

The AAT Level 2 Foundation Certificate in Accounting will be awarded a grade. This grade will be based on performance across the qualification. Unit assessments and synoptic assessments are not individually graded. These assessments are given a mark that is used in calculating the overall grade.

How overall grade is determined

You will be awarded an overall qualification grade (Distinction, Merit, and Pass). If you do not achieve the qualification you will not receive a qualification certificate, and the grade will be shown as unclassified.

The marks of each assessment will be converted into a percentage mark and rounded up or down to the nearest whole number. This percentage mark is then weighted according to the weighting of the unit assessment or synoptic assessment within the qualification. The resulting weighted assessment percentages are combined to arrive at a percentage mark for the whole qualification.

Grade definition	Percentage threshold
Distinction	90–100%
Merit	80–89%
Pass	70–79%
Unclassified	0–69% Or failure to pass one or more assessment/s

Re-sits

Some AAT qualifications such as the AAT Foundation Certificate in Accounting have restrictions in place for how many times you are able to re-sit assessments. Please refer to the AAT website for further details.

You should only be entered for an assessment when you are well prepared and you expect to pass the assessment.

AAT qualifications

The material in this book may support the following AAT qualifications:

AAT Foundation Certificate in Accounting Level 2, AAT Foundation Certificate in Accounting at SCQF Level 5 and Certificate: Accounting Technician (Level 3 AATSA).

Supplements

From time to time we may need to publish supplementary materials to one of our titles. This can be for a variety of reasons. From a small change in the AAT unit guidance to new legislation coming into effect between editions.

You should check our supplements page regularly for anything that may affect your learning materials. All supplements are available free of charge on our supplements page on our website at:

www.bpp.com/learning-media/about/students

Improving material and removing errors

There is a constant need to update and enhance our study materials in line with both regulatory changes and new insights into the assessments.

From our team of authors BPP appoints a subject expert to update and improve these materials for each new edition.

Their updated draft is subsequently technically checked by another author and from time to time non-technically checked by a proof reader.

We are very keen to remove as many numerical errors and narrative typos as we can but given the volume of detailed information being changed in a short space of time we know that a few errors will sometimes get through our net.

We apologise in advance for any inconvenience that an error might cause. We continue to look for new ways to improve these study materials and would welcome your suggestions. If you have any comments about this book, please email nisarahmed@bpp.com or write to Nisar Ahmed, AAT Head of Programme, BPP Learning Media Ltd, BPP House, Aldine Place, London W12 8AA.

Question Bank

Chapter 1 – Business documentation

The tasks in this Question Bank are set in different business situations where the following apply:

- All businesses use a manual bookkeeping system.
- Double entry takes place in the general ledger. Individual accounts of trade receivables and trade payables are kept in the sales and purchases ledgers as subsidiary accounts.
- The cash book and petty cash book should be treated as part of the double entry system unless the task instructions state otherwise.
- The VAT rate is 20%.

Task 1.1

For each of the following transactions state whether they are cash or credit transactions:

	Cash transaction ✓	Credit transaction ✓
Purchase of goods for £200 payable by cash in one week's time		
Writing a cheque for the purchase of a new computer		
Sale of goods to a customer where the invoice accompanies the goods		
Receipt of a cheque from a customer for goods purchased today		
Purchase of goods where payment is due in three weeks' time		

Task 1.2

When a supplier delivers goods to a customer, the customer will expect to receive in due course:

✓	
	A credit note
	A remittance advice
	A petty cash voucher
	An invoice

Task 1.3

A customer wishes to return faulty goods to a credit supplier.

Which document should the customer send with the return?

✓	
	A credit note
	A goods received note
	A goods returned note
	An invoice

Task 1.4

Freddie wishes to purchase some desks from Joe, his credit supplier.

(a) **Which document should Joe issue to Freddie at each stage of this sales process?**

	Document issued by Joe
Freddie asks Joe for a quote on the cost of 14 desks	▼
Joe delivers 14 desks to Freddie	▼
Joe requests payment from Freddie	▼
Freddie pays his invoice and takes a prompt payment discount	▼

Picklist:

Credit note
Customer order
Delivery note
Goods received note
Goods returned note
Invoice
Quotation
Remittance advice

(b) **Which document should Freddie create at each stage of the purchase process?**

	Document created by Freddie
Freddie places an order with Joe for 14 desks	▼
Freddie accepts in to his warehouse delivery of 14 desks from Joe	▼
Freddie returns one faulty desk to Joe	▼
Freddie pays his invoice	▼

Picklist:

Credit note
Customer order
Delivery note
Goods received note
Goods returned note
Invoice
Purchase order
Remittance advice
Sales order

Task 1.5

Ken trades in exotic dress materials. He has a large number of small suppliers. He likes to keep all invoices and credit notes from each supplier together in a file for that supplier.

Which sort of coding system would be most appropriate for Ken to use when devising a unique code number for each supplier?

	✓	
	An alpha-numeric system	
	A numeric system	

Task 1.6

JMC Ltd allocates a customer code to each of its customers as shown below. The codes are made up of the first two letters of the customer's name, followed by the number of the ledger page allocated to each customer in that alphabetical group.

Customer name	Customer code
Baxters Ltd	Ba01
Britoil	Br02
Drumbuie Ltd	Dr01
Drumchapel Ltd	Dr02
Joulie Walker	Jo01
Walkers Ltd	Wa01
William Grant Ltd	Wi02
Whyte and Mackay	Wh03

JMC Ltd has two new credit customers which need to be allocated a customer code.

Insert the relevant customer codes for each customer.

Customer	Customer code
Caledonian Ltd	
Jury's Brewery Ltd	

Task 1.7

Complete the sentence

In order to identify how much is owed to a supplier at any point in time, purchases invoices are coded with a:

▼

Picklist:

Customer code
General ledger code
Product code
Supplier code

Task 1.8

Sumberton Ltd codes all purchase invoices with a supplier code **and** a general ledger code. A selection of the codes used is given below.

Supplier	Supplier Code
Casaubon's	PL012
Frankie's Leatherware	PL128
Jane Peel Ltd	PL244
Trinder and Papp	PL301
Wishburton Ltd	PL666

Item	General Ledger Code
Leather bags	GL001
Canvas bags	GL002
Wheeled cases	GL003
Carry cases	GL004
Accessories	GL005

This is an invoice received from a supplier.

Jane Peel Ltd
56 Ward End Road, Doristown DO9 3YU
VAT Registration No. 134 1452 22

Sumberton Ltd
Sumberton House
10 Main Road
Sawlow
SA7 5LD

23 December 20XX

	£
10 leather bags (product code R245L) @ £17.50 each	175.00
VAT @ 20%	35.00
Total	210.00

(a) **Select which codes would be used to code this invoice.**

Supplier code	▼
General ledger code	▼

Picklist:
GL001
GL002
GL003
GL004
GL005
PL012
PL128
PL244
PL301
PL666

(b) **Complete the sentence.**

In order to identify how much has been spent on a particular product for resale at any point in time, purchases invoices are coded with a

 .

Picklist:
Customer code
General ledger code
Product code
Supplier code

Task 1.9

Ken trades in exotic dress materials. He codes all purchase invoices with a supplier code **and** a general ledger code. A selection of the codes used is given below.

Supplier	Supplier Code
Henderson Co	HEN562
Mack Materials	MAC930
Vinceroy Ltd	VIN234
Streamers	STR220
AVR Partners	AVR001

Product	General Ledger Code
Lace	GL501
Calico	GL502
Seersucker	GL503
Cambric	GL504
Velvet	GL505

This is an invoice received from a supplier.

Vinceroy Ltd
17 Fall Road, Agburton AG5 2WE
VAT Registration No. 783 2873 33
Invoice number: 892

Ken's Exotics
1 Bath Street
5 Feb 20XX
Cembury, CE11 9SD

	£
20 metres .... Velvet @ £7.00 per metre	140.00
VAT @ 20%	28.00
Total	168.00

(a) **Select which codes would be used to code this invoice.**

Supplier account code	▼
General ledger code	▼

Picklist:

AVR001
GL501
GL502
GL503
GL504
GL505
HEN562
MAC930
STR220
VIN234

(b) Why is it necessary to use a general ledger code?

▼

Picklist:

To help trace relevant accounts quickly and easily.
To make sure the correct balances are calculated.
To prevent fraud.

Chapter 2 – The books of prime entry

Task 2.1

Kendo Ltd trades in exotic dress materials. On 7 August, he is preparing an invoice for goods of £100 plus VAT, for a customer, VXT Ltd.

What will be the amounts entered in the sales day book when the invoice has been prepared?

Sales day book

Date 20XX	Details	Invoice number	Total £	VAT £	Net £
7 August	VXT Ltd ▼	172	120	20	100

Picklist:

Kendo Ltd
VXT Ltd

Task 2.2

Kendo has prepared the following invoice.

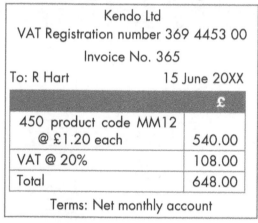

Kendo Ltd VAT Registration number 369 4453 00 Invoice No. 365	
To: R Hart 15 June 20XX	£
450 product code MM12 @ £1.20 each	540.00
VAT @ 20%	108.00
Total	648.00
Terms: Net monthly account	

How will this invoice be entered in to Kendo Ltd's sales day book?

Sales day book

Date 20XX	Details	Invoice number	Total £	VAT £	Net £
15 June	R Hart ▼	365	648	108	540

Picklist:

Kendo Ltd
R Hart

Task 2.3

Natural Productions is a small business that manufactures a variety of soaps and bath products which it sells directly to shops. During January 20XX the following credit sales to customers took place:

Invoice No. 6237 to Hoppers Ltd £547 plus VAT
Invoice No. 6238 to Body Perfect £620 plus VAT
Invoice No. 6239 to Esporta Leisure £346 plus VAT
Invoice No. 6240 to Langans Beauty £228 plus VAT
Invoice No. 6241 to Body Perfect £548 plus VAT
Invoice No. 6242 to Superior Products £221 plus VAT
Invoice No. 6243 to Esporta Leisure £416 plus VAT
Invoice No. 6244 to Hoppers Ltd £238 plus VAT
Invoice No. 6245 to Langans Beauty £274 plus VAT

You are required to:

(a) **Enter these transactions into the sales day book given below.**

(b) **Cast the columns of the sales day book and check that they cross cast.**

Sales day book

Customer	Invoice number	Total £	VAT £	Net £
6237 ▼	6237	656.4	109.4	547
6238 ▼	6238	744	124	620
6239 ▼	6239	415.2	69.2	346
6240 ▼	6240	273.6	45.6	228
6241 ▼	6241	657.6	109.6	548
6242 ▼	6242	265.2	44.2	221
6243 ▼	6243	499.2	83.2	416
6244 ▼	6244	333.2	47.6	238
6245 ▼	6245	328.8	54.8	274

Picklist:

Body Perfect
Esporta Leisure
Hoppers Ltd
Langans Beauty
Natural Productions
Superior Products

Cross-cast check:

	£
Net	
VAT	
Total	

Task 2.4

During January the following credit notes were issued by Natural Productions to various customers:

Credit note No. 1476 to Hoppers Ltd £68.70 plus VAT

Credit note No. 1477 to Esporta Leisure £89.20 plus VAT

Credit note No. 1478 to Superior Products £11.75 plus VAT

Record the credit notes in the appropriate day book by:

- **Selecting the correct daybook title and**
- **Making the necessary entries.**

Day book:	▼

Picklist:

Purchases day book
Purchases returns day book
Sales day book
Sales returns day book

Customer		Credit note number	Total £	VAT £	Net £
	▼	1476			
	▼	1477			
	▼	1478			

Picklist:

Esporta Leisure
Hoppers Ltd
Natural Productions
Superior Products

Task 2.5

Natural Productions manufactures a variety of soaps and bath products. It buys materials for the manufacturing process from a number of suppliers on credit. It also buys other items such as stationery on credit. During January 20XX Natural Productions received the following invoices from credit suppliers:

P J Phillips	
VAT Registration number 436 4472 01	
Invoice No. 03576	
To: Natural Products	4 Jan 20XX
	£
225 soap dispensers	357.00
VAT @ 20%	71.40
Total	428.40
Terms: Net monthly account	

W J Jones	
VAT Registration number 564 4432 89	
Invoice No. 18435	
To: Natural Products	6 Jan 20XX
	£
Stationery	210.00
VAT @ 20%	42.00
Total	252.00
Terms: Net monthly account	

Record the invoices in the appropriate day book by:

- **Selecting the correct day book title and**
- **Making the necessary entries.**

Day book:	▼

Picklist:

Discounts allowed day book
Discounts received day book
Purchases day book
Purchases returns day book
Sales day book
Sales returns day book

Date	Supplier	Invoice number	Total £	VAT £	Purchases (materials) £	Stationery £
	▼					
	▼					

Picklist:

Natural Productions
P J Phillips
W J Jones

Task 2.6

Natural Productions manufactures a variety of soaps and bath products. It buys materials for the manufacturing process from a number of suppliers on credit. It also buys other items such as stationery and packaging on credit. During January 20XX Natural Productions received the following invoices from credit suppliers:

12 Jan Invoice No. 03598 from P J Phillips £413 plus VAT for materials
16 Jan Invoice No. 28423 from Packing Supplies £268 plus VAT for packaging
19 Jan Invoice No. 18478 from Trenter Ltd £521 plus VAT for materials
20 Jan Invoice No. 84335 from O & P Ltd £624 plus VAT for materials
24 Jan Invoice No. 28444 from Packing Supplies £164 plus VAT for packaging
28 Jan Invoice No. 18491 from Trenter Ltd £368 plus VAT for materials
31 Jan Invoice No. 43681 from W J Jones £104 plus VAT for stationery

Record the invoices in the appropriate day book by:

- **Selecting the correct day book title and**
- **Making the necessary entries.**

Day book:	▼

Picklist:

Discounts allowed day book
Discounts received day book
Purchases day book
Purchases returns day book
Sales day book
Sales returns day book

Date	Supplier	Invoice number	Total £	VAT £	Purchases (materials) £	Stationery £	Packaging £
12 Jan	▼	03598					
16 Jan	▼	28423					
19 Jan	▼	18478					
20 Jan	▼	84335					
24 Jan	▼	28444					
28 Jan	▼	18491					
31 Jan	▼	43681					

Picklist:

Natural Productions
O & P Ltd
Packing Supplies
P J Phillips
Trenter Ltd
W J Jones

Task 2.7

During January Natural Productions received the following credit notes from suppliers.

P J Phillips	
VAT Registration number 436 4472 01	
Credit note No. 04216	
To: Natural Products 10 Jan 20XX	
	£
Materials	98.00
VAT @ 20%	19.60
Total	117.60
Terms: Net monthly account	

W J Jones	
VAT Registration number 564 4432 89	
Credit note No. CN 0643	
To: Natural Products 16 Jan 20XX	
	£
Stationery	56.00
VAT @ 20%	11.20
Total	67.20
Terms: Net monthly account	

Record the credit notes in the appropriate day book by:

- **Selecting the correct day book title and**
- **Making the necessary entries.**

Day book:	▼

Picklist:

Discounts allowed day book
Discounts received day book
Purchases day book
Purchases returns day book
Sales day book
Sales returns day book

Date	Supplier	Credit note number	Total £	VAT £	Purchases (materials) £	Stationery £	Packaging £
10 Jan	▼	▼					
16 Jan	▼	▼					

Picklist:

Natural Productions
P J Phillips
W J Jones
04216
CN 0643

Task 2.8

You work in the accounts department of Southfield Electrical. You have been given the two credit notes below.

Southfield Electrical VAT Registration number 569 5242 89	
Credit note No. 08650	
Customer No. SL 44	21 Sept 20XX
To: Whitehill Superstores	
	£
Zanpoint fridge	330.00
Less 10% trade discount	33.00
	297.00
VAT @ 20%	59.40
Total	356.40
Reason: damaged goods	

Southfield Electrical VAT Registration number 569 5242 89	
Credit note No. 08651	
Customer No. SL 15	23 Sept 20XX
To: Dagwell Enterprises	
	£
6 Temax coffee maker @ 40.00 each	240.00
Less 15% trade discount	36.00
	204.00
VAT @ 20%	40.80
Total	244.80
Reason: goods not ordered	

Complete the sales returns day book by:

- **Entering the credit notes.**
- **Totalling the columns.**

Sales returns day book

Date	Customer	Credit note number	Customer code	Gross total £	VAT £	Net £
21 Sep	▼		▼			
23 Sep	▼		▼			
	Totals					

Picklist:

Dagwell Enterprises
Southfield Electrical
Whitehill Superstores
SL 15
SL 44

Task 2.9

Given below are the only four purchase invoices received by Short Furniture in the week ending 27 January 20XX. You are also given an extract from the supplier codes listing.

27 Jan Invoice No. 09642 from Ephraim Supplies £291.00 plus VAT for wood
27 Jan Invoice No. 06932 from Cavendish Woods £705.10 plus VAT for wood
27 Jan Invoice No. 67671 from Calverley Bros £145.60 plus VAT for polish
27 Jan Invoice No. 36004 from Culverden & Co £57.40 plus VAT for other purchases

Supplier codes listing

Calverley Bros	PL03
Cavendish Woods	PL14
Culverden & Co	PL23
Ephraim Supplies	PL39

Complete the purchases day book by:

• **Entering the invoices – note that purchases are analysed into wood, polish and other.**

• **Totalling the columns.**

Purchases day book

Date	Supplier	Invoice number	Supplier code	Total £	VAT £	Net £	Wood Purchases £	Polish purchases £	Other purchases £
	▼		▼						
	▼		▼						
	▼		▼						
	▼		▼						

Picklist:

Calverley Bros
Cavendish Woods
Culverden & Co
Ephraim Supplies
PL03
PL14
PL23
PL39

Task 2.10

You work for Smith & Co. Credit notes to customers have been prepared and partially entered in the sales returns day book, as shown below.

(a) **Complete the entries in the sales returns day book by inserting the appropriate figures for each credit note.**

(b) **Total the last five columns of the sales returns day book.**

Sales returns day book

Date 20XX	Details	Credit note number	Total £	VAT £	Net £	Bags returns £	Suitcases returns £
30 Nov	Shrier Goods	562	624	104	520	520	
30 Nov	Gringles Co	563	408	68	340		340
30 Nov	Lester plc	564	1,068	178	890	890	
	Totals		2,100	350	1,750	1,410	340

Chapter 3 – VAT and discounts

Task 3.1

Ken trades in exotic dress materials. He has many credit customers who operate in the same trade as him and he routinely offers these customers a discount off the list price of his goods in order to maintain good relations.

What type of discount is this an example of?

✓	
✓	A trade discount
	A prompt payment discount
	A bulk discount

Task 3.2

VAT is a tax on consumer expenditure which a VAT registered business must collect from its customers.

Who is VAT paid over to?

✓	
	The Home Office
	The Treasury
	The Inland Revenue
✓	HM Revenue & Customs

Task 3.3

On your desk is a pile of sales invoices that have already had the price of the goods entered onto them and been totalled. The customers are to be given a 15% trade discount.

Calculate the trade discount and net total to be included on each invoice.

Goods total £	Trade discount £	Net total £
416.80	62.52	354.28
105.60	15.84	84.72
96.40	14.46	81.94
263.20	39.48	223.72
351.00	52.65	298.35

Task 3.4

On your desk there is a pile of invoices which have the net total entered.

Calculate the VAT charge and the invoice total to be included on each invoice.

Net total £	VAT £	Gross total £
258.90	51.78	310.68
316.80	63.36	380.16
82.60	16.52	99.12
152.70	30.54	103.24
451.30	90.36	540.56

Task 3.5

The following gross totals include VAT.

Calculate the amount of VAT on each invoice and the net amount of the invoice.

Gross total £	VAT £	Net total £
145.20	24.2	121
66.90	11.15	55.75
246.60	41.1	245.5
35.40	5.9	29.5
125.40	20.4	104.5

Task 3.6

The following purchases have been made for cash inclusive of VAT.

Calculate the amount of VAT on each purchase and the net amount of the purchase.

Gross total £	VAT £	Net total £
252.66	42.11	210.55
169.20	28.2	151
48.60	8.1	40.7
104.28	17.43	86.85
60.48	10.08	50.4
822.60	137.1	685.5

Task 3.7

These customers have all been offered a prompt payment discount of 3% if they pay within 10 days.

Calculate the amount each customer would pay if they pay within 10 days and take the prompt payment discount.

Customer	Gross invoice total £	Amount £
J Smith	258	265.74
Anchorage Ltd	312	321.36
VIP Ltd	84	86.52
Blue House Ltd	150	154.5

Task 3.8

A sales invoice is being prepared for goods supplied, as shown in the customer order below. A bulk discount of 2% is given for all orders where more than 100 products have been ordered.

Customer order

> Jules Ltd
> Order number 8965
>
> Please supply: 2 May 20XX
>
> 200 microwaves
>
> @ £35.00 each less 5% trade discount.

Calculate the amounts to be included in the invoice.

	£
Net amount before discounts	7000
Net amount after discounts	
VAT	
Total	

Task 3.9

An invoice for £1,280 plus VAT has been sent to JKF Ltd offering a prompt payment discount of 10% for payment within 14 days.

(a) What is the amount JKF Ltd will pay if they pay within 14 days?

£ _____

JKF Ltd pays the invoice within 14 days and takes the prompt payment discount.

(b) Complete the table below to show the amounts to be included on the credit note for JKF Ltd.

Credit note

Amount	£
Net amount	
VAT	
Gross amount	

24

Task 3.10

The credit note below has been sent to a customer in respect of a prompt payment discount.

Anchor Supplies Ltd
Horwich Way
Bolton BL8 3XU

VAT Registration No. 424 5242 42

PROMPT PAYMENT DISCOUNT CREDIT NOTE

Shipper Ltd   Customer account code: SHIP001
24 George Street
Rochdale   Invoice no: 298
RC3 4HJ

Credit note no: 223   Date: 15 October 20XX

Net £	VAT £	Gross £
56.00	11.20	67.20

Record the credit note in the appropriate day book by:

- **Selecting the correct daybook title and**
- **Making the necessary entries.**

Day book:	▼

Picklist:

Discounts allowed day book
Discounts received day book
Purchases day book
Purchases returns day book
Sales day book
Sales returns day book

Date 20XX	Details	Credit note number	Total £	VAT £	Net £
15 Oct	▼	223			

Picklist:

Anchor Supplies Ltd
Shipper Ltd

Task 3.11

The credit note below has been received from a supplier in respect of a prompt payment discount.

Rent a Van Ltd
31 Cannon Way, Manchester
MZ2 8BS

VAT Registration No. 569 5242 89

PROMPT PAYMENT DISCOUNT CREDIT NOTE

Pop Ice Cream ltd   Customer account code: POP003
4 Goodge Street
Ainsworth   Invoice no: 569
Lancs AL52 2FC

Credit note no: 11   Date: 10 November 20XX

Net £	VAT £	Gross £
103.00	20.60	123.60

Required

Record the credit note in the appropriate day book by:

- **Selecting the correct day book title and**
- **Making the necessary entries.**

Day book:	▼

Picklist:

Discounts allowed day book
Discounts received day book
Purchases day book
Purchases returns day book
Sales day book
Sales returns day book

Date 20XX	Details	Credit note number	Total £	VAT £	Net £
10 Nov	▼	11			

Picklist:
Pop Ice Cream Ltd
Rent a Van Ltd

Task 3.12

An invoice is being prepared by Sumberton Ltd to be sent to Meering Ltd for £2,000 plus VAT. A prompt payment discount of 4% will be offered for payment within 10 days.

(a) **What is the amount Sumberton Ltd should receive if payment is made within 10 days?**

£

(b) **What is the amount Sumberton Ltd should receive if payment is not made within 10 days?**

£

Task 3.13

Sumberton Ltd offers some established customers a discount of 4% whatever the size of their order and irrespective of when they pay.

What is the name of this type of discount?

▼

Picklist:

Bulk discount
Prompt payment discount
Trade discount

Task 3.14

Show whether the following statements are true or false.

	True ✓	False ✓
The book of prime entry for discounts allowed is the petty cash book.		
Input tax is the VAT suffered on purchases.		
A goods received note is a primary document for recording in the accounting records.		

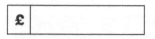

Chapter 4 – Recording credit sales

Task 4.1

Ken trades in exotic dress materials. A new customer has phoned up with an enquiry about buying some materials from Ken.

What should Ken send the customer?

✓	
	A delivery note
	A price list
	A goods received note
	A statement of account

Task 4.2

Ken wishes to analyse his sales so that he can distinguish between those made to UK customers and those from abroad.

What is the best way for him to do this?

✓	
	Analyse every invoice into a separate column of his analysed sales day book
	Allocate one of two sales codes to each invoice and use this to write up the invoices in the analysed sales day book
	Allocate invoice numbers on a randomised basis
	Use a different sequence of invoice numbers for each customer

Task 4.3

On 8 January 20XX, Southfield Electrical received the following purchase order from Whitehill Superstores. The goods were delivered the following day.

Southfield Electrical's customer files show the following information.

Customer name	Customer code	Trade discount	Prompt payment discount
Whitehill Superstores	SL 44	10%	4% – 10 days

Whitehill Superstores
28 Whitehill Park
Benham DR6 5LM

Purchase Order 32431

Southfield Electrical   4 Jan 20XX
Industrial Estate
Benham DR6 2FF

Please supply 8 units of product code 6260 Hosch Tumble
Dryer

@ £300.00 each, plus VAT.

Complete the ten boxes in the sales invoice below.

Southfield Electrical
Industrial Estate
Benham DR6 2FF

VAT registration no: 569 5242 89

SALES INVOICE 57104

Date: [   ] ▼

To: Whitehill Superstores   Customer account code: [   ]
       28 Whitehill Park

       Benham, DR6 5LM   Purchase order no: [   ]

Quantity of units	Product code	Price each £	Total amount after trade discount £	VAT £	Total £

Terms: [   ] ▼

Picklist:

4 Jan 20XX
8 Jan 20XX
9 Jan 20XX
Net monthly account
30 days net
4% prompt payment discount for payment within 10 days
10% trade discount

Task 4.4

On 18 May 20XX, Southfield Electrical received the following purchase order from Harper & Sons Ltd. The goods were delivered the following day.

Southfield Electrical's customer files show the following discount policy.

Customer name	Customer code	Trade discount	Prompt payment discount
Harper & Sons	SL 26	5%	3% – 14 days

Harper & Sons also receives a bulk discount of 5% if the net amount of their order, after deducting trade discount, is over £1,000.

Harper & Sons
30 High Street
Benham DR6 4ST

Purchase Order 04367

Southfield Electrical   16 May 20XX
Industrial Estate
Benham DR6 2FF

Please supply 6 units of product code 6370 Hosch Washing Machine

@ £260.00 each, plus VAT.

Complete the ten boxes in the sales invoice on the following page.

Southfield Electrical
Industrial Estate
Benham DR6 2FF
VAT registration no: 569 5242 89

SALES INVOICE 57105

Date: [▼]

To: Harper & Sons   Customer account code: [ ]
30 High Street

Benham, DR6 4ST   Purchase order no: [ ]

Quantity of units	Product code	Price each £	Total amount after discounts £	VAT £	Total £

Terms: [▼]

Picklist:

16 May 20XX
18 May 20XX
19 May 20XX
Net monthly account
30 days net
3% prompt payment discount for payment within 14 days
5% bulk discount
5% trade discount

Task 4.5

On 20 Oct Whitehill Superstores received an invoice from Southfield Electrical. The invoice is shown below together with the delivery note and the purchase order.

Invoice

Southfield Electrical
Industrial Estate, Benham DR6 2FF
VAT Registration No. 569 5242 89

To: Whitehill Superstores   19 Oct 20XX

Invoice No. 56501

Delivery note 34816
Purchase order 385

	£
15 product 9046 @ £15 each	225.00
VAT @ 20%	45.00
Total	270.00

Terms
Terms: Net monthly account

Delivery note

Southfield Electrical
Industrial Estate, Benham DR6 2FF
VAT Registration No. 569 5242 89

Delivery note 34816

18 Oct 20XX
To:

Whitehill Superstore
28 Whitehill Park
Benham DR6 5LM

Please receive 12 product 9406
Kensharp Toaster.

Purchase order

Whitehill Superstores
Order number 32202

Please supply: 16 Oct 20XX

15 Kensharp Toaster product code 9406

@ £15.00 each less 5% trade discount

As agreed, terms of payment are 3% discount for payment by the end of the month.

(a) **Check the delivery note, the invoice and the purchase order and answer the following questions.**

Questions	Yes ✓	No ✓
Has the correct amount of goods been delivered?		
Has the correct product been delivered?		
Have the correct codes been used on the invoice?		
Has the correct discount been applied?		

(b) **Based on the amounts actually delivered to the customer, what should be the correct amounts of the invoice?**

Net amount £	VAT amount £	Gross amount £

Task 4.6

Given below is a credit note and a goods returned note from a customer, Whitehill Superstores. Whitehill Superstores receives 20% trade discount on all orders.

Credit note

Southfield Electrical
Industrial Estate, Benham DR6 2FF
VAT Registration No. 569 5242 89

To: Whitehill Superstores   22 Oct 20XX

Credit note No. 08669

Purchase order 40102

	£
3 product 4770 @ £220 each	660.00
VAT @ 20%	132.00
Total	792.00

Reason: ordered in error

Goods returned note

Whitehill Superstores
28 Whitehill Park
Benham DR6 5LM

To: Southfield Electrical   19 Oct 20XX

Goods returned note No. 56

Purchase order 40102

4 product 4770 @ £220 each less 20% trade discount

Reason: faulty goods

Identify any discrepancies on the credit note by drawing a line between each left hand box and then the appropriate right hand box.

Reason for return		Not shown on credit note
VAT rate		Incorrectly shown on credit note
Trade discount		Correctly shown on credit note
Quantity		

Task 4.7

Southfield Electrical received a cheque for £516.10 from a credit customer, Hayworth Ltd, on 20 November 20XX. There was no document included with the cheque to show what transactions were included in the payment.

(a) **Show what document the customer should have included with the cheque by circling one document name.**

Document names			
Delivery note	Petty cash voucher	Purchase order	Remittance advice note

After contacting Hayworth Ltd, you identify that the payment covers the invoice shown below.

Invoice number	30227	
Date:	7 November 20XX	
To:	Hayworth Ltd	
		£
Goods value		448.00
VAT		89.60
Invoice total		537.60
4% prompt payment discount for payment received within 10 days of invoice date, otherwise 30 days net		

(b) **Using the picklist below, complete the following statement.**

The cheque from Hayworth Ltd for £516.10 has resulted in an

[▼]

This is because Hayworth has taken the [▼] offered.

This should not have been taken as the cheque arrived [▼] after the invoice date.

In order to resolve the problem Southfield Electrical should

[▼] from Hayworth Ltd for £ [   ] which will clear the outstanding balance.

Picklist:

13 days
14 days
less than 10 days
overpayment
prompt payment discount
request a credit note
request an invoice
request another cheque
trade discount
underpayment

Task 4.8

Southfield Electrical received a cheque for £709.48 from a credit customer, Harper & Sons, with a remittance advice stating the payment was for invoice **30256**, shown below. The cheque was received on 19 November 20XX.

Invoice number	30256	
Date:	12 November XX	
To:	Harper & Sons	
		£
Goods value		620.00
VAT		124.00
Invoice total		744.00
4% prompt payment discount for payment received within 10 days of invoice date, otherwise 30 days net		

Using the picklist below, complete the following statement.

The cheque from Harper & Sons for £709.48 has resulted in an [▼] .

Harper & Sons paid within the time limit for the [▼] offered by Southfield Electrical.

However, they [▼] the discount.

In order to resolve the problem Southfield Electrical should [▼] from Harper & Sons for £ [ ] which will clear the outstanding balance.

Picklist:

correctly calculated
incorrectly calculated
overpayment
prompt payment discount
request a credit note
request an invoice
request another cheque
trade discount
underpayment

Task 4.9

On 21 December Sumberton Ltd delivered the following goods to a credit customer, Gringles Co.

Sumberton Ltd
Sumberton House
10 Main Road
Sawlow
SA7 5LD

Delivery note No. 6734527
21 December 20XX

Gringles Co   Customer account code: SL637
Unit 18 Radley Estate
Sawlow
SA7 7VB

80 leather shoulder bags, product code L736B.

The list price of the goods was £100 per box of five bags plus VAT. Gringles Co is to be given a 15% bulk discount and a 4% discount if the invoice is paid within 10 days.

Complete the invoice below.

Sumberton Ltd
Sumberton House,
10 Main Road
Sawlow
SA7 5LD

VAT Registration No. 536 3723 77

Gringles Co   Customer account code: SL637
Unit 18 Radley Estate
Sawlow
SA7 7VB

Date: 22 December 20XX

Invoice No: 12901
Delivery note number: 6734527

Quantity of goods	Product code	Total list price £	Net amount after bulk discount £	VAT £	Gross £

Task 4.10

The account shown below is in the sales ledger of Sumberton Ltd. A remittance advice for an automated payment of £2,807 has now been received from this customer.

Meering Ltd

Date 20XX	Details	Amount £	Date 20XX	Details	Amount £
6 October	Sales invoice 12624	1,756	10 October	Sales returns credit note 501	78
11 November	Sales invoice 12711	2,918	17 November	Sales returns credit note 555	111
7 December	Sales invoice 12813	2,384	30 November	Bank	1,678

Which outstanding item has not been included in the payment of £2,807?

▼

Picklist:

Bank
Sales invoice 12624
Sales invoice 12711
Sales invoice 12813
Sales returns credit note 501
Sales returns credit note 555

Chapter 5 – Recording credit purchases

Task 5.1

Ken trades in exotic dress materials.

Complete the following statement:

When a supplier delivers materials to him he retains the supplier's delivery note and also prepares [▼] once he has had a chance to inspect the quality of the items.

Picklist:

an invoice
a goods received note
a remittance advice

Task 5.2

Complete the following statement:

A code which will help Ken to classify the different types of material purchase when completing his analysed purchases day book is:

	✓
A supplier code	
A product code	

Task 5.3

Ken has been offered a prompt payment discount by one of his suppliers of '2% for payment within 10 days'. He receives an invoice dated 10 June on 12 June with a total of £239.20, excluding VAT. He wishes to take advantage of the discount.

(a)   By what date must the supplier receive the payment?

[▼]

Picklist:

19 June
20 June
21 June
22 June

(b) **How much should Ken pay the supplier on that date?**

£ [   ]

Task 5.4

You work for Newmans, a music shop, in the accounts department and one of your responsibilities is to organise the payments to suppliers. You have been off sick for the last week and a half and therefore it is urgent that you consider the invoices that are on your desk requiring payment.

Newmans' policy is to pay any invoices that are due each Friday. When a cheque is written on a Friday it does not then reach the supplier until Monday, ie three days later. If a prompt payment discount is offered by a supplier then this is taken if the discount will still be valid on the Monday. Otherwise the policy is to take the maximum amount of credit available.

Today's date is Friday 27 January 20XX. Thereafter, the following payment dates are 3 February, 10 February and 17 February. Remember that, as payments take three days to reach the supplier, any invoice dated earlier than 7 January with a 30-day period must be paid today, because if they are delayed until 3 February then the payments will not be received until 6 February, more than 30 days after they are due.

The invoices that are on your desk are scheduled below:

Invoice date	Supplier name	Terms	Total £	VAT £	Net £
5 Jan	Henson Press	30 days	336.00	56.00	280.00
8 Jan	GH Publications	30 days	136.80	22.80	114.00
12 Jan	Ely Instruments	20 days 2% discount otherwise 30 days	765.00	127.50	637.50
15 Jan	Hams Instruments	14 days 2.5% discount otherwise 30 days	372.00	62.00	310.00
19 Jan	CD Supplies	10 days 3% discount otherwise 30 days	138.72	23.12	115.60
22 Jan	Jester Press	10 days 3.5% discount otherwise 30 days	156.00	26.00	130.00
22 Jan	Henson Press	30 days	306.00	51.00	255.00

In the schedule given below show the date that each invoice should be paid and the amount for which the cheque should be written out.

Invoice date	Supplier name	Payment date	Amount of cheque £
5 Jan	Henson Press	▼	
8 Jan	GH Publications	▼	
12 Jan	Ely Instruments	▼	
15 Jan	Hams Instruments	▼	
19 Jan	CD Supplies	▼	
22 Jan	Jester Press	▼	
22 Jan	Henson Press	▼	

Picklist:

27 Jan
3 Feb
10 Feb
17 Feb

Task 5.5

Given below is a statement received by your organisation, Edgehill Designs, from one of its credit suppliers, P T Supplies, as at 31 January 20XX. You are instructed to pay all of the invoices less credit notes up to 10 January. Today's date is 7 February.

PT Supplies 149 Field Road, Darton, DF12 8GH

STATEMENT OF ACCOUNT

To: Edgehill Designs   31 January 20XX

Date 20XX	Invoice/credit note number	Details	Amount £
6 Jan	Inv 20671	Goods	107
8 Jan	Inv 20692	Goods	157
10 Jan	CN 04722	Goods returned	28
27 Jan	Inv 20718	Goods	120
30 Jan	CN 04786	Goods returned	16
6 Jan	Inv 20671	Goods	107

(a) **Complete the remittance advice below by:**

- **Selecting the date from the picklist in the first column**
- **Dragging and dropping the appropriate details and transaction amount below into the second column**

You only need to enter the relevant invoices and credit notes. Leave blank any rows that are not needed.

Remittance advice	
To: PT Supplies	From: Edgehill Designs
Date: 7 February 20XX	

Date 20XX	Details and transaction amount £
▼	
▼	
▼	
▼	
▼	

Picklist:

6 Jan
8 Jan
10 Jan
27 Jan
30 Jan
7 Feb

Details and transaction amount (£):

Inv 20671 – £107	Inv 20692 – £157	CN 04722 – £28
Inv 20718 – £120	CN 04786 – £16	

(b) **What is the total payment amount to accompany this remittance advice note?**

£ [   ]

Task 5.6

On 12 July Whitehill Superstores ordered goods from Southfield Electrical who agreed a 10% trade discount and payment terms of 30 days net. The goods were delivered on 15 July and the invoice and goods received note are shown below.

Invoice

<table>
<tr><td colspan="2" align="center">Southfield Electrical
Industrial Estate Benham DR6 2FF
VAT Registration No. 569 5242 89</td></tr>
<tr><td>To: Whitehill Superstores   Invoice No. 56389</td><td align="right">15 Jun 20XX</td></tr>
<tr><td></td><td align="right">£</td></tr>
<tr><td>10 product code 9116 @ £24 each</td><td align="right">240.00</td></tr>
<tr><td>VAT @ 20%</td><td align="right">48.00</td></tr>
<tr><td>Total</td><td align="right">288.00</td></tr>
</table>

Terms: Cash on delivery

Goods received note

Whitehill Superstores

Goods received note GRN47422

15 July 20XX

Received from: Southfield Electrical

10 product code 9116 in good condition

(a) **Refer to the information above and the goods received note and identify any discrepancies on the invoice by drawing a line between each left hand box and then the appropriate right hand box.**

Terms of payment	Not shown on invoice
Customer name	
VAT rate	Incorrectly shown on invoice
Trade discount	
Quantity of goods delivered	Correctly shown on invoice
Date	

(b) **What will be the correct amounts on the invoice?**

Net amount £	VAT amount £	Gross amount £

Task 5.7

Given below is an invoice received by Dartmouth Supplies and the related purchase order.

Invoice

Dan Industries
Park Rise
Fenbridge DR2 7AD
VAT Registration No. 0621 3384 20

To: Dartmouth Supplies   7 Oct 20XX

Invoice No. 77412

Delivery note 34816
Purchase order 317428

	£
16 product D5345 Rocking chair @ £96.00 each	1,536.00
Less trade discount @ 5%	76.80
	1,459.20
VAT @ 20%	291.84
Total	1,600.04

Terms: 30 days net

Purchase order

Dan Industries
Order number 317428

20 Sept 20XX

Please supply 16 product D4632 Rocking chair @ £96.00 each plus VAT

Discount: 10% trade discount, as agreed

(a) **Check the invoice and the purchase order and answer the following questions.**

	Yes ✓	No ✓
Has the correct purchase price of the rocking chairs been charged?		
Has the correct discount been applied?		
Has the invoice been correctly cast?		
Has the correct product code been used on the invoice?		
Has VAT been charged at the correct rate?		

(b) **What will be the correct amounts on the invoice?**

Net amount £	VAT amount £	Gross amount £

Task 5.8

You work for Bailie Ltd. Shown below is a statement of account received from a credit supplier, Dazzle Ltd, and the supplier's account as shown in the purchases ledger of Bailie Ltd.

Dazzle Ltd
21 Albert Street
Keeley
KE4 7AB

To: Bailie Ltd
5 Purley Road
Keeley
KE5 7LW

STATEMENT OF ACCOUNT

Date 20XX	Reference	Details	Debit £	Credit £	Balance £
1 July	8371	Goods	335		335
3 July	8412	Goods	420		755
7 July	8515	Goods	723		1,478
10 July	CN 3215	Goods returned		250	1,228
16 July		Cheque		485	743

45

Purchases ledger – Dazzle Ltd

Date 20XX	Details	Amount £	Date 20XX	Details	Amount £
15 July	Bank – cheque	485	1 July	PDB 8371	335
15 July	Discount received	20	3 July	PDB 8412	420
			7 July	PDB 8515	723

(a) **Which item is missing from the statement of account from Dazzle Ltd?**

Picklist:

Bank – cheque £485
Credit note 3215 £250
Discount received £20
Invoice 8371 £335
Invoice 8412 £420
Invoice 8515 £723

(b) **Which item is missing from the supplier account in Bailie Ltd's purchases ledger?**

Picklist:

Cheque £485
Credit note 3215 £250
Discount received £20
Invoice 8371 £335
Invoice 8412 £420
Invoice 8515 £723

(c) **Assuming any differences between the statement of account from Dazzle Ltd and the supplier account in Bailie Ltd's purchases ledger are simply due to omission errors, what is the amount owing to Dazzle Ltd?**

£

Task 5.9

A supply of nails has been delivered to Acute Carpentry by Carbon Irons. The purchase order sent from Acute Carpentry, and the invoice from Carbon Irons, are shown below.

Acute Carpentry
Purchase Order No. 78639

To: Carbon Irons

Date: 16 June

Please supply 30 boxes 6 inch nails product code N1106
Purchase price: £20 per box, plus VAT
Discount: less 10% trade discount, as agreed.

Carbon Irons
Invoice No. 2318

Acute Carpentry

18 June

	£
30 .... boxes product code N1106 @ £25 each	750.00
VAT @ 20%	150.00
Total	900.00

Terms: 30 days net

Check the invoice against the purchase order and answer the following questions.

	Yes ✓	No ✓
Has the correct purchase price of the cardboard boxes been charged?		
Has the correct discount been applied?		

	Amount £
What would be the VAT amount charged if the invoice was correct?	
What would be the total amount charged if the invoice was correct?	

Task 5.10

Ken runs a business trading in exotic dress materials. He sends out cheques to suppliers on the last day of the month following the month of invoice. Below is an extract from Ken's purchases ledger for his supplier, Mack Materials.

Mack Materials

Date 20XX	Details	Amount £	Date 20XX	Details	Amount £
31 May	Bank	890	1 May	Balance b/d	890
19 May	Purchases returns Credit note 43	31	7 May	Purchases Invoice 901	760
			3 June	Purchases Invoice 963	189

(a) **Complete the remittance advice note below. Leave any spare lines blank. Enter all amounts as positive values.**

Ken's Exotics
1 Bath Street

Cembury, CE11 9SD

REMITTANCE ADVICE

To: Mack Materials   Date: 30 June 20XX

Please find attached our cheque in payment of the following amounts.

Invoice number	Credit note number	Amount £
▼	▼	
▼	▼	
▼	▼	
▼	▼	
Total amount paid		

Picklist:

Balance b/d
Bank
Credit note 43
Invoice 901
Invoice 903

(b) **Which of the following statements is true?**

	✓
The remittance advice note will be sent to the accounts department at Mack Materials to request that a cheque is raised.	
The remittance advice note will be sent to Mack Materials's bank to advise them of the amount being paid.	
The remittance advice note will be sent to the customer to advise them of the amount being paid.	
The remittance advice note will be sent to the supplier to advise them of the amount being paid.	

Task 5.11

Ken has received a statement from a supplier which shows that, as at the end of June 20XX, he owes the supplier £2,876. The purchases ledger account for this supplier shows that at that date Ken only owed £1,290.

Which of the following items would explain the difference?

	✓
Ken has requested a credit note from the supplier for £1,586 which he has not yet received.	
Ken sent a cheque for £1,586 to the supplier on 30 June 20XX.	
Ken ordered some items from the supplier on 30 June for £1,586 but the goods have not yet been delivered and an invoice has not yet been raised.	

Task 5.12

A supply of suitcases has been delivered to Sumberton Ltd by Casaubon's. The purchase order sent from Sumberton Ltd, and the invoice from Casaubon's, are shown below.

Sumberton Ltd
Sumberton House, 10 Main Road
Sawlow
SA7 5LD

Purchase Order No. 7683247

To: Casaubon's

Date: 17 December 20XX

Please supply 15 small wheeled cabin cases, product code WCC625
Purchase price: £23 each, plus VAT
Discount: less 15% trade discount, as agreed.

Casaubon's
80 Eliot Street, Sawlow SA9 4AC
VAT Registration No. 983 3933 83

Invoice No. 782736

Sumberton Ltd
Sumberton House, 10 Main Road
Sawlow
SA7 5LD

22 December 20XX

	£
15 small wheeled cabin cases product code WCC625 @ £25 each	375.00
Less trade discount at 5%	18.75
Net amount	356.25
VAT @ 20%	71.25
Total	427.50
Terms: 30 days net	

Check the invoice against the purchase order and answer the following questions.

	Yes ✓	No ✓
Has the correct purchase price of the cabin cases been charged?		
Has the correct discount been applied?		

	Amount £
What would be the VAT amount charged if the invoice was correct?	
What would be the total amount charged if the invoice was correct?	

Task 5.13

Shown below is a statement of account received from a credit supplier, and the supplier's account as shown in the purchases ledger of Sumberton Ltd.

Trinder and Papp
54 Vallais Road
Gosfirth
GO9 5VV

To: Sumberton Ltd
Sumberton House
10 Main Road
Sawlow
SA7 5LD

STATEMENT OF ACCOUNT

Date 20XX	Number	Details	Amount £	Balance £
20 October	10923	Invoice	2,109	2,109
4 November		Payment	–2,099	10
8 November	11004	Invoice	3,188	3,198
10 November	C536	Credit note	–156	3,042
26 November	11342	Invoice	2,185	5,227
28 November	11378	Invoice	1,244	6,471
30 November	C579	Credit note	–320	6,151

Trinder and Papp

Date 20XX	Details	Amount £	Date 20XX	Details	Amount £
4 Nov	Bank – BACS	2,099	20 Oct	Purchases	2,109
4 Nov	Discount	10	8 Nov	Purchases	3,188
10 Nov	Purchases returns	156	26 Nov	Purchases	2,185
			28 Nov	Purchases	1,244

(a) **Which item is missing from the statement of account from Trinder and Papp?**

Picklist:

Credit note C536
Credit note C579
Discount of £10
Invoice 10923
Invoice 11004
Invoice 11342
Invoice 11378
Payment for £2,099

(b) **Which item is missing from the supplier account in Sumberton Ltd's purchases ledger?**

Picklist:

Credit note C536
Credit note C579
Discount of £10
Invoice 10923
Invoice 11004
Invoice 11342
Invoice 11378
Payment for £2,099

(c) **Assuming any differences between the statement of account from Trinder and Papp and the supplier account in Sumberton Ltd's purchases ledger are simply due to omission errors, what is the amount owing to Trinder and Papp?**

£

(d) **Which of the following statements is true?**

	✓
A credit note adds to the amount owed to the supplier	
A remittance advice note adds to the amount owed to the supplier	
A goods received note adds to the amount owed to the supplier	
An invoice adds to the amount owed to the supplier	

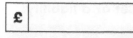

Chapter 6 – Double entry bookkeeping (part 1)

Task 6.1

Identify whether each of the following is an asset or a liability:

	Asset ✓	Liability ✓
A trade receivable		
A car used in the business		
A loan from the bank		
A bank overdraft		
Cash in hand		
VAT owed to HMRC		
A trade payable		
Inventory of raw materials		

Task 6.2

Complete the following statements using the word 'debit' or 'credit' in each case:

An increase in an expense is a [   ] .

A decrease in a liability is a [   ] .

An increase in income is a [   ] .

An increase in an asset is a [   ] .

An increase in capital is a [   ] .

A decrease in an asset is a [   ] .

An increase in a liability is a [   ] .

A decrease in capital is a [   ] .

Task 6.3

(a)   Insert the two effects of each of these transactions in the space given below.

(i)   James paid £20,000 into a business bank account in order to start his business.

Effect 1	Effect 2
▼	▼

Picklist:

Decrease in capital
Decrease in cash
Decrease in liabilities
Increase in cash
Increase in capital
Increase in liabilities (trade payables)

(ii)   He paid an initial rental of £2,500 by cheque for the shop that he is to trade from.

Effect 1	Effect 2
▼	▼

Picklist:

Decrease in capital
Decrease in cash
Increase in assets
Increase in cash
Increase in liabilities (trade payables)
Rent expense incurred

(iii)   He purchased a van by cheque for £7,400.

Effect 1	Effect 2
▼	▼

Picklist:

Decrease in capital
Decrease in cash
Decrease in liabilities (trade payables)
Increase in assets
Increase in cash
Van expense incurred

(iv) He purchased £6,000 of goods for resale on credit.

Effect 1	Effect 2
▼	▼

Picklist:

Decrease in cash
Decrease in liabilities (trade payables)
Increase in assets (trade receivables)
Increase in cash
Increase in liabilities (trade payables)
Increase in purchases

(v) He sold goods for £1,000 – the customer paid by cheque.

Effect 1	Effect 2
▼	▼

Picklist:

Decrease in cash
Decrease in purchases
Increase in assets (trade receivables)
Increase in cash
Increase in liabilities (trade payables)
Increase in sales

(vi) He sold goods on credit for £4,800.

Effect 1	Effect 2
▼	▼

Picklist:

Decrease in cash
Decrease in purchases
Increase in assets (trade receivables)
Increase in cash
Increase in liabilities (trade payables)
Increase in sales

(vii) He paid shop assistants' wages by cheque totalling £2,100.

Effect 1	Effect 2
▼	▼

Picklist:

Decrease in cash
Decrease in liabilities (trade payables)
Increase in cash
Increase in drawings
Increase in purchases
Wages expenses incurred

(viii) He made further sales on credit for £3,900.

Effect 1	Effect 2
▼	▼

Picklist:

Decrease in cash
Decrease in purchases
Increase in assets (trade receivables)
Increase in cash
Increase in liabilities (trade payables)
Increase in sales

(ix) He purchased a further £1,400 of goods for resale by cheque.

Effect 1	Effect 2
▼	▼

Picklist:

Decrease in cash
Decrease in liabilities (trade payables)
Increase in assets (trade receivables)
Increase in cash
Increase in liabilities (trade payables)
Increase in purchases

(x) £3,700 was received from credit customers.

Effect 1	Effect 2
▼	▼

Picklist:

Decrease in assets (trade receivables)
Decrease in liabilities (trade payables)
Decrease in sales
Increase in assets (trade receivables)
Increase in cash
Increase in purchases

(xi) He paid £3,300 to credit suppliers.

Effect 1	Effect 2
▼	▼

Picklist:

Decrease in assets (trade receivables)
Decrease in cash
Decrease in liabilities (trade payables)
Increase in assets (trade receivables)
Increase in cash
Increase in purchases

(xii) He withdrew £800 from the business for his living expenses.

Effect 1	Effect 2
▼	▼

Picklist:

Decrease in cash
Decrease in liabilities (trade payables)
Increase in cash
Increase in drawings
Increase in purchases
Wages expenses incurred

(b) **Enter James's transactions above in to his ledger accounts. You do not need to balance off the ledger accounts.**

Bank

Details		£	Details		£
	▼			▼	
	▼			▼	
	▼			▼	
	▼			▼	
	▼			▼	
	▼			▼	

Picklist:

Capital
Drawings
Purchases
Purchases ledger control
Sales
Sales ledger control
Rent
Van
Wages

Capital

Details		£	Details		£
	▼			▼	
	▼			▼	

Picklist:

Bank
Capital
Drawings
Purchases
Purchases ledger control
Sales
Sales ledger control
Rent
Van
Wages

Rent

Details	£	Details	£
▼		▼	
▼		▼	

Picklist:

Bank
Capital
Drawings
Purchases
Purchases ledger control
Sales
Sales ledger control
Rent
Van
Wages

Van

Details	£	Details	£
▼		▼	
▼		▼	

Picklist:

Bank
Capital
Drawings
Purchases
Purchases ledger control
Sales
Sales ledger control
Rent
Van
Wages

Purchases

Details		£	Details		£
	▼			▼	
	▼			▼	

Picklist:

Bank
Capital
Drawings
Purchases
Purchases ledger control
Sales
Sales ledger control
Rent
Van
Wages

Purchases ledger control

Details		£	Details		£
	▼			▼	
	▼			▼	

Picklist:

Bank
Capital
Drawings
Purchases
Purchases ledger control
Sales
Sales ledger control
Rent
Van
Wages

Sales account

Details		£	Details		£
	▼			▼	
	▼			▼	
	▼			▼	

Picklist:

Bank
Capital
Drawings
Purchases
Purchases ledger control
Sales
Sales ledger control
Rent
Van
Wages

Sales ledger control

Details		£	Details		£
	▼			▼	
	▼			▼	
	▼			▼	

Picklist:

Bank
Capital
Drawings
Purchases
Purchases ledger control
Sales
Sales ledger control
Rent
Van
Wages

Wages

Details	£	Details	£
▼		▼	
▼		▼	
▼		▼	

Picklist:

Bank
Capital
Drawings
Purchases
Purchases ledger control
Sales
Sales ledger control
Rent
Van
Wages

Drawings

Details	£	Details	£
▼		▼	
▼		▼	
▼		▼	

Picklist:

Bank
Capital
Dawings
Purchases
Purchases ledger control
Sales
Sales ledger control
Rent
Van
Wages

Task 6.4

In this task, assume the business is NOT registered for VAT.

(a) **What is the double entry required for discounts allowed to customers?**

	Debit ✓	Credit ✓
Discounts allowed		
Sales ledger control		

(b) **What is the double entry required for discounts received from suppliers?**

	Debit ✓	Credit ✓
Discounts received		
Purchases ledger control		

(c) **What is the double entry required for a purchase of goods for resale made on credit?**

	Debit ✓	Credit ✓
Purchases		
Purchases ledger control		

(d) **What is the double entry required for a sale made on credit?**

	Debit ✓	Credit ✓
Sales		
Sales ledger control		

(e) **What is the double entry required for a sale made for cash?**

	Debit ✓	Credit ✓
Cash		
Sales		

(f) **What is the double entry required for cash received from a credit customer?**

	Debit ✓	Credit ✓
Cash		
Sales ledger control		

(g) **What is the double entry required for drawings made by the owner of a business?**

	Debit ✓	Credit ✓
Drawings		
Cash		

(h) **What is the double entry required for wages paid in cash to employees?**

	Debit ✓	Credit ✓
Wages		
Cash		

Task 7.1

The following account is in the sales ledger of Smith & Co at the close of day on 31 May.

(a) **Insert the balance carried down together with date and details.**

(b) **Insert the totals.**

(c) **Insert the balance brought down together with date and details.**

TN Designs

Date 20XX	Details	Amount £	Date 20XX	Details	Amount £
1 May	Balance b/f	2,643	8 May	Bank	1,473
11 May	Invoice 27491	1,804	24 May	Credit note 381	265
18 May	Invoice 27513	1,088			
▼	▼		▼	▼	
	Total			Total	
▼	▼		▼	▼	

Picklist:

31 May
1 June
Balance b/d
Balance c/d
Smith & Co
TN Designs

Task 7.2

The following account is in the purchases ledger of Smith & Co at the close of day on 30 September.

(a) **Insert the balance carried down together with date and details.**

(b) **Insert the totals.**

(c) **Insert the balance brought down together with date and details.**

Harold & Partners

Date 20XX	Details	Amount £	Date 20XX	Details	Amount £
7 Sept	Bank	635	1 Sept	Balance b/f	1,367
7 Sept	Discount	33	5 Sept	Invoice 27465	998
30 Sept	Credit note 364	106	12 Sept	Invoice 27499	478
▼	▼		▼	▼	
	Total			Total	
▼	▼		▼	▼	

Picklist:

30 Sept
1 Oct
Balance b/d
Balance c/d
Harold & Partners
Smith & Co

Task 7.3

A payment by cheque is made to a supplier for £367.48.

What is the double entry for this transaction?

Account name		Debit £	Credit £
	▼		
	▼		

Picklist:

Bank
Purchases
Purchases ledger control
Sales
Sales ledger control

Task 7.4

For each of the following, indicate whether they are capital or revenue transactions:

	Capital ✓	Revenue ✓
Purchase of a new computer paid for by cheque		
Purchase of printer paper by cheque		
Purchase of a new business car on credit		
Payment of road tax on a new business car		
Payment of rent for the business premises		

Task 7.5

The following three accounts are in the general ledger at the close of day on 31 October.

Complete the accounts below by:

- Inserting the balance carried down together with date and details.

- Inserting the totals.

- Inserting the balance brought down together with date and details.

(a) Purchases ledger control

Date	Details	Amount £	Date	Details	Amount £
31 Oct	Purchases returns	4,467	1 Oct	Balance b/f	41,204
31 Oct	Bank	36,409	31 Oct	Purchases	52,390
31 Oct	Discounts received	125			
▼	▼		▼	▼	
	Total			Total	
▼	▼		▼	▼	

Picklist:

31 Oct
1 Nov
Balance b/d
Balance c/d
Purchases ledger control
Petty cash
VAT

(b) Petty cash

Date	Details	Amount £	Date	Details	Amount £
1 Oct	Balance b/f	200.00	31 Oct	Expenses	183.25
31 Oct	Bank	183.25			
▼	▼		▼	▼	
	Total			Total	
▼	▼		▼	▼	

Picklist:

31 Oct
1 Nov
Balance b/d
Balance c/d
Petty cash
Purchases ledger control
VAT

(c) VAT

Date	Details	£	Date	Details	£
31 Oct	Sales returns	40.00	1 Oct	Balance b/f	183.25
31 Oct	Purchases	1,900.00	31 Oct	Purchases returns	62.00
			31 Oct	Sales	3,250.00
▼	▼		▼	▼	
	Total			Total	
▼	▼		▼	▼	

Picklist:

31 Oct
1 Nov
Balance b/d
Balance c/d
Petty cash
Purchases ledger control
VAT

Task 7.6

For each of the following, indicate whether they are capital or revenue transactions:

	Capital ✓	Revenue ✓
Purchase of goods for resale on credit from a supplier		
Receipt of proceeds from sale of car used in the business		
Payment of drawings to the business owner		
Acquisition of new machine for use over five years		
Payment by a cash customer for goods		

Task 7.7

The following two accounts are in the general ledger at the close of day on 30 November.

Complete the accounts below by:

- **Inserting the balance carried down together with date and details;**

- **Inserting the totals; and**

- **Inserting the balance brought down together with date and details.**

(a) Purchases

Date 20XX	Details	Amount £	Date 20XX	Details	Amount £
01 Nov	Balance b/f	140,389		▼	
15 Nov	Purchases ledger control	14,388		▼	
30 Nov	Purchases ledger control	52,389		▼	
▼		▼	▼	▼	
	Total			Total	
▼		▼	▼	▼	

Picklist:

30 Nov
1 Dec
Balance b/d
Balance c/d
Bank
Purchases
Purchases ledger control
Sales ledger control

(b) Bank interest received

Date 20XX	Details	Amount £	Date 20XX	Details	Amount £
		▼	01 Nov	Balance b/f	32
		▼	15 Nov	Bank	14
		▼	30 Nov	Bank	22
▼	▼		▼		▼
	Total			Total	
▼	▼		▼		▼

Picklist:

30 Nov
1 Dec
Balance b/d
Balance c/d
Bank
Bank interest received
Purchases ledger control
Sales ledger control

Task 7.8

It is important to understand the difference between capital expenditure, revenue expenditure, capital income and revenue income.

Select one option in each instance below to show whether the item will be capital expenditure, revenue expenditure, capital income or revenue income.

Item	Capital expenditure ✓	Revenue expenditure ✓	Capital income ✓	Revenue income ✓
Purchase of airline tickets for business travel				
Proceeds from sale of machinery				
Sale of goods to a customer for cash				

Item	Capital expenditure ✓	Revenue expenditure ✓	Capital income ✓	Revenue income ✓
Receipt of interest on the business's savings account from the bank				
Purchase of a shop building				
Petty cash payment for stationery				

Task 7.9

For each of the items below, identify an example from the picklist provided.

Item	Example
Asset	▼
Liability	▼
Capital transaction	▼

Picklist:

Bank overdraft
Drawings
Trade receivables

Chapter 8 – Maintaining the cash book

Task 8.1

There are four payments to be entered in the credit side of Natural Production's cash book during one week.

Cash purchases listing

Suppliers paid in cash	Net £	VAT £	Gross £
Mendip plc	115	23	138

Trade payables listing

Credit suppliers paid by cheque	Amount paid £
W J Jones	521
Trenter Ltd	358
Packing Supplies	754

(a) **Enter the details from the cash purchases listing and the trade payables listing into the credit side of the cash book shown below and total each column.**

Details	Cash £	Bank £	VAT £	Cash purchases £	Trade payables £
Balance b/f		735			
▼					
▼					
▼					
▼					
Total					

Picklist:

Bank
Cash
Cash purchases

Mendip plc
Packing Supplies
Trade payables
Trenter Ltd
VAT
W J Jones

The debit side of the cash book shows the cash balance brought forward at the beginning of the week was £200 and a further £319 has been received during the week.

(b) **Using your answer to (a) above, calculate the cash balance.**

£ |

The debit side of the cash book shows the total amount of money banked during the week was £560.

(c) **Using your answer to (a) above, calculate the bank balance. If your calculations show that the bank account is overdrawn, your answer should start with a minus sign, for example – 123.**

£ |

(d) **Is the balance at bank calculated in (c) above a debit or a credit balance?**

	✓
Debit	
Credit	

Task 8.2

Given below are the cheque stubs for the two payments made by Newmans on 27 January.

You have also looked at the standing order and direct debit instruction file and noted that there is a standing order due to be paid to the local council for business rates of £255 on the 27th of each month, and a direct debit for rent of £500 also due on 27th of the month.

Cheque book stubs

Henson Press	Ely Instruments
(Purchases ledger account HEN006)	(Purchases ledger account ELY003)
£329	£736
000168	000169

Make the necessary entries in the cash book and total each column.

Cash book – credit side

Details		Cash £	Bank £	VAT £	Trade payables £	Cash purchases £	Rent & rates £
	▼						
	▼						
	▼						
	▼						
Total							

Picklist:

Cash purchases
Ely Instruments
Henson Press
Newmans
Rates
Rent
Trade payables

Task 8.3

The two amounts shown below have been received from customers and are ready to be entered in the cash book.

Receipt 56
11 July 20XX
Cheque for £500 and cash £334 received from Hoppers Ltd plc for goods supplied today – £834 including VAT.

Body Perfect Remittance advice
13 July 20XX
An amount of £542 will be transferred to your bank account today by BACS, in full settlement of our May account.

Make the necessary entries in the cash book and total each column.

Cash book – debit side

Details	Cash £	Bank £	VAT £	Trade receivables £	Cash sales £
Balance b/f	120	1,520			
▼					
▼					
Totals					

Picklist:

Bank
Body Perfect
Cash
Hoppers Ltd
Trade receivables
VAT

Task 8.4

The two amounts shown below have been received from customers and are ready to be entered in the cash book.

Receipt 56	Esporta Leisure
14 Oct 20XX	Remittance advice
	14 Oct 20XX
Cash £210 received from Howsham Ltd plc for goods supplied today – £210 including VAT.	Please find enclosed a cheque for £958 in full settlement of invoice 2457.

Make the necessary entries in the cash book and total each column.

Cash book – debit side

Details	Cash £	Bank £	VAT £	Trade receivables £	Cash sales £
Balance b/f	56	1,805			
▼					
▼					
Totals					

Picklist:

Bank
Cash
Esporta Leisure
Howsham Ltd
Trade receivables
VAT

Task 8.5

There are five payments to be entered in Canlan Ltd's cash book.

Receipts from suppliers for Canlan Ltd's cash purchases

Supplier: Dubai Dreams	
Received cash with thanks for goods bought.	
	£
Net	270
VAT	54
Total	324

Supplier: Walter Enterprises	
Received cash with thanks for goods bought.	
	£
Net	190
VAT	38
Total	228

Supplier: Sinead Reilly

Received cash with thanks for goods bought.

Net   £56
(No VAT)

Stubs from Canlan Ltd's cheque book

Payee: Sumatra Trading (Purchases ledger account PLO26)	Payee: SHSK Co
	For stationery (Canlan Ltd has no credit account with this supplier)
£7,265	£378 including VAT
Cheque number 093673	Cheque number 093674

(a) **Enter the details of the three receipts from suppliers and two cheque book stubs into the credit side of the cash book shown below. Total each column.**

Cash book – credit side

Details	Cash £	Bank £	VAT £	Trade payables £	Cash purchases £	Stationery £
Balance b/f		236				
Dubai Dreams						
Walter Enterprises						
Sinead Reilly						
Sumatra Trading						
SHSK Co						
Total						

(b) **There are two cheques from credit customers to be entered in the cash book:**

Park Farm Stores £2,576

Tristram Pale Ltd £4,233

Enter these details into the debit side of the cash book and total each column.

Cash book – debit side

Details	Cash £	Bank £	VAT £	Trade receivables £
Balance b/f	1,228			
Park Farm Stores				
Tristram Pale Ltd				
Total				

(c) **Using your answers to (a) and (b) above, calculate the cash balance.**

£ [ ]

(d) **Using your answers to (a) and (b) above, calculate the bank balance.**

£	

(e) **Is the bank balance calculated in (d) above a debit or credit balance?**

	✓
Debit	
Credit	

Task 8.6

There are five payments to be entered in Kitchen Kuts's cash book.

Receipts

Received cash with thanks for goods bought

From Kitchen Kuts, a customer without a credit account.

	£
Net	200
VAT	40
Total	240

B Smithson Ltd

Received cash with thanks for goods bought.

From Kitchen Kuts, a customer without a credit account.

	£
Net	160
VAT	32
Total	192

H Hamnet

Received cash with thanks for goods bought.

From Kitchen Kuts, a customer without a credit account.

Net   £320
(No VAT)

Renee Reid

Cheque book stubs

Tenon Ltd
(Purchase ledger account TEN006)

£3,600

000168

Vernon Motor Repairs
(We have no credit account with this supplier)

£48 including VAT

000169

(a) Enter the details from the three receipts and two cheque book stubs into the credit side of the cash book shown below and total each column.

Cash book – credit side

Details	Cash £	Bank £	VAT £	Trade payables £	Cash purchases £	Motor expenses £
Balance b/f		16,942				
B Smithson Ltd						
H Hamnet						
Renee Reid						
Tenon Ltd						
Vernon Motor Repairs						
Total						

There are two cheques from credit customers to be entered in Kitchen Kuts' cash book:

G Brownlow	£749
S Barnett	£300

(b) Enter the above details into the debit side of the cash book and total each column.

Cash book – debit side

Details	Cash £	Bank £	VAT £	Trade receivables £
Balance b/f	1,325			
G Brownlow				
S Barnett				
Total				

(c) Using your answers to (a) and (b) above, calculate the cash balance.

£ [ ]

(d) Using your answers to (a) and (b) above, calculate the bank balance.

£ [ ]

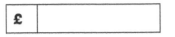

(e) **Will the bank balance calculated in (d) above be a debit or credit balance?**

	✓
Debit	
Credit	

Task 8.7

Shown below are the debit and credit sides of Halliday Ltd's cash book.

You are required to balance off Halliday Ltd's cash book.

Cash book – debit side

Details	Cash £	Bank £	VAT £	Trade receivables £	Cash sales £
Balance b/f	55	1,300			
Whippet's	210		35		175
Ragdoll Ltd		958		958	
▼					
Totals					
▼					

Picklist:

Balance b/d
Balance c/d
Halliday Ltd
Ragdoll Ltd
Whippet's

Cash book – credit side

Details	Cash £	Bank £	VAT £	Trade payables £	Cash purchases £
Hornsea Ltd		355		355	
Lyndon Plc		738		738	
▼					
Totals					
▼					

Picklist:

Balance b/d
Balance c/d
Halliday Ltd
Ragdoll Ltd
Whippet's

Task 8.8

There are three receipts to be entered in the debit side of the cash-book during one week.

Cash sales listing

Sale made for cash	Net £	VAT £	Gross £
Humber & Co	485	97	582

Trade receivables listing

Credit customers paying by cheque	Amount paid £
Ridgely Ltd	2,150
Watts Partners	978

(a)   Enter the details from the cash sales listing and the trade receivables listing into the debit side of the cash-book shown below and total each column.

Cash book – debit side

Details	Cash £	Bank £	VAT £	Trade receivables £	Cash sales £
Balance b/f	159	844			
Humber & Co					
Ridgely Ltd					
Watts Partners					
Total					

The credit side of the cash-book shows cash spent on cash purchases of £561 during the week.

(b)   Using your answer to (a) above, calculate the cash balance.

£

The credit side of the cash-book shows the total amount of cheques sent during the week was £4,085.

(c)   Using your answer to (a) above, calculate the bank balance. If your calculations show that the bank account is overdrawn, your answer should start with a minus sign, for example – 123.

£

Chapter 9 – Double entry for sales and trade receivables

Task 9.1

The following credit transactions have been entered into the sales day book as shown below. No entries have yet been made into the ledgers.

Sales day book

Date 20XX	Customer	Invoice number	Customer code	Total £	VAT £	Net £
Dec	S Himms	00011	SL 18	900	150	750
Dec	G Pood	00012	SL 13	1,500	250	1,250
Dec	M Kitchell	00013	SL 04	456	76	380
Dec	B Crown	00014	SL 15	1,392	232	1,160
Totals				4,248	708	3,540

(a) **What will be the entries in the sales ledger?**

Sales ledger

Account name		Amount £	Debit ✓	Credit ✓
	▼			
	▼			
	▼			
	▼			

Picklist:

B Crown
G Pood
M Kitchell
Purchases
Purchases ledger control
Purchases returns
S Himms
Sales
Sales ledger control
Sales returns
VAT

(b) **What will be the entries in the general ledger?**

General ledger

Account name		Amount £	Debit ✓	Credit ✓
	▼			
	▼			
	▼			

Picklist:

B Crown
G Pood
M Kitchell
Purchases
Purchases ledger control
Purchases returns
S Himms
Sales
Sales ledger control
Sales returns
VAT

Task 9.2

The following credit transactions have been entered into the sales day book as shown below. No entries have yet been made into the ledgers.

Sales day book

Date 20XX	Customer	Invoice number	Customer code	Total £	VAT £	Net £
Jan	H Simms	0001	SL 45	1,800	300	1,500
Jan	P Good	0002	SL 21	3,000	500	2,500
Jan	K Mitchell	0003	SL 30	912	152	760
Jan	C Brown	0004	SL 05	2,790	465	2,325
Totals				8,502	1,417	7,085

(a) **Post these transactions to the general ledger accounts shown below.**

GENERAL LEDGER

Sales ledger control

Details		Amount £	Details		Amount £
	▼			▼	
	▼			▼	
	▼			▼	

Picklist:

Bank
Cash
C Brown
H Simms
K Mitchell
P Good
Purchases
Purchases ledger control
Sales
Sales ledger control
VAT

Sales

Details		Amount £	Details		Amount £
	▼			▼	
	▼			▼	

Picklist:

Bank
Cash
C Brown
H Simms
K Mitchell
P Good
Purchases
Purchases ledger control
Sales
Sales ledger control
VAT

VAT

Details		Amount £	Details		Amount £
	▼			▼	
	▼			▼	

Picklist:

Bank
Cash
H Simms
K Mitchell
Sales
Sales ledger control
VAT

(b) **Post the transactions with H Simms and K Mitchell to the relevant accounts in the Sales ledger.**

Sales ledger

H Simms   **SL 45**

Details		Amount £	Details		Amount £
	▼			▼	

Picklist:

Bank
Cash
H Simms
Invoice 0001
Sales ledger control

K Mitchell   **SL 30**

Details		Amount £	Details		Amount £
	▼			▼	

Picklist:

Bank
Cash
Invoice 0003
K Mitchell
Sales ledger control

Task 9.3

The following credit transactions have been entered into Natural Production's sales day book as shown below. No entries have yet been made into the ledgers.

Sales day book

Date 20XX	Customer	Invoice number	Total £	VAT £	Net £
2 Jan	Hoppers Ltd	6237	656.40	109.40	547.00
5 Jan	Body Perfect	6238	744.00	124.00	620.00
		Totals	1,400.40	233.40	1,167.00

(a) **What will be the entries in the sales ledger?**

Sales ledger

Account name	Amount £	Debit ✓	Credit ✓
▼			
▼			

Picklist:

Body Perfect
Hoppers Ltd
Natural Productions
Purchases returns
Sales
Sales ledger control
Sales returns
VAT

(b) **What will be the entries in the general ledger?**

General ledger

Account name		Amount £	Debit ✓	Credit ✓
	▼			
	▼			
	▼			

Picklist:

Body Perfect
Hoppers Ltd
Natural Productions
Purchases
Purchases ledger control
Purchases returns
Sales
Sales ledger control
Sales returns
VAT

Task 9.4

The following credit transactions have been entered into Natural Production's sales day book as shown below. No entries have yet been made into the ledgers.

Sales day book

Date 20XX	Customer	Invoice number	Total £	VAT £	Net £
21 Jan	Esporta Leisure	6239	415.20	69.20	346.00
25 Jan	Langans Beauty	6240	273.60	45.60	228.00
		Totals	688.80	114.80	574.00

(a) **Post the totals of the sales day book to the general ledger accounts given.**

GENERAL LEDGER

Sales ledger control

Details		Amount £	Details		Amount £
	▼			▼	
	▼			▼	
	▼			▼	

Sales

Details	Amount £	Details	Amount £
▼		▼	
▼		▼	

VAT

Details	Amount £	Details	Amount £
▼		▼	
▼		▼	

(b) **Post the individual entries to the sales ledger.**

SALES LEDGER

Langans Beauty

Details		Amount £	Details		Amount £
▼				▼	

Picklist:

Bank
Cash
Invoice 6240
Langans Beauty
Sales ledger control

Esporta Leisure

Details		Amount £	Details		Amount £
▼				▼	

Picklist:

Bank
Cash
Esporta Leisure
Invoice 6239
Sales day book

Task 9.5

The following credit transactions have been entered into Short Furniture's sales day book as shown below. No entries have yet been made into the ledgers.

Sales day book

Customer	Invoice number	Customer code	Invoice total £	VAT £	Net £
Rocks Garden Suppliers	08663	SL22	701.76	116.96	584.80
Eridge Nurseries	08664	SL07	429.30	71.55	357.75
Abergaven GC	08665	SL16	923.40	153.90	769.50
Rother Nurseries	08666	SL13	756.00	126.00	630.00
		Totals	2,810.46	468.41	2,342.05

(a) **What will be the entries in the sales ledger?**

Sales ledger

Account name		Amount £	Debit ✓	Credit ✓
	▼			
	▼			
	▼			
	▼			

Picklist:

Abergaven GC
Eridge Nurseries
Purchases returns
Rocks Garden Suppliers
Rother Nurseries
Sales
Sales ledger control
Sales returns
Short Furniture
VAT

(b) **What will be the entries in the general ledger?**

General ledger

Account name		Amount £	Debit ✓	Credit ✓
	▼			
	▼			
	▼			

Picklist:

Abergaven GC
Eridge Nurseries
Purchases returns
Rocks Garden Suppliers
Rother Nurseries
Sales
Sales ledger control
Sales returns
Short Furniture
VAT

Task 9.6

During January, Natural Productions issued some credit notes as shown in the sales returns day book below. No entries have yet been made into the ledgers.

Sales returns day book

Date 20XX	Customer	Credit note number	Total £	VAT £	Net £
17 Jan	Hoppers Ltd	1476	82.44	13.74	68.70
23 Jan	Esporta Leisure	1477	107.04	17.84	89.20
30 Jan	Superior Products	1478	14.16	2.36	11.80
		Totals	203.64	33.94	169.70

(a) **What will be the entries in the sales ledger?**

Sales ledger

Account name		Amount £	Debit ✓	Credit ✓
	▼			
	▼			
	▼			

Picklist:

Esporta Leisure
Hoppers Ltd
Natural Productions
Purchases
Purchases ledger control
Purchases returns
Sales
Sales ledger control
Sales returns
Superior Products
VAT

(b) **What will be the entries in the general ledger?**

General ledger

Account name		Amount £	Debit ✓	Credit ✓
	▼			
	▼			
	▼			

Picklist:

Esporta Leisure
Hoppers Ltd
Natural Productions
Purchases
Purchases ledger control
Purchases returns
Sales
Sales ledger control
Sales returns
Superior Products
VAT

....

Task 9.7

Natural Productions discounts allowed day book is shown below. No entries have yet been made into the ledgers.

Discounts allowed day book

Date 20XX	Customer	Credit note number	Total £	VAT £	Net £
1 Feb	Hoppers Ltd	1501	36	6	30
25 Feb	Esporta Leisure	1502	72	12	60
		Totals	108	18	90

(a) What will be the entries in the sales ledger?

Sales ledger

Account name		Amount £	Debit ✓	Credit ✓
	▼			
	▼			

Picklist:

Discounts allowed
Discounts received
Esporta Leisure
Hoppers Ltd
Purchases
Purchases ledger control
Purchases returns
Sales
Sales ledger control
Sales returns
VAT

(b) What will be the entries in the general ledger?
General ledger

Account name		Amount £	Debit ✓	Credit ✓
	▼			
	▼			
	▼			

Picklist:

Discounts allowed
Discounts received
Purchases
Purchases ledger control
Purchases returns
Sales
Sales ledger control
Sales returns
VAT

Task 9.8

You work for Short Furniture. A remittance advice and cheque for £1,112.17 has been received from Rother Nurseries which they state is in full settlement of the account at 31 January. The remittance advice and the customer's account in the sales ledger is shown below.

Rother Nurseries
REMITTANCE ADVICE

To: Short Furniture   Date: 1 Feb 20XX

Please find attached our cheque for full settlement of our account as at 31 January 20XX

Invoice number	Credit note number	Amount £
08666		756.00
08674		114.78
	1470	(96.50)
08681		337.89
Total amount paid		£1,112.17

SALES LEDGER

Rother Nurseries   **SL 16**

Date	Details	£	Date	Details	£
9 Jan	Invoice 08666	756.00	20 Jan	Credit note 1470	96.50
16 Jan	Invoice 08674	214.78			
24 Jan	Invoice 08681	337.89			
5 Feb	Invoice 08695	265.98			

(a) **Check the remittance advice against the customer's account in the sales ledger and state whether the following statements are true or false.**

	True ✓	False ✓
Rother Nurseries has fully settled their account at 31 January 20XX.		
Rother Nurseries should have included invoice 08695 with their payment in order to fully settle their account at 31 January.		
The remittance advice note has been correctly cast.		
The invoice amounts are included correctly on the remittance advice note.		

(b) **What amount should Rother Nurseries have paid to fully settle their account as at 31 January?**

Task 9.9

A remittance advice and cheque for £2,279.30 has been received from Abergaven Garden Centre which they state is in full settlement of the account at 9 February. The remittance advice and the customer's account in the sales ledger is shown below.

Abergaven Garden Centre
REMITTANCE ADVICE

To: Short Furniture

Date: 9 Feb 20XX

Please find attached our cheque for full settlement of our account as at 31 January 20XX

Invoice number	Credit note number	Amount £
08665		923.40
08672		623.56
08685		316.58
08692		415.76
Total amount paid		**£1,863.54**

Abergaven Garden Centre   **SL 17**

Date	Details	£	Date	Details	£
7 Jan	Invoice 08665	923.40	13 Jan	Credit note 1471	32.50
13 Jan	Invoice 08672	623.56	2 Feb	Credit note 1476	110.23
26 Jan	Invoice 08685	316.58			
3 Feb	Invoice 08692	415.76			

(a) **Check the remittance advice against the customer's account in the sales ledger and state whether the following statements are true or false.**

	True ✓	False ✓
Abergaven Garden Centre has included on the remittance advice note all relevant transactions up to 9 February.		
The remittance advice note has been correctly cast.		
The invoice amounts are included correctly on the remittance advice note.		

(b) **What amount should Abergaven Garden Centre have paid to fully settle their account as at 9 February?**

£

Task 9.10

Shown below are the totals of Natural Productions's cash book – debit side, at the end of the week.

Cash book – debit side

Date	Details	Cash £	Bank £	VAT £	Cash sales £	Trade receivables £
		279.84	2,018.10	46.64	233.20	2,018.10

What will be the entries in the general ledger?

Account name	Amount £	Debit ✓	Credit ✓
▼			
▼			
▼			

Picklist:

Bank
Cash
Cash purchases
Cash sales
Purchases ledger control
Sales ledger control
VAT

Task 9.11

Natural Productions' cash book – debit side, is shown below. The cash book is not part of the general ledger.

Date	Details	Cash £	Bank £	VAT £	Cash sales £	Trade receivables £
23 Jan	Hoppers Ltd		553.96			553.96
23 Jan	Superior Products		116.70			116.70
24 Jan	Cash sales	131.16		21.86	109.30	
25 Jan	Esporta Leisure		367.20			367.20
27 Jan	Cash sales	88.56		14.76	73.80	
27 Jan	Body Perfect		706.64			706.64
27 Jan	Cash sales	60.12		10.02	50.10	
27 Jan	Langans Beauty		273.60			273.60
	Totals	279.84	2,018.10	46.64	233.20	2,018.10

(a) **Post the entries to the individual accounts in the sales ledger shown below.**

SALES LEDGER

Hoppers Ltd

Details	Amount £	Details	Amount £
Invoice 6237	656.40	Credit note 1476	82.44
▼		▼	

Picklist:

Bank
Cash sales
Hoppers Ltd
Natural Productions
Purchases
Purchases ledger control
Sales
Sales ledger control
Trade receivables
VAT

Body Perfect

Details	Amount £	Details	Amount £
Invoice 6238	744.00	▼	
▼			

Picklist:

Bank
Body Perfect
Cash sales
Natural Productions
Purchases
Purchases ledger control
Sales
Sales ledger control
Trade receivables
VAT

Esporta Leisure

Details	Amount £	Details	Amount £
Invoice 6239	415.20	Credit note 1477	107.04
▼		▼	

Picklist:

Bank
Cash sales
Esporta Leisure
Natural Productions
Purchases
Purchases ledger control
Sales
Sales ledger control
Trade receivables
VAT

Langans Beauty

Details	Amount £	Details	Amount £
Invoice 6240	273.60		
▼		▼	

Picklist:

Bank
Cash sales
Langans Beauty
Natural Productions
Purchases
Purchases ledger control
Sales
Sales ledger control
Trade receivables
VAT

Superior Products

Details	Amount £	Details	Amount £
Invoice 6242	265.20	Credit note 1478	14.16
▼		▼	

Picklist:

Bank
Cash sales
Natural Productions
Purchases
Purchases ledger control
Sales
Sales ledger control
Superior Products
Trade receivables
VAT

(b) Post the totals to the general ledger accounts shown below.

GENERAL LEDGER

Cash

Details	Amount £	Details	Amount £
▼		▼	
▼		▼	

Picklist:

Bank
Body Perfect
Cash
Esporta Leisure
Hoppers Ltd
Langans Beauty
Sales
Sales ledger control
Superior Products
VAT

Bank

Details	Amount £	Details	Amount £
▼		▼	
▼		▼	

Picklist:

Bank
Body Perfect
Cash
Esporta Leisure
Hoppers Ltd
Langans Beauty
Sales
Sales ledger control
Superior Products
VAT

Sales ledger control

Details	Amount £	Details	Amount £
Sales	3,438.00	Sales returns	169.70
VAT	687.60	VAT	33.94
▼		▼	
▼		▼	

Picklist:

Bank
Body Perfect
Cash
Esporta Leisure
Hoppers Ltd
Langans Beauty
Sales
Sales ledger control
Superior Products
VAT

Sales

Details	Amount £	Details	Amount £
▼		Sales ledger control	3,438.00
▼		▼	

Picklist:

Bank
Body Perfect
Cash
Esporta Leisure
Hoppers Ltd
Langans Beauty
Sales
Sales ledger control
Superior Products
VAT

VAT

Details	Amount £	Details	Amount £
Sales ledger control	33.94	Sales ledger control	687.60
▼		▼	

Picklist:

Bank
Body Perfect
Cash
Esporta Leisure
Hoppers Ltd
Langans Beauty
Sales
Sales ledger control
Superior Products
VAT

Task 9.12

The following transactions all took place on 30 June and have been entered in the debit side of the cash book as shown below. No entries have yet been made in the ledgers.

Cash book – debit side

Date 20XX	Details	Cash £	Bank £	VAT £	Cash sales £	Trade receivables £
30 Jun	Henderson & Co		7,349			7,349
30 Jun	Cash sale	426		71	355	

(a) **What will be the entry in the sales ledger?**

Sales ledger

Account name	Amount £	Debit ✓	Credit ✓
▼			

Picklist:

Bank
Cash
Henderson & Co
Purchases ledger control
Sales
Sales ledger control
VAT

(b) **What will be the three entries in the general ledger?**

General ledger

Account name		Amount £	Debit ✓	Credit ✓
	▼			
	▼			
	▼			

Picklist:

Bank
Cash
Henderson & Co
Purchases ledger control
Sales
Sales ledger control
VAT

Task 9.13

You work in the accounts department of Southfield Electrical. The following are extracts from the day books relating to transactions in May 20XX with Alpha Services & Co together with a remittance advice note for a cheque payment received in May 20XX from the customer.

Sales day book – extract

Date 20XX	Customer	Invoice number	Customer code	Total £	VAT £	Net £
7 May	Alpha Services	715	SL10	5,190.00	865.00	4,325.00
17 May	Alpha Services	787	SL10	10,020.00	1,670.00	8,350.00

Sales returns day book – extract

Date 20XX	Customer	Credit note number	Customer code	Total £	VAT £	Net £
12 May	Alpha Services	551	SL10	624.00	104.00	520.00

REMITTANCE ADVICE NOTE Alpha Services	Remittance advice note number 013278	
Supplier:	Southfield Electrical	
Account number (supplier code)	PL 821	
Date	**Transaction reference**	**Amount £**
21/04/XX	Invoice 600	289.50
27/04/XX	Credit note 401	(35.87)
1/5/XX	Payment made – cheque enclosed	253.63

Enter the transactions from the day books and the remittance advice into the customer's account in the sales ledger. You do not need to balance off the account.

SALES LEDGER

Alpha Services   **SL 10**

Details	Amount £	Details	Amount £
Balance b/d	253.63	▼	
▼		▼	
▼		▼	
▼		▼	

Picklist:

Alpha Services
Bank
Cash sales
Invoice 715
Invoice 787
Credit note 551
Purchases
Purchases ledger control
Sales
Sales ledger control
Southfield Electrical
Trade receivables
VAT

Task 9.14

The following transactions all took place on 30 November and have been entered into the sales day book as shown below. No entries have yet been made into the ledger system.

Sales day book

Date 20XX	Details	Invoice number	Total £	VAT £	Net £
30 Nov	Gringles Co	12786	300	50	250
30 Nov	Lester plc	12787	1,308	218	1,090
30 Nov	Shrier Goods	12788	2,676	446	2,230
30 Nov	Abunda Bags	12789	1,992	332	1,660
		Totals	6,276	1,046	5,230

(a) **What will be the entries in the sales ledger?**

Sales ledger

Account name	Amount £	Debit ✓	Credit ✓
▼			
▼			
▼			
▼			

(b) **What will be the entries in the general ledger?**

General ledger

Account name		Amount £	Debit ✓	Credit ✓
	▼			
	▼			
	▼			

Chapter 10 – Double entry for purchases and trade payables

Task 10.1

You have been given an extract from your organisation's purchases day book in respect of credit transactions in June. No entries have yet been made in the ledgers.

(a) **Complete and total the purchases day book shown below.**

Purchases day book

Date 20XX	Details	Invoice number	Total £	VAT £	Net £
30 June	Seashell Ltd	8971			3,211.00
30 June	Opal & Co	05119	4,800.00		
		Totals			

(b) **Using your answer from (a) above, record the transactions in the purchases ledger.**

Purchases ledger

Account name		Amount £	Debit ✓	Credit ✓
	▼			
	▼			

Picklist:

Net
Opal & Co
Purchases
Purchases ledger control
Purchases returns
Sales
Sales ledger control
Sales returns
Seashell Ltd
Total
VAT

Task 10.2

These are the totals of the purchases day book at the end of the month.

Purchases day book

Details	Total £	VAT £	Net £	Purchases £	Stationery £	Packaging £
Totals	4,148.40	691.40	3,457.00	2,711.00	314.00	432.00

(a) **What will be the entries in the general ledger?**

Account name		Amount £	Debit ✓	Credit ✓
	▼			
	▼			
	▼			
	▼			
	▼			

Picklist:

Packaging
Purchases
Purchases ledger control
Purchases returns
Sales
Sales ledger control
Sales returns
Stationery
VAT

One of the entries in the purchases day book is for an invoice from W J Jones for £210 plus VAT.

(b) **What will be the entry in the purchases ledger?**

Account name		Amount £	Debit ✓	Credit ✓
	▼			

Picklist:

Discounts allowed
Discounts received
Purchases
Purchases ledger control
Purchases returns
Sales
Sales ledger control
Sales returns
VAT
W J Jones

Task 10.3

Natural Productions' purchases day book is shown below.

Purchases day book

Date	Supplier	Invoice number	Total £	VAT £	Net £	Purchases £	Packaging £
31 Jan	P J Phillips	03576	428.40	71.40	357.00	357.00	
31 Jan	Packing Supplies Ltd	28423	321.60	53.60	268.00		268.00
			750.00	125.00	625.00	357.00	268.00

(a) Post the totals of the purchases day book to the general ledger accounts given.

GENERAL LEDGER

Purchases ledger control

Details	Amount £	Details	Amount £
▼		▼	
▼		▼	
▼		▼	

VAT

Details	Amount £	Details	Amount £
▼		▼	
▼		▼	

Purchases

Details	Amount £	Details	Amount £
▼		▼	
▼		▼	

Picklist:

Packing Supplies Ltd
PJ Phillips
Purchases
Purchases ledger control
Purchases returns
Sales
Sales ledger control
Sales returns
VAT

Packaging

Details		Amount £	Details		Amount £
	▼			▼	
	▼			▼	

Picklist:

Packing Supplies Ltd
PJ Phillips
Purchases
Purchases ledger control
Purchases returns
Sales
Sales ledger control
Sales returns
VAT

(b) **Post the individual entries to the purchases ledger accounts given.**

PURCHASES LEDGER

PJ Phillips

Details		Amount £	Details		Amount £
	▼			▼	

Picklist:

Invoice 03576
Invoice 28423
Packing Supplies Ltd
PJ Phillips
VAT

Packing Supplies Ltd

Details	Amount £	Details	Amount £
▼		▼	

Picklist:

Invoice 03576
Invoice 28423
Packing Supplies Ltd
PJ Phillips
VAT

Task 10.4

Given below is Short Furniture's purchases day book as at 27 January.

Purchases day book

Date	Supplier	Invoice number	Supplier code	Total £	VAT £	Net £	Wood purchases £	Polish/ varnish purchases £	Other purchases £
27 Jan	Ephraim Supplies	09642	PL39	349.20	58.20	291.00	291.00		
27 Jan	Cavendish Woods	06932	PL14	846.12	141.02	705.10	705.10		
27 Jan	Calverley Bros	67671	PL03	174.72	29.12	145.60		145.60	
27 Jan	Culverden & Co	36004	PL23	68.88	11.48	57.40			57.40
			Totals	1,438.92	239.82	1,199.10	996.10	145.60	57.40

(a) **What will be the entries in the general ledger?**

General ledger

Account name		Amount £	Debit ✓	Credit ✓
	▼			
	▼			
	▼			
	▼			
	▼			

Picklist:

Other purchases
Polish/varnish purchases
Purchases ledger control
Purchases returns
Sales
Sales ledger control
Sales returns
Stationery
Wood purchases
VAT

(b) **What will be the entries in the purchases ledger?**

Purchases ledger

Account name		Amount £	Debit ✓	Credit ✓
	▼			
	▼			
	▼			
	▼			

Picklist:

Calverley Bros
Cavendish Woods
Culverden & Co
Ephraim Supplies
Discounts received
Other purchases
Polish/varnish purchases
Purchases day book
Purchases ledger control
Purchases returns
VAT
Wood purchases

Task 10.5

Shown below is Thimble's purchases returns day book.

Purchases returns day book

Date	Supplier	Credit note number	Total £	VAT £	Net £	Purchases £	Stationery £
10 Mar	K Mates	0326	235.20	39.20	196.00	196.00	
16 Mar	R Jones	C55	134.40	22.40	112.00		112.00
30 Mar	X & Y Ltd	563	297.60	49.60	248.00	248.00	
		Totals	667.20	111.20	556.00	444.00	112.00

(a) **What will be the entries in the general ledger?**

General ledger

Account name		Amount £	Debit ✓	Credit ✓
	▼			
	▼			
	▼			
	▼			

Picklist:

Packaging
Purchases
Purchases ledger control
Purchases returns
Sales
Sales ledger control
Sales returns
Stationery
VAT

(b) **What will be the entries in the purchases ledger?**

Purchases ledger

Account name		Amount £	Debit ✓	Credit ✓
	▼			
	▼			
	▼			

Picklist:

K Mates
Purchases
Purchases ledger control
Purchases returns
R Jones
Sales
Sales ledger control
Sales returns
VAT
X & Y Ltd

Task 10.6

Shown below is Norris Day's purchases returns day book.

Purchases returns day book

Date	Supplier	Credit note number	Total £	VAT £	Net £	Purchases £	Stationery £
10 Jan	Phillips	04216	117.60	19.60	98.00	98.00	
16 Jan	Wallace	CN0643	67.20	11.20	56.00		56.00
30 Jan	Olivia Ltd	CN1102	148.80	24.80	124.00	124.00	
		Totals	333.60	55.60	278.00	222.00	56.00

(a) **Post the totals of the purchases returns day book to the general ledger accounts given.**

GENERAL LEDGER

Purchases ledger control

Details		Amount £	Details	Amount £
	▼		Purchases	2,711.00
	▼		Stationery	314.00
	▼		Packaging	432.00
	▼		VAT	691.40
	▼		▼	
	▼		▼	

Picklist:

Purchases
Purchases ledger control
Purchases returns
Sales
Sales ledger control
Sales returns
Stationery
VAT

VAT

Details	Amount £	Details	Amount £
Purchases ledger control	691.40	▼	
▼		▼	

Picklist:

Purchases
Purchases ledger control
Purchases returns
Sales
Sales ledger control
Sales returns
Stationery
VAT

Purchases returns

Details	Amount £	Details	Amount £
▼		▼	
▼		▼	

Picklist:

Purchases
Purchases ledger control
Purchases returns
Sales
Sales ledger control
Sales returns
Stationery
VAT

Stationery

Details	Amount £	Details		Amount £
Purchases ledger control	314.00		▼	
	▼		▼	

Picklist:

Purchases
Purchases ledger control
Purchases returns
Sales
Sales ledger control
Sales returns
Stationery
VAT

(b) **Post the individual entries to the purchases ledger accounts also given below.**

PURCHASES LEDGER

Phillips

Details		Amount £	Details		Amount £
	▼		Invoice 0357		428.40
	▼		Invoice 0358		495.60
	▼			▼	

Picklist:

Credit note 04216
Credit note CN0643
Credit note CN1102
Phillips
VAT

Wallace

Details		Amount £	Details		Amount £
	▼		Invoice I342		252.00
	▼		Invoice I350		124.80
	▼			▼	

Picklist:

Credit note 04216
Credit note CN0643
Credit note CN1102
VAT
Wallace

Olivia Ltd

Details	Amount £	Details	Amount £
▼		Invoice 55773	748.80
▼		▼	

Picklist:

Credit note 04216
Credit note CN0643
Credit note CN1102
Olivia Ltd
VAT

Task 10.7

You work for Mountain Ltd and one of your duties is to transfer data from the cash book to the ledgers. Most of the payments are to credit suppliers but there are some cash purchases of materials from small suppliers which include VAT. The cash book – credit side is shown below.

Cash book – credit side

Date	Details	Cash £	Bank £	VAT £	Cash purchases £	Trade payables £
23 Jan	Time Ltd		1,105.07			1,105.07
23 Jan	Cash purchase	108.00		18.00	90.00	
24 Jan	WFF Ltd		252.00			252.00
	Totals	108.00	1,357.07	18.00	90.00	1,357.07

(a) **What will be the entries in the general ledger?**

Account name		Amount £	Debit ✓	Credit ✓
	▼			
	▼			
	▼			

Picklist:

Cash
Bank
Purchases
Purchases ledger control
Purchases returns
Sales
Sales ledger control
Sales returns
Trade payables
VAT

(b) **What will be the entries in the purchases ledger?**

Account name		Amount £	Debit ✓	Credit ✓
	▼			
	▼			

Picklist:

Purchases
Purchases ledger control
Purchases returns
Sales
Sales ledger control
Sales returns
Time Ltd
VAT
WFF Ltd

Task 10.8

The following credit transactions all took place on 30 November and have been entered into the purchases day book as shown below. No entries have yet been made in the ledgers.

Purchases day book

Date 20XX	Details	Invoice number	Total £	VAT @ 20% £	Net £
30 Nov	Frankie's Leatherware	0923	12,348	2,058	10,290
30 Nov	Casaubon's	C6478	3,924	654	3,270
		Totals	16,272	2,712	13,560

(a)   What will be the entries in the purchases ledger?

Purchases ledger

Account name	Amount £	Debit ✓	Credit ✓
▼			
▼			

Picklist:

Casaubon's
Frankie's Leatherware
Purchases
Purchases ledger control
Purchases returns
Sales
Sales ledger control
Sales returns
VAT

(b) **What will be the entries in the general ledger?**

General ledger

Account name		Amount £	Debit ✓	Credit ✓
	▼			
	▼			
	▼			

Picklist:

Casaubon's
Frankie's Leatherware
Purchases
Purchases ledger control
Purchases returns
Sales
Sales ledger control
Sales returns
VAT

Task 10.9

Natural Productions' discounts received day book is shown below. No entries have yet been made into the ledgers.

Discounts received day book

Date 20XX	Customer	Credit note number	Total £	VAT £	Net £
3 May	Trenter Ltd	1501	36	6	30
10 May	WJ Jones	1502	72	12	60
			108	18	90

(a) **What will be the entries in the purchases ledger?**

Purchases ledger

Account name		Amount £	Debit ✓	Credit ✓
	▼			
	▼			

Picklist:

Discounts allowed
Discounts received
Purchases
Purchases ledger control
Purchases returns
Sales
Sales ledger control
Sales returns
Trenter Ltd
VAT
WJ Jones

(b) **What will be the entries in the general ledger?**

General ledger

Account name		Amount £	Debit ✓	Credit ✓
	▼			
	▼			
	▼			

Picklist:

Discounts allowed
Discounts received
Purchases
Purchases ledger control
Purchases returns
Sales
Sales ledger control
Sales returns
Trenter Ltd
VAT
WJ Jones

Task 10.10

The following transactions all took place on 30 November and have been entered in the credit side of the cash book as shown below. No entries have yet been made in the ledgers.

Cash book – Credit side

Date 20XX	Details	Cash £	Bank £	VAT £	Cash purchases £	Trade payables £
30 Nov	Cash purchase	612		102	510	
30 Nov	Casaubon's		2,445			2,445

(a)   What will be the entry in the purchases ledger?

Purchases ledger

Account name		Amount £	Debit ✓	Credit ✓
	▼			

Picklist:

Bank
Casaubon's
Discounts allowed
Discounts received
Purchases
Purchases ledger control
Sales
Sales ledger control
VAT

(b)   What will be the three entries in the general ledger?

General ledger

Account name		Amount £	Debit ✓	Credit ✓
	▼			
	▼			
	▼			

Picklist:

Bank

Casaubon's

Discounts allowed

Discounts received

Purchases

Purchases ledger control

Sales

Sales ledger control

VAT

Task 10.11

These are totals of the cash book at the end of the month.

Cash book

Cash £	Bank £	VAT £	Trade receivables £	Cash sales £	Cash £	Bank £	VAT £	Trade payables £	Cash purchases £
550	6,893	59	4,368	295	550	6,893	–	2,492	–

What will be the entries in the general ledger?

Account name		Amount £	Debit ✓	Credit ✓
	▼			
	▼			
	▼			
	▼			

Picklist:

Bank

Cash

Cash purchases

Cash sales

Purchases ledger control

Sales ledger control

VAT

Chapter 11 – Accounting for petty cash

Task 11.1

Natural Productions has a petty cash system based on an imprest amount of £100 which is replenished weekly. On Friday 20 January the total of the vouchers in the petty cash box was £68.34.

How much cash is required to replenish the petty cash box?

£

··

Task 11.2

Newmans, the music shop, has an imprest petty cash system based upon an imprest amount of £120.00. During the week ending 29 January the petty cash vouchers given below were presented, authorised and paid.

Petty cash voucher 0721	
29 January 20XX	
	£
Coffee	3.99
VAT is not applicable.	

Petty cash voucher 0722	
29 January 20XX	
	£
Taxi	8.94
VAT @ 20%	1.78
Total	10.72

(a) **Complete the petty cash book by:**

- **Entering both transactions into the petty cash book below.**

- **Totalling the petty cash book and inserting the balance carried down at 29 January.**

Petty cash book

Date 20XX	Details	Amount £	Date 20XX	Details	Amount £	VAT £	Travel £	Office expenses £
24 Jan	Balance b/f	120.00	27 Jan	Paper	7.12	1.18		5.94
			29 Jan	▼				
			29 Jan	▼				
			29 Jan	▼				
	Total			Totals				

Picklist:

Balance b/f
Balance c/d
Coffee
Office expenses
Taxi
Travel
VAT

(b) **What will be the amount of cash withdrawn from the bank to restore the imprest level of £120.00?**

£	

Task 11.3

On the first day of every month cash is drawn from the bank to restore the petty cash imprest level to £75.

A summary of petty cash transactions during November is shown below:

Opening balance on 01 November	£22
Cash from bank on 01 November	£53
Expenditure during month	£16

(a) **What will be the amount required to restore the imprest level on 01 December?**

£	

(b) **Will the receipt from the bank on 01 December be a debit or credit entry in the petty cash book?**

	✓
Debit	
Credit	

Task 11.4

Short Furniture has a monthly petty cash imprest system based upon an imprest amount of £150.00. The total amount of cash in the petty cash box at 31 January is £48.50.

The petty cash control account in the general ledger is given below. You are to balance the petty cash control account (this should be the same as the balance of cash in the petty cash box on 31 January).

Petty cash control

Date	Details	Amount £	Date	Details	Amount £
1 Jan	Balance b/f	150.00	31 Jan	Expenditure	101.50
▼	▼		▼	▼	
	Total			Total	
▼	▼		▼	▼	

Picklist:
31 Jan
1 Feb
Balance b/d
Balance c/d
Petty cash
VAT

Task 11.5

A business which is not registered for VAT has partially completed its petty cash book for November, as shown below.

(a) **Complete the analysis columns for the four items purchased from petty cash.**

(b) **Total and balance the petty cash book, showing clearly the balance carried down at 30 November.**

(c) **Enter the balance brought down at 01 December, showing clearly the date, details, and amount. You do NOT need to restore the imprest amount.**

Petty cash book

Debit side			Credit side					
Date	Details	Amount £	Date	Details	Total £	Stationery £	Postage £	Motor fuel £
1 Nov	Bal b/f	100	7 Nov	Postage stamps	20			
			15 Nov	Pens & pencils	18			
			22 Nov	Petrol	10			
			30 Nov	Envelopes	15			
▼	▼		▼	▼				
	Total			Total				
▼	▼		▼	▼				

Picklist:

30 Nov
1 Dec
Balance b/d
Balance c/d
Envelopes
Pens & pencils
Petrol
Postage stamps
VAT

Task 11.6

This is a summary of petty cash payments made by your business.

Post Office paid	£30.00 (no VAT)
Window cleaning paid	£25.60 plus VAT
MegaBus paid	£29.50 (no VAT)

(a)   **Enter the above transactions in the petty cash book.**
(b)   **Total the petty cash book and show the balance carried down.**

Petty cash book

Debit side		Credit side					
Details	**Amount £**	**Details**	**Amount £**	**VAT £**	**Postage £**	**Travel £**	**Cleaning £**
Bal b/f	175.00	▼					
		▼					
		▼					
▼		▼					
Total		Total					

Picklist:

Balance b/d
Balance c/d
Cleaning
MegaBus
Post Office
Postage
Travel
VAT
Window cleaning

Task 11.7

At the end of September the cash in the petty cash box was £9.76.

Complete the petty cash reimbursement document below to restore the imprest amount of £250.

Petty cash reimbursement		
Date: 30.09.20XX		
Amount required to restore the cash in the petty cash box	£	

BPP
LEARNING MEDIA

Task 11.8

This is a summary of petty cash payments made by Kitchen Kuts.

Tom's Taxi paid	£18.00 (no VAT)
Post Office paid	£30.00 (no VAT)
SMP Stationery paid	£36.00 plus VAT

(a) **Enter the above transactions, in the order in which they are shown, in the petty cash book below.**

(b) **Total the petty cash book and show the balance carried down.**

Petty cash book

Debit side			Credit side					
Details	Amount £	Details	Amount £	VAT £	Postage £	Travel £	Stationery £	
Bal b/f	150.00	▼						
		▼						
		▼						
▼		▼						
Total		Total						

Picklist:

Balance b/f
Balance c/d
Post Office
Postage
SMP Stationery
Stationery
Tom's Taxi
Travel
VAT

- -

Task 11.9

At the end of the month the cash in the petty cash box was £3.45.

Complete the petty cash reimbursement document below to restore the imprest amount of £200.

Petty cash reimbursement		
Date: 31.07.20XX		
Amount required to restore the cash in the petty cash box	£	

Task 11.10

Ken trades in exotic dress materials. The following is the credit side of Ken's Petty Cash Book, which acts only as a book of prime entry.

Petty cash book – credit side

Details	Voucher number	Total £	VAT £	Office expenses £	Stationery £	Maintenance £
Tea, coffee and milk for office	1234	15.20		15.20		
Printer cartridge	1235	39.12	6.52		32.60	
Repair to fire extinguisher	1236	54.00	9.00			45.00
Totals		108.32	15.52	15.20	32.60	45.00

(a) What will be the five entries in the general ledger?

General ledger

Account name		Amount £	Debit ✓	Credit ✓
	▼			
	▼			
	▼			
	▼			
	▼			

Picklist:

Bank
Cash
Maintenance
Office expenses
Petty cash
Purchases
Stationery
VAT

(b)   Which entry would be omitted if Ken's Petty Cash Book operated as a general ledger account as well?

▼

Picklist:

Bank
Cash
Maintenance
Office expenses
Petty cash
Purchases
Stationery
VAT

Task 11.11

Benjamin operates a petty cash system whereby each week he withdraws £50 from the bank and puts it in the petty cash tin.

What type of system is this?

	✓
Imprest system	
Non-imprest system	

Task 11.12

Lucy operates a petty cash system whereby each Friday afternoon she puts £60 in to the petty cash tin. At the start of the week, Lucy had £75.23 in notes and coins in her petty cash tin.

This is a summary of petty cash payments made by Lucy during the week.

Taxi paid	£9.00 (no VAT)
Post Office paid	£15.00 (no VAT)
Suzie's Stationery paid	£36.00 plus VAT

On Friday afternoon, Lucy withdrew £60 from the bank and put it in the petty cash tin.

(a)   Enter the above transactions, in the order in which they are shown, in the petty cash book below.

(b)   Total the petty cash book and show the balance carried down.

Petty cash book

Debit side			Credit side					
Details	**Amount £**	**Details**	**Amount £**	**VAT £**	**Postage £**	**Travel £**	**Stationery £**
Balance b/f	75.23	▼					
		▼					
		▼					
▼		▼					
Total		Total					

Picklist:

Balance b/f
Balance c/d
Bank
Post Office
Postage
Stationery
Suzie's Stationery
Taxi
Travel
VAT

(c) **What is the balance in notes and coins in the petty cash tin on Friday after Lucy has added the £60 withdrawn from the bank?**

£ [   ]

Task 11.13

Sumberton Ltd maintains a petty cash-book as a book of prime entry and part of the double entry bookkeeping system. This is a summary of petty cash transactions in a week.

Stamps bought for £12.60, VAT not applicable.
Staplers bought for £18.90, including VAT.

(a) **Enter the above transactions into the partially completed petty cash-book below.**

(b) **Total the petty cash-book and show the balance carried down.**

Petty cash book

Details	Amount £	Details	Amount £	VAT £	Postage £	Stationery £
Balance b/f	175.00	Printer cartridges	17.40	2.90		14.50
Total		Totals				

Picklist:

Balance b/f
Balance c/d
Postage
Stamps
Staplers
Stationery
VAT

(c) **What will be the three accounts in the general ledger which will record the above transactions?**

General ledger accounts	✓
Stamps	
Stationery	
Petty cash-book	
Petty cash control	
Postage	
Staplers	
VAT	

(d) **Complete the following statement by choosing one word.**

In order to top up the petty cash to the imprest amount, the petty cashier needs to prepare a:

	✓
Remittance advice note	
Cheque requisition form	
Petty cash claim	
Customer statement	

At the start of the next week cash was withdrawn from the bank to restore the imprest level of £175.

(e) **What is the amount of cash that would have been withdrawn from the bank to restore the imprest level?**

£	

Chapter 12 – Initial trial balance

Task 12.1

You are given the following account balances from the general ledger of your organisation.

Would each balance be a debit or a credit balance in the trial balance?

Ledger account	Balance	Debit ✓	Credit ✓
Sales	592,513		
Telephone	1,295		
Sales ledger control	52,375		
Wages	104,288		
Purchases returns	8,229		
Bank overdraft	17,339		
Purchases	372,589		
Drawings	71,604		
Sales returns	32,800		
Car	14,700		
Purchases ledger control	31,570		

Task 12.2

Below are two general ledger accounts and a partially completed trial balance at 31 January 20XX.

Complete the trial balance by:

- **Transferring the balances of the two general ledger accounts to the debit or credit column of the trial balance;**

- **Entering the amounts shown against each of the other account names into the debit or credit column of the trial balance; and**

- **Totalling both columns of the trial balance.**

Do not enter figures with decimal places in this task and do not enter a zero in unused column cells.

BPP
LEARNING MEDIA

Office equipment

Date 20XX	Details	Amount £	Date 20XX	Details	Amount £
9 Jan	Balance b/f	29,502	1 Jan	Journal	350
31Jan	Bank	7,288	21 Jan	Balance c/d	36,440
		36,790			36,790

Purchases

Date 20XX	Details	Amount £	Date 20XX	Details	Amount £
1 Jan	Balance b/f	89,920	30 Jan	Balance c/d	196,800
30 Jan	Purchases ledger control	106,880			
		196,800			196,800

	£	Debit £	Credit £
Office equipment			
Purchases			
Motor vehicles	76,800		
Sales	285,600		
Bank (overdraft)	2,016		
Petty cash	36		
Capital	90,000		
Sales returns	5,640		
Purchases returns	4,320		
Sales ledger control	42,960		
Purchases ledger control	36,120		
VAT (owed to HMRC)	15,540		
Drawings	12,040		
Telephone	1,920		
Electricity	3,360		

	£	Debit £	Credit £
Wages	74,520		
Loan from bank	36,000		
Discounts allowed	7,680		
Discounts received	4,680		
Rent expense	16,080		
Totals			

Task 12.3

The double-entry system of bookkeeping normally results in which of the following balances on the ledger accounts? Tick ONE.

Debit balances	Credit balances	✓
Assets and income	Liabilities, capital and expenses	
Income, capital and liabilities	Assets and expenses	
Assets and expenses	Liabilities, capital and income	
Assets, expenses and capital	Liabilities and income	

Task 12.4

What does a credit balance on a ledger account indicate? Tick ONE.

	✓
An asset or an expense	
A liability or an expense	
An amount owing to the organisation	
A liability or income	

Task 12.5

Which of the following balances would be a credit balance on a trial balance?

	✓
Non-current assets	
Sales returns	
Discounts allowed	
Bank overdraft	

....

Task 12.6

Given below is the list of ledger balances for your organisation at 31 August.

You are required to prepare a trial balance as at 31 August.

	£	Debit £	Credit £
Bank (overdraft)	4,838		
Capital	216,000		
Discounts allowed	18,432		
Discounts received	11,232		
Drawings	28,896		
Electricity	8,064		
Loan from bank	86,400		
Motor vehicles	184,320		
Office equipment	87,456		
Petty cash	100		
Purchases	472,320		
Purchases ledger control	86,688		
Purchases returns	10,368		
Rent expense	38,592		

	£	Debit £	Credit £
Sales	685,440		
Sales ledger control	103,104		
Sales returns	13,536		
Telephone	4,608		
VAT (owed to HMRC)	37,310		
Wages	178,848		
Totals			

Answer Bank

Chapter 1

Task 1.1

	Cash transaction ✓	Credit transaction ✓
Purchase of goods for £200 payable by cash in one week's time		✓
Writing a cheque for the purchase of a new computer	✓	
Sale of goods to a customer where the invoice accompanies the goods		✓
Receipt of a cheque from a customer for goods purchased today	✓	
Purchase of goods where payment is due in three weeks' time		✓

Task 1.2

✓	
	A credit note
	A remittance advice
	A petty cash voucher
✓	An invoice

Task 1.3

✓	
	A credit note
	A goods received note
✓	A goods returned note
	An invoice

Task 1.4

(a)

	Document issued by Joe
Freddie asks Joe for a quote for 14 desks	Quotation
Joe delivers 14 desks to Freddie	Delivery note
Joe requests payment from Freddie	Invoice
Freddie pays his invoice and takes a prompt payment discount	Credit note

(b)

	Document issued by Freddie
Freddie places an order with Joe for 14 desks	Purchase order
Freddie accepts in to his warehouse delivery of 14 desks from Joe	Goods received note
Freddie returns one faulty desk to Joe	Goods returned note
Freddie pays his invoice	Remittance advice

Task 1.5

✓	
✓	An alpha-numeric system
	A numeric system

Task 1.6

Customer	Customer code
Caledonian Ltd	Ca01
Jury's Brewery Ltd	Ju02

Task 1.7

The correct answer is: | Supplier code |

Task 1.8

(a)

Supplier code	PL244
General ledger code	GL001

(b) The correct answer is: | Product code |

Task 1.9

(a)

Supplier account code	VIN234
General ledger code	GL505

(b) The correct answer is: | To help trace relevant accounts quickly and easily |

Chapter 2

Task 2.1

Date 20XX	Details	Invoice number	Total £	VAT £	Net £
7 August	VXT Ltd	172	120	20	100

Working: VAT = 100 × 20%, Gross amount = 100 + 20 = 120

Task 2.2

Date 20XX	Details	Invoice number	Total £	VAT £	Net £
15 June	R Hart	365	648.00	108.00	540.00

Task 2.3

(a) – (b) Sales day book

Customer	Invoice number	Total £	VAT £	Net £
Hoppers Ltd	6237	656.40	109.40	547.00
Body Perfect	6238	744.00	124.00	620.00
Esporta Leisure	6239	415.20	69.20	346.00
Langans Beauty	6240	273.60	45.60	228.00
Body Perfect	6241	657.60	109.60	548.00
Superior Products	6242	265.20	44.20	221.00
Esporta Leisure	6243	499.20	83.20	416.00
Hoppers Ltd	6244	285.60	47.60	238.00
Langans Beauty	6245	328.80	54.80	274.00
		4,125.60	687.60	3,438.00

Cross-cast check:

	£
Net	3,438.00
VAT	687.60
Total	4,125.60

Task 2.4

Day book:	Sales returns day book

Customer	Credit note number	Total £	VAT £	Net £
Hoppers Ltd	1476	82.44	13.74	68.70
Esporta Leisure	1477	107.04	17.84	89.20
Superior Products	1478	14.10	2.35	11.75

Task 2.5

Day book:	Purchases day book

Date	Supplier	Invoice number	Total £	VAT £	Purchases (materials) £	Stationery £
4 Jan	P J Phillips	03576	428.40	71.40	357.00	
6 Jan	W J Jones	18435	252.00	42.00		210.00

Task 2.6

| Day book: | | Purchases day book | | | | | |

Date	Supplier	Invoice number	Total £	VAT £	Purchases (materials) £	Stationery £	Packaging £
12 Jan	P J Phillips	03598	495.60	82.60	413.00		
16 Jan	Packing Supplies	28423	321.60	53.60			268.00
19 Jan	Trenter Ltd	18478	625.20	104.20	521.00		
20 Jan	O & P Ltd	84335	748.80	124.80	624.00		
24 Jan	Packing Supplies	28444	196.80	32.80			164.00
28 Jan	Trenter Ltd	18491	441.60	73.60	368.00		
31 Jan	W J Jones	43681	124.80	20.80		104.00	

Task 2.7

| Day book: | | Purchases returns day book | | | | | |

Date	Supplier	Credit note number	Total £	VAT £	Purchases (materials) £	Stationery £	Packaging £
10 Jan	P J Phillips	04216	117.60	19.60	98.00		
16 Jan	W J Jones	CN 0643	67.20	11.20		56.00	

Task 2.8

Date	Customer	Credit note number	Customer code	Gross total £	VAT £	Net £
21 Sep	Whitehill Superstores	08650	SL 44	356.40	59.40	297.00
23 Sep	Dagwell Enterprises	08651	SL 15	244.80	40.80	204.00
	Totals			601.20	100.20	501.00

Task 2.9

Date	Supplier	Invoice number	Supplier code	Total £	VAT £	Net £	Wood purchases £	Polish/ varnish purchases £	Other purchases £
27 Jan	Ephraim Supplies	09642	PL39	349.20	58.20	291.00	291.00		
27 Jan	Cavendish Woods	06932	PL14	846.12	141.02	705.10	705.10		
27 Jan	Calverley Bros	67671	PL03	174.72	29.12	145.60		145.60	
27 Jan	Culverden & Co	36004	PL23	68.88	11.48	57.40			57.40
				1,438.92	239.82	1,199.10	996.10	145.60	57.40

Task 2.10

(a) – (b)

Sales returns day book

Date 20XX	Details	Credit note number	Total £	VAT @ 20% £	Net £	Bags returns £	Suitcases returns £
30 Nov	Shrier Goods	562	624	104	520	520	
30 Nov	Gringles Co	563	408	68	340		340
30 Nov	Lester plc	564	1,068	178	890	890	
	Totals		2,100	350	1,750	1,410	340

Chapter 3

Task 3.1

✓	A trade discount
	A prompt payment discount
	A bulk discount

Task 3.2

	The Home Office
	The Treasury
	The Inland Revenue
✓	HM Revenue & Customs

Task 3.3

Goods total £	Trade discount (15% × price) £	Net total £
416.80	62.52	354.28
105.60	15.84	89.76
96.40	14.46	81.94
263.20	39.48	223.72
351.00	52.65	298.35

Task 3.4

Net total £	VAT (Net × 20%) £	Gross total £
258.90	51.78	310.68
316.80	63.36	380.16
82.60	16.52	99.12
152.70	30.54	183.24
451.30	90.26	541.56

Task 3.5

Gross total £	VAT (Invoice total × 20/120) £	Net total £
145.20	24.20	121.00
66.90	11.15	55.75
246.60	41.10	205.50
35.40	5.90	29.50
125.40	20.90	104.50

Task 3.6

Invoice total £	VAT (Invoice total × 20/120) £	Net total £
252.66	42.11	210.55
169.20	28.20	141.00
48.60	8.10	40.50
104.28	17.38	86.90
60.48	10.08	50.40
822.60	137.10	685.50

Task 3.7

Customer	Gross invoice total £	Amount £
J Smith	258	250.26
Anchorage Ltd	312	302.64
VIP Ltd	84	81.48
Blue House Ltd	150	145.50

Tutorial note. Multiply the gross total by 97% to give the amount payable by each customer.

Task 3.8

	£
Net amount before discounts	7,000
Net amount after discounts	6,517
VAT	1,303.4
Total	7,820.4

Workings

	£
Net amount before discounts	200 × 35.00 = 7,000
Net amount after discounts:	
Trade discount	7,000 × 5% = 350
After trade discount	6,650
Bulk discount	6,650 × 2% = 133
Net amount after trade and bulk discounts	6,517
VAT @ 20%	6,517 × 20% = 1,303.4
Total	7,820.4

Task 3.9

(a)

£	1,382.40

Working 1,280 × 1.2 × 90% = 1,382.40

(b)

Amount	£
Net amount	128.00
VAT	25.60
Gross amount	153.60

Working

Discount: 1,280 × 1.2 × 10% = 153.60, VAT = 153.60/6 = 25.60, Net amount = 153.60 − 25.60 = 128.00

Task 3.10

Day book:		Discounts allowed day book			

Date 20XX	Details	Credit note number	Total £	VAT £	Net £
15 Oct	Shipper Ltd	223	67.20	11.20	56.00

Tutorial note. The credit note should be recorded in Anchor Supplies Ltd's discounts allowed day book as it is a discount allowed to a customer.

The name of the customer (Shipper Ltd) should be recorded in the 'details' column.

....

Task 3.11

Day book:		Discounts received day book			

Date 20XX	Details	Credit note number	Total £	VAT £	Net £
10 Nov	Rent a Van Ltd	11	123.60	20.60	103.00

Tutorial note. The credit note should be recorded in Pop Ice Cream Ltd's discounts received day book as it is a discount received from a supplier.

The name of the supplier (Rent a Van Ltd) should be recorded in the 'details' column.

....

Task 3.12

(a) The correct answer is: | £ | 2,304 |

Working Gross amount = ((£2,000 × 20%) + £2,000) = £2,400

Amount after discount = £2,400 × 96% = £2,304

(b) The correct answer is: | £ | 2,400 | (£2,000 + £400)

....

Task 3.13

The correct answer is: | Trade discount |

....

Task 3.14

	True ✓	False ✓
The book of prime entry for discounts allowed is the petty cash book.		✓
Input tax is the VAT suffered on purchases.	✓	
A goods received note is a primary document for recording in the accounting records.		✓

Chapter 4

Task 4.1

	A delivery note
✓	A price list
	A goods received note
	A statement of account

Task 4.2

	Analyse every invoice into a separate column of his analysed sales day book
✓	Allocate one of two sales codes to each invoice and use this to write up the invoices in the analysed sales day book
	Allocate invoice numbers on a randomised basis
	Use a different sequence of invoice numbers for each customer

Task 4.3

Southfield Electrical
Industrial Estate
Benham DR6 2FF

SALES INVOICE 57104

Date: 9 Jan 20XX

To: Whitehill Superstores   Customer account code: SL 44
      28 Whitehill Park
      Benham, DR6 5LM   Purchase order no: 32431

Quantity of units	Product code	Price each £	Total amount after trade discount £	VAT £	Total £
8	6260	300	2,160	432	2,592

Terms: 4% prompt payment discount for payment within 10 days

Tutorial note. The invoice is dated 9 Jan 20XX as the goods are delivered on this date.

Workings

	Calculation	£
Total list price	8 × 300	2,400
Trade discount	2,400 × 10%	240
Net amount	2,400 – 240	2,160
VAT	2,160 × 20%	432
Total	2,160 + 432	2,592

Task 4.4

Southfield Electrical
Industrial Estate
Benham DR6 2FF

SALES INVOICE 57105

Date: 19 May 20XX

To: Harper & Sons   Customer account code: SL 26
      30 High Street
      Benham, DR6 4ST   Purchase order no: 04367

Quantity of units	Product code	Price each £	Total amount after discounts £	VAT £	Total £
6	6370	260	1,407.9	281.58	1,689.48

Terms: 3% prompt payment discount for payment within 14 days

Tutorial note. The invoice is dated 19 May 20XX as this is the date the goods are delivered.

Workings

	Calculation	£
Total list price	6 × 260	1,560
Trade discount	1,560 × 5%	78
Net	1,560 – 78	1,482
Bulk discount	1,482 × 5%	74.1
Net after discounts	1,482 – 74.1	1,407.9
VAT	1,407.9 × 20%	281.58
Total	1,407.9 + 281.58	1,689.48

Task 4.5

(a)

Questions	Yes ✓	No ✓
Has the correct amount of goods been delivered?		✓
Has the correct product been delivered?	✓	
Have the correct codes been used on the invoice?		✓
Has the correct discount been applied?		✓

Tutorial note.

The invoice is for 15 toasters (as ordered) whereas the delivery note shows that only 12 were delivered. The correct product has been delivered, but the wrong product code has been used on the invoice (9046 instead of 9406), the purchase order number on the invoice is also incorrect, it should be 32202.

The customer was entitled to a 5% trade discount which has not been applied to the invoice. Additionally the invoice should state that the customer has been offered a 3% prompt payment discount.

(b)

Net amount £	VAT amount £	Gross amount £
171.00	34.20	205.20

Workings

	Calculation	£
Total list price	12 × 15	180.00
Trade discount	180 × 5%	9.00
Net	180 − 9	171.00
VAT	171 × 20%	34.20
Total	171.00 + 34.20	205.20

Task 4.6

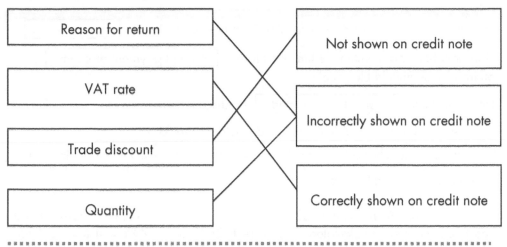

Reason for return	Not shown on credit note
VAT rate	Incorrectly shown on credit note
Trade discount	Correctly shown on credit note
Quantity	

··

Task 4.7

(a)

Document names
Delivery note   Petty cash voucher   Purchase order   ⟨Remittance advice note⟩

(b)

The cheque from Hayworth Ltd for £516.10 has resulted in an
underpayment .

This is because Hayworth has taken the prompt payment discount
offered.

This should not have been taken as the cheque arrived 13 days after the
invoice date.

In order to resolve the problem Southfield Electrical should
request another cheque from Hayworth Ltd for £ 21.50 which will
clear the outstanding balance.

Workings

Prompt payment discount: £537.60 × 4% = £21.50 has been deducted:
£537.60 − £21.50 = £516.10. This should not have been taken as the
cheque arrived 13 days after the invoice date.

··

Task 4.8

The cheque from Harper & Sons for £709.48 has resulted in an underpayment .

Harper & Sons paid within the time limit for the prompt payment discount offered by Southfield Electrical.

However, they incorrectly calculated the discount.

In order to resolve the problem Southfield Electrical should

request another cheque from Harper & Sons for £ 4.76 which will clear the outstanding balance.

Tutorial note. A discount of £34.52 (£744 – £709.48) has been taken, but it has been incorrectly calculated. The correct discount is £744 × 4% = £29.76. Therefore the cheque should have been made out for £34.52 – £29.76 = £4.76.

Task 4.9

Sumberton Ltd
Sumberton House,
10 Main Road
Sawlow
SA7 5LD

VAT Registration No. 536 3723 77

Gringles Co   Customer account code: SL637
Unit 18 Radley Estate
Sawlow
SA7 7VB

Date: 22 December 20XX

Invoice No: 12901
Delivery note number: 6734527

Quantity of goods	Product code	Total list price £	Net amount after bulk discount £	VAT £	Gross £
80	L736B	1,600	1,360	272	1,632

Tutorial note. Total list price: 80/5 × £100 = £1,600, Net amount after bulk discount = 1,600 × 85% = £1,360, VAT = 20% × £1,360 = £272, Gross = £1,360 + £272 = £1,632

Task 4.10

The correct answer is: | Sales invoice 12813 |

Chapter 5

Task 5.1

When a supplier delivers materials to him he retains the supplier's delivery note and also prepares ┃ a goods received note ┃ once he has had a chance to inspect the quality of the items.

Task 5.2

The correct answer is: ┃ A product code ┃

Task 5.3

(a) The correct answer is: ┃ 20 June ┃

(b) The correct answer is: ┃ £ ┃ 281.30 ┃

Workings

VAT: £239.20 × 20% = £47.84

Invoice total: £239.20 + £47.84 = £287.04

Discount: £287.04 × 2% = £5.74

Payment: £287.04 – £5.74 = £281.30

Task 5.4

Invoice date	Supplier name	Payment date	Workings	Amount of cheque £
5 Jan	Henson Press	27 Jan		336.00
8 Jan	GH Publications	3 Feb		136.80
12 Jan	Ely Instruments	27 Jan	765 × 98%	749.70
15 Jan	Hams Instruments	10 Feb		372.00
19 Jan	CD Supplies	10 Feb		138.72
22 Jan	Jester Press	27 Jan	156 × 96.5%	150.54
22 Jan	Henson Press	17 Feb		306.00

Task 5.5

(a)

Remittance advice	
To: PT Supplies	**From: Edgehill Designs**
Date: 7 February 20XX	

Date 20XX	Details and transaction amount £
6 Jan	Inv 20671 – £107
8 Jan	Inv 20692 – £157
10 Jan	CN 04722 – £28

(b)

£	236

Working

£107 + £157 – £28 = £236

Task 5.6

(a)

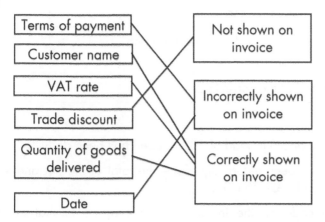

(b)

Net amount £	VAT amount £	Gross amount £
216.00	43.20	259.20

Working

	Calculation	£
Net before discount	10 × 24	240
Trade discount	240 × 10%	24
Net amount	240 – 24	216
VAT	216 × 20%	43.20
Total	216 + 43.2	259.20

Task 5.7

(a)

	Yes ✓	No ✓
Has the correct purchase price of the rocking chairs been charged?	✓	
Has the correct discount been applied?		✓
Has the invoice been correctly cast?		✓
Has the correct product code been used on the invoice?		✓
Has VAT been charged at the correct rate?	✓	

Tutorial note.

- Trade discount of 5% instead of 10% agreed has been deducted.

- The invoice has been incorrectly cast – the total of the net and VAT amounts should be £1,751.04.

- The product code on the invoice does not agree to that on the purchase order.

(b)

Net amount £	VAT amount £	Gross amount £
1,382.40	276.48	1,658.88

Working

	Calculation	£
Net before discount	16 × 96.00	1,536.00
Trade discount	1,536.00 × 10%	153.60
Net amount	1,536.00 – 153.60	1,382.40
VAT	1,382.40 × 20%	276.48
Total	1,382.40 + 276.48	1,658.88

Task 5.8

(a) The correct answer is: | Discount received £20 |

(b) The correct answer is: | Credit note 3215 £250 |

(c) The correct answer is: | £ | 723 |

Working

£743 – £20 = £723

Task 5.9

	Yes ✓	No ✓
Has the correct purchase price of the cardboard boxes been charged?		✓
Has the correct discount been applied?		✓

	Amount £
What would be the VAT amount charged if the invoice was correct?	108.00
What would be the total amount charged if the invoice was correct?	648.00

Working

	Calculation	£
Net before discount	30 × 20	600
Trade discount	600 × 10%	60
Net amount	600 – 60	540
VAT	540 × 20%	108
Total	540 + 108	648

Task 5.10

(a)

Ken's Exotics
1 Bath Street

Cembury, CE11 9SD

REMITTANCE ADVICE

To: Mack Materials   Date: 30 June 20XX

Please find attached our cheque in payment of the following amounts.

Invoice number	Credit note number	Amount £
Invoice 901		760
	Credit note 43	31
Total amount paid		729

(b)

	✓
The remittance advice note will be sent to the accounts department at Mack Materials to request that a cheque is raised.	
The remittance advice note will be sent to Mack Materials's bank to advise them of the amount being paid.	
The remittance advice note will be sent to the customer to advise them of the amount being paid.	
The remittance advice note will be sent to the supplier to advise them of the amount being paid.	✓

Task 5.11

	✓
Ken has requested a credit note from the supplier for £1,586 which he has not yet received.	
Ken sent a cheque for £1,586 to the supplier on 30 June 20XX.	✓
Ken ordered some items from the supplier on 30 June for £1,586 but the goods have not yet been delivered and an invoice has not yet been raised.	

Task 5.12

	Yes ✓	No ✓
Has the correct purchase price of the cabin cases been charged?		✓
Has the correct discount been applied?		✓

	Amount £
What would be the VAT amount charged if the invoice was correct?	58.65
What would be the total amount charged if the invoice was correct?	351.90

BPP
LEARNING MEDIA

Workings

VAT: (15 × £23) × 0.85 × 0.2 = £58.65

Total: (15 × £23 × 0.85) + £58.65 = £351.90

Task 5.13

(a) The correct answer is: | Discount of £10 |

(b) The correct answer is: | Credit note C579 |

(c) The correct answer is: | £ | 6,141 |

Working

(£6,151 – £10)

(d)

	✓
A credit note adds to the amount owed to the supplier	
A remittance advice note adds to the amount owed to the supplier	
A goods received note adds to the amount owed to the supplier	
An invoice adds to the amount owed to the supplier	✓

Chapter 6

Task 6.1

	Asset ✓	Liability ✓
A trade receivable	✓	
A car used in the business	✓	
A loan from the bank		✓
A bank overdraft		✓
Cash in hand	✓	
VAT owed to HMRC		✓
A trade payable		✓
Inventory of raw materials	✓	

Task 6.2

An increase in an expense is a	debit
A decrease in a liability is a	debit
An increase in income is a	credit
An increase in an asset is a	debit
An increase in capital is a	credit
A decrease in an asset is a	credit
An increase in a liability is a	credit
A decrease in capital is a	debit

Task 6.3

(a) **(i)** James paid £20,000 into a business bank account in order to start the business.

Effect 1	Effect 2
Increase in cash	Increase in capital

(ii) He paid an initial rental of £2,500 by cheque for the shop that he is to trade from.

Effect 1	Effect 2
Decrease in cash	Rent expense incurred

(iii) He purchased a van by cheque for £7,400.

Effect 1	Effect 2
Decrease in cash	Increase in assets

(iv) He purchased £6,000 of goods for resale on credit.

Effect 1	Effect 2
Increase in purchases	Increase in liabilities (trade payables)

(v) He sold goods for £1,000 - the customer paid by cheque.

Effect 1	Effect 2
Increase in cash	Increase in sales

(vi) He sold goods on credit for £4,800.

Effect 1	Effect 2
Increase in assets (trade receivables)	Increase in sales

(vii) He paid shop assistants' wages by cheque totalling £2,100.

Effect 1	Effect 2
Decrease in cash	Wages expense incurred

(viii) He made further sales on credit for £3,900.

Effect 1	Effect 2
Increase in assets (trade receivables)	Increase in sales

(ix) He purchased a further £1,400 of goods for resale by cheque.

Effect 1	Effect 2
Decrease in cash	Increase in purchases

(x) £3,700 was received from credit customers.

Effect 1	Effect 2
Increase in cash	Decrease in assets (trade receivables)

(xi) He paid £3,300 to credit suppliers.

Effect 1	Effect 2
Decrease in cash	Decrease in liabilities (trade payables)

(xii) He withdrew £800 from the business for his living expenses.

Effect 1	Effect 2
Decrease in cash	Increase in drawings

(b)

Bank

Details	£	Details	£
Capital (i)	20,000	Rent (ii)	2,500
Sales (v)	1,000	Van (iii)	7,400
Sales ledger control (x)	3,700	Wages (vii)	2,100
		Purchases (ix)	1,400
		Purchases ledger control (xi)	3,300
		Drawings (xii)	800

Capital

Details	£	Details	£
		Bank (i)	20,000

Rent

Details	£	Details	£
Bank (ii)	2,500		

Van

Details	£	Details	£
Bank (iii)	7,400		

Purchases

Details	£	Details	£
Purchases ledger control (iv)	6,000		
Bank (ix)	1,400		

Purchases ledger control

Details	£	Details	£
Bank (xi)	3,300	Purchases (iv)	6,000

Sales account

Details	£	Details	£
		Bank (v)	1,000
		Sales ledger control (vi)	4,800
		Sales ledger control (viii)	3,900

Sales ledger control

Details	£	Details	£
Sales (vi)	4,800	Bank (x)	3,700
Sales (viii)	3,900		

Wages

Details	£	Details	£
Bank (vii)	2,100		

Drawings

Details	£	Details	£
Bank (xii)	800		

Task 6.4

(a)

	Debit ✓	Credit ✓
Discounts allowed	✓	
Sales ledger control		✓

(b)

	Debit ✓	Credit ✓
Discounts received		✓
Purchases ledger control	✓	

(c)

	Debit ✓	Credit ✓
Purchases	✓	
Purchases ledger control		✓

(d)

	Debit ✓	Credit ✓
Sales		✓
Sales ledger control	✓	

(e)

	Debit ✓	Credit ✓
Cash	✓	
Sales		✓

(f)

	Debit ✓	Credit ✓
Cash	✓	
Sales ledger control		✓

(g)

	Debit ✓	Credit ✓
Drawings	✓	
Cash		✓

(h)

	Debit ✓	Credit ✓
Wages	✓	
Cash		✓

Chapter 7

Task 7.1

TN Designs

Date 20XX	Details	Amount £	Date 20XX	Details	Amount £
1 May	Balance b/f	2,643	8 May	Bank	1,473
11 May	Invoice 27491	1,804	24 May	Credit note 381	265
18 May	Invoice 27513	1,088			
			31 May	Balance c/d	3,797
	Total	5,535		Total	5,535
1 June	Balance b/d	3,797			

Task 7.2

Harold & Partners

Date 20XX	Details	Amount £	Date 20XX	Details	Amount £
7 Sept	Bank	635	1 Sept	Balance b/f	1,367
7 Sept	Discount	33	5 Sept	Invoice 27465	998
30 Sept	Credit note 364	106	12 Sept	Invoice 27499	478
30 Sept	Balance c/d	2,069			
	Total	2,843		Total	2,843
			1 Oct	Balance b/d	2,069

Task 7.3

Account name	Debit £	Credit £
Purchases ledger control	367.48	
Bank		367.48

Task 7.4

	Capital ✓	Revenue ✓
Purchase of a new computer paid for by cheque	✓	
Purchase of printer paper by cheque		✓
Purchase of a new business car on credit	✓	
Payment of road tax on a new business car		✓
Payment of rent for the business premises		✓

Task 7.5

(a) Purchases ledger control

Date	Details	Amount £	Date	Details	Amount £
31 Oct	Purchases returns	4,467	1 Oct	Balance b/f	41,204
31 Oct	Bank	36,409	31 Oct	Purchases	52,390
31 Oct	Discounts received	125			
31 Oct	Balance c/d	52,593			
	Total	93,594		Total	93,594
			1 Nov	Balance b/d	52,593

(b) Petty cash

Date	Details	Amount £	Date	Details	Amount £
1 Oct	Balance b/f	200.00	31 Oct	Expenses	183.25
31 Oct	Bank	183.25	31 Oct	Balance c/d	200.00
	Total	383.25		Total	383.25
1 Nov	Balance b/d	200.00			

(c) VAT

Date	Details	Amount £	Date	Details	Amount £
31 Oct	Sales returns	40.00	1 Oct	Balance b/f	183.25
31 Oct	Purchases	1,900.00	31 Oct	Purchases returns	62.00
31 Oct	Balance c/d	1,555.25	31 Oct	Sales	3,250.00
	Total	3,495.25		Total	3,495.25
			1 Nov	Balance b/d	1,555.25

Task 7.6

	Capital ✓	Revenue ✓
Purchase of goods for resale on credit from a supplier		✓
Receipt of proceeds from sale of car used in the business	✓	
Payment of drawings to the business owner	✓	
Acquisition of new machine for use over five years	✓	
Payment by a cash customer for goods		✓

Task 7.7

(a) Purchases

Date 20XX	Details	Amount £	Date 20XX	Details	Amount £
01 Nov	Balance b/f	140,389			
15 Nov	Purchases ledger control	14,388			
30 Nov	Purchases ledger control	52,389			
			30 Nov	Balance c/d	207,166
	Total	207,166		Total	207,166
1 Dec	Balance b/d	207,166			

(b) Bank interest received

Date 20XX	Details	Amount £	Date 20XX	Details	Amount £
			01 Nov	Balance b/f	32
			15 Nov	Bank	14
			30 Nov	Bank	22
30 Nov	Balance c/d	68			
	Total	68		Total	68
			1 Dec	Balance b/d	68

Task 7.8

Item	Capital expenditure ✓	Revenue expenditure ✓	Capital income ✓	Revenue income ✓
Purchase of airline tickets for business travel		✓		
Proceeds from sale of machinery			✓	
Sale of goods to a customer for cash				✓
Received interest on the business's savings account from the bank				✓
Purchase of a shop building	✓			
Petty cash payment for stationery		✓		

Task 7.9

Item	Example
Asset	Trade receivables
Liability	Bank overdraft
Capital transaction	Drawings

Chapter 8

Task 8.1

(a)

Details	Cash £	Bank £	VAT £	Cash purchases £	Trade payables £
Balance b/f		735			
Mendip plc	138		23	115	
W J Jones		521			521
Trenter Ltd		358			358
Packing Supplies		754			754
Totals	138	2,368	23	115	1,633

(b) Cash balance is £ | 381

Working £200 + £319 – £138

(c) Bank balance is £1,808

Working £560 – £2,368

(d)

	✓
Debit	
Credit	✓

Task 8.2

Cash book – credit side

Details	Cash £	Bank £	VAT £	Trade payables £	Cash purchases £	Rent & rates £
Henson Press		329		329		
Ely Instruments		736		736		
Rates		255				255
Rent		500				500
Total		1,820		1,065		755

Task 8.3

Cash book – debit side

Details	Cash £	Bank £	VAT £	Trade receivables £	Cash sales £
Balance b/f	120	1,520			
Hoppers Ltd	334	500	139		695
Body Perfect		542		542	
Totals	454	2,562	139	542	695

Task 8.4

Cash book – debit side

Details	Cash £	Bank £	VAT £	Trade receivables £	Cash sales £
Balance b/f	56	1,805			
Howsham Ltd	210		35		175
Esporta Leisure		958		958	
Totals	266	2,763	35	958	175

Task 8.5

(a) Cash book – credit side

Details	Cash £	Bank £	VAT £	Trade payables £	Cash purchases £	Stationery £
Balance b/f		236				
Dubai Dreams	324		54		270	
Walter Enterprises	228		38		190	
Sinead Reilly	56				56	
Sumatra Trading		7,265		7,265		
SHSK Co		378	63			315
Total	608	7,879	155	7,265	516	315

(b) Cash book – debit side

Details	Cash £	Bank £	VAT £	Trade receivables £
Balance b/f	1,228			
Park Farm Stores		2,576		2,576
Tristram Pale Ltd		4,233		4,233
Total	1,228	6,809		6,809

(c) The correct answer is: £ | 620

Working

(1,228 – 608)

(d) The correct answer is: £ | 1,070

Working

(7,879 – 6,809)

(e)

	✓
Debit	
Credit	✓

Task 8.6

(a) Cash book – credit side

Details	Cash £	Bank £	VAT £	Trade payables £	Cash purchases £	Motor expenses £
Balance b/f		16,942				
B Smithson Ltd	240		40		200	
H Hamnet	192		32		160	
Renee Reid	320				320	
Tenon Ltd		3,600		3,600		
Vernon Motor Repairs		48	8			40
Total	752	20,590	80	3,600	680	40

(b) Cash book – debit side

Details	Cash £	Bank £	VAT £	Trade receivables £
Balance b/f	1,325			
G Brownlow		749		749
S Barnett		300		300
Total	1,325	1,049		1,049

(c) The correct answer is: £ 573

Working

(1,325 – 752 = 573)

(d) The correct answer is: £ 19,541

Working

(20,590 – 1,049 = 19,541)

(e)

	✓
Debit	
Credit	✓

Task 8.7

Cash book – debit side

Details	Cash £	Bank £	VAT £	Trade receivables £	Cash sales £
Balance b/f	55	1,300			
Whippet's	210		35		175
Ragdoll Ltd		958		958	
Totals	265	2,258	35	958	175
Balance b/d	265	1,165			

Cash book – credit side

Details	Cash £	Bank £	VAT £	Trade payables £	Cash purchases £
Hornsea Ltd		355		355	
Lyndon Plc		738		738	
Balance c/d	265	1,165			
Total	265	2,258		1,093	

Task 8.8

(a) **Cash book – debit side**

Details	Cash £	Bank £	VAT £	Trade receivables £	Cash sales £
Balance b/f	159	844			
Humber & Co	582		97		485
Ridgely Ltd		2,150		2,150	
Watts Partners		978		978	
Total	741	3,972	97	3,128	485

(b) The correct answer is: £ | 180   (£741 – £561)

(c) The correct answer is: £ | –113   (£3,972 – £4,085)

Chapter 9

Task 9.1

(a) Sales ledger

Account name	Amount £	Debit ✓	Credit ✓
S Himms	900	✓	
G Pood	1,500	✓	
M Kitchell	456	✓	
B Crown	1,392	✓	

(b) General ledger

Account name	Amount £	Debit ✓	Credit ✓
Sales	3,540		✓
VAT	708		✓
Sales ledger control	4,248	✓	

Task 9.2

(a) General ledger

Sales ledger control

Details	Amount £	Details	Amount £
Sales	7,085		
VAT	1,417		

Sales

Details	Amount £	Details	Amount £
		Sales ledger control	7,085

VAT

Details	Amount £	Details	Amount £
		Sales ledger control	1,417

(b) **Sales ledger**

H Simms   **SL 45**

Details	Amount £	Details	Amount £
Invoice 0001	1,800		

K Mitchell   **SL 30**

Details	Amount £	Details	Amount £
Invoice 0003	912		

Task 9.3

(a) **Sales ledger**

Account name	Amount £	Debit ✓	Credit ✓
Hoppers Ltd	656.40	✓	
Body Perfect	744.00	✓	

(b) **General ledger**

Account name	Amount £	Debit ✓	Credit ✓
Sales	1,167.00		✓
VAT	233.40		✓
Sales ledger control	1,400.40	✓	

Task 9.4

(a) GENERAL LEDGER

Sales ledger control

Details	Amount £	Details	Amount £
Sales	574.00		
VAT	114.80		

Sales

Details	Amount £	Details	Amount £
		Sales ledger control	574.00

VAT

Details	Amount £	Details	Amount £
		Sales ledger control	114.80

(b) SALES LEDGER

Langans Beauty

Details	Amount £	Details	Amount £
Invoice 6240	273.60		

Esporta Leisure

Details	Amount £	Details	Amount £
Invoice 6239	415.20		

Task 9.5

(a) Sales ledger

Account name	Amount £	Debit ✓	Credit ✓
Rocks Garden Suppliers	701.76	✓	
Eridge Nurseries	429.30	✓	
Abergaven GC	923.40	✓	
Rother Nurseries	756.00	✓	

(b) General ledger

Account name	Amount £	Debit ✓	Credit ✓
Sales	2,342.05		✓
VAT	468.41		✓
Sales ledger control	2,810.46	✓	

Task 9.6

(a) Sales ledger

Account name	Amount £	Debit ✓	Credit ✓
Hoppers Ltd	82.44		✓
Esporta Leisure	107.04		✓
Superior Products	14.16		✓

(b) General ledger

Account name	Amount £	Debit ✓	Credit ✓
Sales returns	169.70	✓	
VAT	33.94	✓	
Sales ledger control	203.64		✓

Task 9.7

(a)

Account name	Amount £	Debit ✓	Credit ✓
Hoppers Ltd	36		✓
Esporta Leisure	72		✓

(b)

Account name	Amount £	Debit ✓	Credit ✓
Discounts allowed	90	✓	
VAT	18	✓	
Sales ledger control	108		✓

Task 9.8

(a)

	True ✓	False ✓
Rother Nurseries has fully settled their account at 31 January 20XX.		✓
Invoice 08695 should have been included in the payment in order to fully settle the account at 31 January.		✓
The remittance advice has been correctly cast.	✓	
The invoice amounts are included correctly on the remittance advice note.		✓

Tutorial note. Rother Nurseries has not fully settled its account as at 31 January because it has made a mistake in the amount included for invoice 08674. It has included this invoice as £114.78 instead of £214.78, therefore it still owes £100. Invoice 08695 is dated 5 February, so did not form part of the account as at 31 January and was correctly excluded from the payment.

(b)

£	1,212.17

Working

£756.00 + £214.78 + £337.89 – £96.50 = £1,212.17

....

Task 9.9

(a)

	True ✓	False ✓
Abergaven Garden Centre has included on the remittance advice note all relevant transactions up to 9 February.		✓
The remittance advice note has been correctly cast.		✓
The invoice amounts are included correctly on the remittance advice note.	✓	

Tutorial note. Abergaven Garden Centre has not included its credit notes with its payment. Therefore it has paid too much. The remittance advice has not been correctly cast as the final invoice has been excluded from the casting.

(b)

£	2,136.57

Working

923.40 + 623.56 + 316.58 + 415.76 – 32.50 – 110.23 = £2,136.57

....

Task 9.10

Account name	Amount £	Debit ✓	Credit ✓
VAT	46.64		✓
Cash sales	233.20		✓
Sales ledger control	2,018.10		✓

....

Task 9.11

(a) SALES LEDGER

Hoppers Ltd

Details	Amount £	Details	Amount £
Invoice 6237	656.40	Credit note 1476	82.44
		Bank	553.96

Body Perfect

Details	Amount £		Amount £
Invoice 6238	744.00	Bank	706.64

Esporta Leisure

Details	Amount £	Details	Amount £
Invoice 6239	415.20	Credit note 1477	107.04
		Bank	367.20

Langans Beauty

Details	Amount £	Details	Amount £
Invoice 6240	273.60	Bank	273.60

Superior Products

Details	Amount £	Details	Amount £
Invoice 6242	265.20	Credit note 1478	14.16
		Bank	116.70

(b) GENERAL LEDGER

Cash

Details	Amount £	Details	Amount £
Sales	233.20		
VAT	46.64		

Bank

Details	Amount £	Details	Amount £
Sales ledger control	2,018.10		

Sales ledger control

Details	Amount £	Details	Amount £
Sales	3,438.00	Sales returns	169.70
VAT	687.60	VAT	33.94
		Bank	2,018.10

Sales

Details	Amount £	Details	Amount £
		Sales ledger control	3,438.00
		Cash	233.20

VAT

Details	Amount £	Details	Amount £
Sales ledger control	33.94	Sales ledger control	687.60
		Cash	46.64

Task 9.12

(a) Sales ledger

Account name	Amount £	Debit ✓	Credit ✓
Henderson & Co	7,349		✓

(b) General ledger

Account name	Amount £	Debit ✓	Credit ✓
Sales ledger control	7,349		✓
Sales	355		✓
VAT	71		✓

Task 9.13

SALES LEDGER

Alpha Services   **SL 10**

Details	Amount £	Details	Amount £
Balance b/d	253.63	Credit note 551	624.00
Invoice 715	5,190.00	Bank	253.63
Invoice 787	10,020.00		

Task 9.14

(a) Sales ledger

Account name	Amount £	Debit ✓	Credit ✓
Gringles Co	300	✓	
Lester plc	1,308	✓	
Shrier Goods	2,676	✓	
Abunda Bags	1,992	✓	

(b)   General ledger

Account name	Amount £	Debit ✓	Credit ✓
Sales ledger control	6,276	✓	
Sales	5,230		✓
VAT	1,046		✓

Chapter 10

Task 10.1

(a) Purchases day book

Date 20XX	Details	Invoice number	Total £	VAT £	Net £
30 June	Seashell Ltd	8971	3,853.20	642.20	3,211.00
30 June	Opal & Co	05119	4,800.00	800.00	4,000.00
		Totals	8,653.20	1,422.20	7,211.00

Workings

Seashell Ltd VAT = 3,211 × 20% = 642.20, Gross = 3,211 + 642.20 = 3,853.20

Opal & Co VAT = 4,800/6 = 800, Net = 4,800 - 800 = 4,000

(b) Purchases ledger

Account name	Amount £	Debit ✓	Credit ✓
Seashell Ltd	3,853.20		✓
Opal & Co	4,800.00		✓

Task 10.2

(a)

Account name	Amount £	Debit ✓	Credit ✓
Purchases	2,711.00	✓	
Stationery	314.00	✓	
Packaging	432.00	✓	
VAT	691.40	✓	
Purchases ledger control	4,148.40		✓

(b)

Account name	Amount £	Debit ✓	Credit ✓
W J Jones	252		✓

Working

£210 × 20 % = £42, gross = £210 + £42 = £252

Task 10.3

(a)   GENERAL LEDGER

Purchases ledger control

Details	Amount £	Details	Amount £
		Purchases	357.00
		Packaging	268.00
		VAT	125.00

VAT

Details	Amount £	Details	Amount £
Purchases ledger control	125.00		

Purchases

Details	Amount £	Details	Amount £
Purchases ledger control	357.00		

Packaging

Details	Amount £	Details	Amount £
Purchases ledger control	268.00		

(b) PURCHASES LEDGER   PJ Phillips

Details	Amount £	Details	Amount £
		Invoice 03576	428.40

Packing Supplies

Details	Amount £	Details	Amount £
		Invoice 28423	321.60

Task 10.4

(a) General ledger

Account name	Amount £	Debit ✓	Credit ✓
Wood purchases	996.10	✓	
Polish/varnish purchases	145.60	✓	
Other purchases	57.40	✓	
VAT	239.82	✓	
Purchases ledger control	1,438.92		✓

(b) Purchases ledger

Account name	Amount £	Debit ✓	Credit ✓
Calverley Bros	174.72		✓
Cavendish Woods	846.12		✓
Culverden & Co	68.88		✓
Ephraim Supplies	349.20		✓

Task 10.5

(a) General ledger

Account name	Amount £	Debit ✓	Credit ✓
Purchases ledger control	667.20	✓	
Purchases returns	444.00		✓
Stationery	112.00		✓
VAT	111.20		✓

(b) Purchases ledger

Account name	Amount £	Debit ✓	Credit ✓
K Mates	235.20	✓	
R Jones	134.40	✓	
X & Y Ltd	297.60	✓	

Task 10.6

(a) GENERAL LEDGER

Purchases ledger control

Details	Amount £	Details	Amount £
Purchases returns	222.00	Purchases	2,711.00
Stationery	56.00	Stationery	314.00
VAT	55.60	Packaging	432.00
		VAT	691.40

VAT

Details	Amount £	Details	Amount £
Purchases ledger control	691.40	Purchases ledger control	55.60

Purchases returns

Details	Amount £	Details	Amount £
		Purchases ledger control	222.00

Stationery

Details	Amount £	Details	Amount £
Purchases ledger control	314.00	Purchases ledger control	56.00

(b) PURCHASES LEDGER

Phillips

Details	Amount £	Details	Amount £
Credit note 04216	117.60	Invoice 0357	428.40
		Invoice 0358	495.60

Wallace

Details	£	Details	£
Credit note CN0643	67.20	Invoice I342	252.00
		Invoice I350	124.80

Olivia Ltd

Details	£	Details	£
Credit note CN1102	148.80	Invoice 55773	748.80

Task 10.7

(a)

Account name	Amount £	Debit ✓	Credit ✓
Purchases	90.00	✓	
VAT	18.00	✓	
Purchases ledger control	1,357.07	✓	

(b)

Account name	Amount £	Debit ✓	Credit ✓
Time Ltd	1,105.07	✓	
WFF Ltd	252.00	✓	

Task 10.8

(a) **Purchases ledger**

Account name	Amount £	Debit ✓	Credit ✓
Frankie's Leatherware	12,348		✓
Casaubon's	3,924		✓

(b) **General ledger**

Account name	Amount £	Debit ✓	Credit ✓
Purchases	13,560	✓	
VAT	2,712	✓	
Purchases ledger control	16,272		✓

Task 10.9

(a) **Purchases ledger**

Account name	Amount £	Debit ✓	Credit ✓
Trenter Ltd	36	✓	
WJ Jones	72	✓	

(b) **General ledger**

Account name	Amount £	Debit ✓	Credit ✓
Purchases ledger control	108	✓	
Discounts received	90		✓
VAT	18		✓

Task 10.10

(a) Purchases ledger

Account name	Amount £	Debit ✓	Credit ✓
Casaubon's	2,445	✓	

(b) General ledger

Account name	Amount £	Debit ✓	Credit ✓
Purchases ledger control	2,445	✓	
Purchases	510	✓	
VAT	102	✓	

Task 10.11

What will be the entries in the general ledger?

Account name	Amount £	Debit ✓	Credit ✓
Purchases ledger control	2,492	✓	
Sales ledger control	4,368		✓
Cash sales	295		✓
VAT	59		✓

Chapter 11

Task 11.1

£	68.34

Tutorial note. The cash required to replenish the petty cash box is equal to the total of the vouchers in the petty cash box.

Task 11.2

(a) Petty cash book

Date 20XX	Details	Amount £	Date 20XX	Details	Amount £	VAT £	Travel £	Office expenses £
24 Jan	Balance b/f	120.00	27 Jan	Paper	7.12	1.18		5.94
			29 Jan	Coffee	3.99			3.99
			29 Jan	Taxi	10.72	1.78	8.94	
			29 Jan	Balance c/d	98.17			
	Total	120.00		Totals	120.00	2.96	8.94	9.93

(b)

£	21.83

Working £120 – £98.17 = £21.83

Task 11.3

(a)

£	16

Working

	£
Opening balance	22
Cash from bank	53
Less: expenditure during month	(16)
balance at end of month	59

Therefore 75 – 59 = £16 required to restore the imprest level

(b)

	✓
Debit	✓
Credit	

Task 11.4

Petty cash control

Date	Details	Amount £	Date	Details	Amount £
1 Jan	Balance b/f	150.00	31 Jan	Expenditure	101.50
			31 Jan	Balance c/d	48.50
	Total	150.00		Total	150.00
1 Feb	Balance b/d	48.50			

Task 11.5

(a) – (c)

Petty cash book

Date	Details	Amount £	Date	Details	Total £	Stationery £	Postage £	Motor fuel £
1 Nov	Bal b/f	100	7 Nov	Postage stamps	20		20	
			15 Nov	Pens and pencils	18	18		
			22 Nov	Petrol	10			10
			30 Nov	Envelopes	15	15		
					63			
			30 Nov	Bal c/d	37			
	Total	100		Total	100	33	20	10
1 Dec	Bal b/d	37						

Task 11.6

(a) – (b)

Petty cash book

Debit side		Credit side					
Details	Amount £	Details	Amount £	VAT £	Postage £	Travel £	Cleaning £
Bal b/f	175.00	Post Office	30.00		30.00		
		Window cleaning	30.72	5.12			25.60
		MegaBus	29.50			29.50	
		Balance c/d	84.78				
Total	175.00	Total	175.00	5.12	30.00	29.50	25.60

Task 11.7

Petty cash reimbursement		
Date: 30.09.20XX		
Amount required to restore the cash in the petty cash box	£	240.24

Tutorial note. The amount of cash required to restore the petty cash is the imprest amount less the cash remaining in the box: £250 – £9.76 = £240.24.

Task 11.8

(a) – (b)

Petty cash book

Debit side		Credit side					
Details	**Amount £**	**Details**	**Amount £**	**VAT £**	**Postage £**	**Travel £**	**Stationery £**
Balance b/f	150.00	Tom's Taxi	18.00			18.00	
		Post Office	30.00		30.00		
		SMP Stationery	43.20	7.20			36.00
		Balance c/d	58.80				
Total	150.00	Total	150.00	7.20	30.00	18.00	36.00

Task 11.9

Petty cash reimbursement		
Date: 31.07.20XX		
Amount required to restore the cash in the petty cash box	£	196.55

Task 11.10

(a) General ledger

Account name	Amount £	Debit ✓	Credit ✓
Petty cash	108.32		✓
VAT	15.52	✓	
Office expenses	15.20	✓	
Stationery	32.60	✓	
Maintenance	45.00	✓	

(b) The answer is: | Petty cash |

Tutorial note. The credit entry to petty cash would not be needed if the petty cash book was itself part of the general ledger double entry system.

Task 11.11

	✓
Imprest system	
Non-imprest system	✓

Task 11.12

(a) – (b)

Petty cash book

Debit side		Credit side					
Details	Amount £	Details	Amount £	VAT £	Postage £	Travel £	Stationery £
Balance b/f	75.23	Taxi	9.00			9.00	
Bank	60.00	Post Office	15.00		15.00		
		Suzie's Stationery	43.20	7.20			36.00
Balance b/d		Balance c/d	68.03				
Total	135.23	Total	135.23	7.20	15.00	9.00	36.00

(c) The correct answer is: | £ | 68.03 |

Tutorial note. The balance c/d on the petty cash book above is the amount of cash remaining in the petty cash tin on Friday. This is a **non-imprest** system of managing petty cash because Lucy tops up the balance by £60 each week independently of the petty cash expenditure.

Task 11.13

(a) – (b)

Petty cash-book

Details	Amount £	Details	Amount £	VAT £	Postage £	Stationery £
Balance b/f	175.00	Printer cartridges	17.40	2.90		14.50
		Stamps	12.60		12.60	
		Staplers	18.90	3.15		15.75
		Balance c/d	126.10			
Total	175.00	Totals	175.00	6.05	12.60	30.25

Working £18.90 × 20/120 = £3.15 VAT

(c)

General ledger accounts	✓
Stamps	
Stationery	✓
Petty cash-book	
Petty cash control	
Postage	✓
Staplers	
VAT	✓

(d)

	✓
Remittance advice note	
Cheque requisition form	✓
Petty cash claim	
Customer statement	

(e)

£	48.90

Working £17.40 + £12.60 + £18.90 = £48.90

Chapter 12

Task 12.1

Ledger account	Balance	Debit ✓	Credit ✓
Sales	592,513		✓
Telephone	1,295	✓	
Sales ledger control	52,375	✓	
Wages	104,288	✓	
Purchases returns	8,229		✓
Bank overdraft	17,339		✓
Purchases	372,589	✓	
Drawings	71,604	✓	
Sales returns	32,800	✓	
Car	14,700	✓	
Purchases ledger control	31,570		✓

Task 12.2

	£	Debit £	Credit £
Office equipment		36,440	
Purchases		196,800	
Motor vehicles	76,800	76,800	
Sales	285,600		285,600
Bank (overdraft)	2,016		2,016
Petty cash	36	36	
Capital	90,000		90,000
Sales returns	5,640	5,640	
Purchases returns	4,320		4,320
Sales ledger control	42,960	42,960	
Purchases ledger control	36,120		36,120
VAT (owed to HMRC)	15,540		15,540
Drawings	12,040	12,040	
Telephone	1,920	1,920	
Electricity	3,360	3,360	
Wages	74,520	74,520	
Loan from bank	36,000		36,000
Discounts allowed	7,680	7,680	
Discounts received	4,680		4,680
Rent expense	16,080	16,080	
Totals		474,276	474,276

Task 12.3

Debit balances	Credit balances	✓
Assets and income	Liabilities, capital and expenses	
Income, capital and liabilities	Assets and expenses	
Assets and expenses	Liabilities, capital and income	✓
Assets, expenses and capital	Liabilities and income	

Task 12.4

	✓
An asset or an expense	
A liability or an expense	
An amount owing to the organisation	
A liability or income	✓

Task 12.5

	✓
Non-current assets	
Sales returns	
Discounts allowed	
Bank overdraft	✓

Task 12.6

	£	Debit £	Credit £
Bank (overdraft)	4,838		4,838
Capital	216,000		216,000
Discounts allowed	18,432	18,432	
Discounts received	11,232		11,232
Drawings	28,896	28,896	
Electricity	8,064	8,064	
Loan from bank	86,400		86,400
Motor vehicles	184,320	184,320	
Office equipment	87,456	87,456	
Petty cash	100	100	
Purchases	472,320	472,320	
Purchases ledger control	86,688		86,688
Purchases returns	10,368		10,368
Rent expense	38,592	38,592	
Sales	685,440		685,440
Sales ledger control	103,104	103,104	
Sales returns	13,536	13,536	
Telephone	4,608	4,608	
VAT (owed to HMRC)	37,310		37,310
Wages	178,848	178,848	
Totals		1,138,276	1,138,276

AAT AQ2016 ASSESSMENT 1
BOOKKEEPING TRANSACTIONS

Time allowed: 1.5 hours

Bookkeeping Transactions (BTRN)
AAT practice assessment 1

Introduction

The tasks in this assessment are set in different business situations where the following apply:

All businesses use a manual bookkeeping system.

Double entry takes place in the general ledger. Individual accounts of trade receivables and trade payables are kept in the sales and purchases ledgers as subsidiary accounts.

The cash book and petty cash book should be treated as part of the double entry system unless the task instructions state otherwise.

The VAT rate is 20%.

Task 1 (12 marks)

A sales invoice is being prepared for goods supplied, as shown in the customer order below.

Customer order

> JABC Ltd
> Order number 3971
>
> Please supply: 12 March 20XX
>
> 120 units of product JBZ
>
> @ £3.60 each less 7.5% trade discount.

(a) Calculate the amounts to be included in the invoice.   (4 marks)

	£
Net amount before discount	
Net amount after discount	
VAT	
Total	

(b) **What will be the amounts entered in the sales daybook when the invoice in (a) has been prepared?** **(3 marks)**

Sales daybook

Date 20XX	Details	Invoice number	Total £	VAT £	Net £
12 Mar	JABC Ltd	1320			

A cheque for £1,567 has been received from JABC Ltd which they incorrectly state is in full settlement of the account at 28 February. The customer's account in the sales ledger is shown below.

JABC Ltd

Date 20XX	Details	Amount £	Date 20XX	Details	Amount £
1 Feb	Balance b/f	1,349	1 Feb	Credit note 88	480
8 Feb	Invoice 1223	270	4 Feb	Bank	869
17 Feb	Invoice 1250	1,208	13 Feb	Credit note 91	32
23 Feb	Invoice 1268	391	25 Feb	Credit note 96	110
28 Feb	Invoice 1281	3,420			

(c) **Show which THREE transactions are still outstanding by circling the relevant transactions below.** **(3 marks)**

Transactions
Balance b/f   Invoice 1223   Invoice 1250   Invoice 1268   Invoice 1281
Credit note 88   Bank   Credit note 91   Credit note 96

A quotation to supply goods for £3,550.00 plus VAT has been sent to JABC Ltd offering a prompt payment discount of 2% for payment within 10 days.

(d) **What will be the amount JABC Ltd will pay if they purchase the goods and pay within 10 days?** **(2 marks)**

£ [   ]

BPP
LEARNING MEDIA

Task 2 (9 marks)

The invoice and purchase order below relate to goods received from ABC Ltd.

Invoice

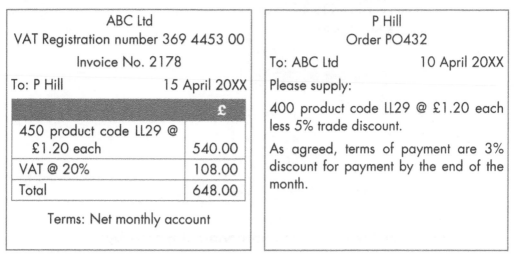

Invoice

ABC Ltd
VAT Registration number 369 4453 00
Invoice No. 2178

To: P Hill   15 April 20XX

	£
450 product code LL29 @ £1.20 each	540.00
VAT @ 20%	108.00
Total	648.00

Terms: Net monthly account

Purchase order

P Hill
Order PO432

To: ABC Ltd   10 April 20XX

Please supply:

400 product code LL29 @ £1.20 each less 5% trade discount.

As agreed, terms of payment are 3% discount for payment by the end of the month.

(a) **Identify any discrepancies on the invoice by drawing a line from each left hand box to the appropriate right hand box.**

(4 marks)

| Terms of payment | | Not shown on invoice |
| Terms of payment | | Not shown on invoice |

| VAT rate | | Incorrectly shown on invoice |

| Trade discount | |

| Quantity | | Correctly shown on invoice |

The invoice below has been received from Benton plc.

Invoice

Benton plc
VAT Registration number 436 4472 01
Invoice No. 13985

To: P Hill   15 April 20XX

	£
225 product code XX42 @ £0.95 each	213.75
VAT @ 20%	42.75
Total	256.50

Terms: Net monthly account

(b) Record the invoice in the appropriate daybook by:

- **Selecting the correct daybook title; and**
- **Making the necessary entries.**   **(5 marks)**

▼

Drop-down list:

Discounts allowed daybook
Discounts received daybook
Purchases daybook
Purchases returns daybook
Sales daybook
Sales returns daybook

Date 20XX	Details	Invoice number	Total £	VAT £	Net £
15 Apr	▼	13985			

Drop-down list:

Benton plc
P Hill

Task 3 (9 marks)

It is the policy of Cross plc to check statements of account when they are received and pay only those transactions that are included in the supplier's account in the purchases ledger. This is the account of DBL Ltd in the purchases ledger and the statement of account received from them.

(a) **Place a tick next to the three items in the statement of account that are not to be paid because they are missing from the supplier's account.** **(3 marks)**

DBL Ltd

Date 20XX	Details	Amount £	Date 20XX	Details	Amount £
1 Jun	Credit note C33	150	1 Jun	Balance b/f	12,946
4 Jun	Bank	12,946	10 Jun	Invoice 3921	462
			15 Jun	Invoice 4003	9,216
			21 Jun	Invoice 4079	1,543

Statement of account

DBL Ltd
149 Field Road, Darton, DF12 8GH

STATEMENT OF ACCOUNT

To: Cross plc   30 June 20XX

Date 20XX	Invoice/credit note number	Details	Amount £	Not to be paid ✓
1 Jun	C33	Goods returned	150	☐
10 Jun	3921	Goods	462	☐
15 Jun	4003	Goods	9,216	☐
16 Jun	C37	Goods returned	129	☐
17 Jun	4034	Goods	1,187	☐
21 Jun	4079	Goods	1,543	☐
29 Jun	4170	Goods	3,926	☐

(b) **What will be the amount paid?** (1 mark)

£ ☐

This is the account of Stone plc in the purchases ledger and a credit note that has been received from the supplier but not yet entered into their account.

Stone plc

Date 20XX	Details	Amount £	Date 20XX	Details	Amount £
1 Jul	Bank	3,684	1 Jul	Balance b/f	3,882
1 Jul	Credit note S74	482	3 Jul	Invoice S2227	917
			4 Jul	Invoice S2243	1,446
			4 Jul	Invoice S2260	352

Credit note

Stone plc

VAT Registration number 412 3297 00

Credit note No. S81

To: Cross plc   5 July 20XX

	£
To correct overcharge on Invoice S2156	165.00
VAT @ 20%	33.00
Total	198.00

Terms: Net monthly account

(c) **What will be the amount to be paid to Stone plc once the credit note has been entered into their account?** (1 mark)

£ ☐

The two invoices below were received on 6 July from credit suppliers who offer a prompt payment discount.

BPP
LEARNING MEDIA

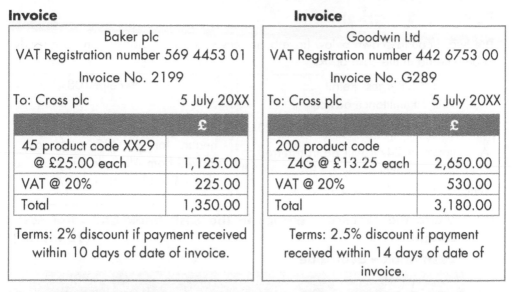

Invoice

Baker plc	
VAT Registration number 569 4453 01	
Invoice No. 2199	
To: Cross plc	5 July 20XX
	£
45 product code XX29 @ £25.00 each	1,125.00
VAT @ 20%	225.00
Total	1,350.00

Terms: 2% discount if payment received within 10 days of date of invoice.

Invoice

Goodwin Ltd	
VAT Registration number 442 6753 00	
Invoice No. G289	
To: Cross plc	5 July 20XX
	£
200 product code Z4G @ £13.25 each	2,650.00
VAT @ 20%	530.00
Total	3,180.00

Terms: 2.5% discount if payment received within 14 days of date of invoice.

(d) **Calculate the amount to be paid to each supplier if the discount is taken and show the date by which the supplier should receive the payment.** **(4 marks)**

Supplier	£	Date by which payment should be received by supplier
Baker plc		▼
Goodwin Ltd		▼

Drop-down list:

5 July 20XX
6 July 20XX
15 July 20XX
16 July 20XX
19 July 20XX
20 July 20XX

Task 4 (15 marks)

The two amounts shown below have been received from customers and are ready to be entered in the cash book.

Burgess Retail Remittance advice 1 August 20XX An amount of £474 will be transferred to your bank account today by BACS, in full settlement of our June account.	Receipt 108 1 August 20XX Cheque for £1,000 and cash £326 received from Alba plc for goods supplied today – £1,326 including VAT.

(a) **Make the necessary entries in the cash book and total each column.** **(13 marks)**

Cash book – debit side

Details	Cash £	Bank £	VAT £	Trade receivables £	Cash sales £
Balance b/f	183	3,220			
▼					
▼					
Totals					

Drop-down list:

Alba plc
Bank
Burgess Retail
Cash
Trade receivables
VAT

The credit side of the cash book shows total cash payments during the week were £342.

(b) **Using your answer to (a), calculate the cash balance.** **(1 mark)**

£ [   ]

The credit side of the cash book shows total bank payments during the week were £1,743.

(c) **Using your answer to (a), calculate the bank balance. Use a minus sign if your calculations indicate an overdrawn bank balance, eg –123.** **(1 mark)**

£ [   ]

Task 5 (15 marks)

An organisation restores the petty cash imprest level of £175.00 on the last day of each month.

The petty cash book below shows all of the petty cash payments in August.

Date 20XX	Details	Amount £	Date 20XX	Details	Amount £	VAT £	Office expenses £	Postage and carriage £	Miscellaneous expenses £
1 Aug	Bal/bf	175.00	10 Aug	Compton Craft	30.66	5.11	25.55		
			18 Aug	Hughes Ltd	46.50	7.75			
			29 Aug	Jay Jones	37.20	6.20		31.00	38.75
			29 Aug	D Holmes	15.92		15.92		

(a) **What will be the entry in the petty cash book to restore the imprest level on 31 August?** **(3 marks)**

Details £	Amount £	Debit	Credit
▼		☐	☐

Drop-down list:

Balance b/d
Balance c/d
Cash from bank

(b) **What will be the entry in the petty cash book to record the closing balance on 31 August after the imprest level has been restored?** **(3 marks)**

Details £	Amount £	Debit	Credit
▼		☐	☐

Drop-down list:

Balance b/d
Balance c/d
Cash from bank

(c) **What will be the total of the VAT coloumn in the petty cash book?** (1 mark)

£ [   ]

On 2 September the petty cash vouchers below are ready to be recorded.

Petty cash voucher 317	
2 September 20XX	
	£
Parcel delivery to customer by courier	41.55 plus VAT

Petty cash voucher 318	
2 September 20XX	
	£
Keys for car park gate	35.28 including VAT

(d) **What will be the total, VAT and net amounts to be entered in the petty cash book?** (6 marks)

Petty cash voucher number	Total £	VAT £	Net £
317			
318			

(e) **Which analysis columns in the petty cash book will be used to record the net amounts of the petty cash payments in (d)?** (2 marks)

Petty cash voucher number	Analysis column
317	[▼]
318	[▼]

Drop-down list:

Amount
Miscellaneous expenses
Office expenses
Postage and carriage
VAT

Task 6 (12 marks)

These are the totals of the discounts allowed daybook at the end of the month.

Discounts allowed daybook

Details	Total £	VAT £	Net £
Totals	510	85	425

(a) **What will be the entries in the general ledger?** **(9 marks)**

Account name	Amount £	Debit ✓	Credit ✓
▼			
▼			
▼			

Drop-down list:

Discounts allowed
Discounts received
Purchases
Purchases ledger control
Purchases returns
Sales
Sales ledger control
Sales returns
VAT

One of the entries in the discounts allowed daybook is for a credit note sent to Jackson Jones for £70 plus VAT.

(b) **What will be the entry in the sales ledger?** **(3 marks)**

Account name	Amount £	Debit ✓	Credit ✓
▼			

Drop-down list:

Discounts allowed
Discounts received
Jackson Jones

Purchases
Purchases ledger control
Purchases returns
Sales
Sales ledger control
Sales returns
VAT

Task 7 (12 marks)

These are totals of the cash book at the end of the month.

Cash book

Cash £	Bank £	VAT £	Trade receivables £	Cash sales £	Cash £	Bank £	VAT £	Trade payables £	Cash purchases £
854	16,370	—	16,370	—	854	16,370	59	9,942	295

What will be the entries in the general ledger?   **(12 marks)**

Account name	Amount £	Debit ✓	Credit ✓
▼			
▼			
▼			
▼			

Drop-down list:

Bank
Cash
Cash purchases
Cash sales
Purchases ledger control
Sales ledger control
VAT

Task 8 (12 marks)

The following two accounts are in the general ledger at close of day on 31 October.

Loan from bank

Date 20XX	Details	Amount £	Date 20XX	Details	Amount £
15 Oct	Bank	1,270	1 Oct	Balance b/f	26,725
			31 Oct	Bank	10,000

Office equipment

Date 20XX	Details	Amount £	Date 20XX	Details	Amount £
1 Oct	Balance b/f	13,924	30 Oct	Journal	200
8 Oct	Bank	865			

(a) **What will be the balance brought down at 1 November on each account?** **(4 marks)**

Account	Balance b/d at 1 November	Debit ✓	Credit ✓
Loan from bank			
Office equipment			

The following account is in the sales ledger at the close of day on 31 October.

(b) **Complete the account below by:** **(8 marks)**

- **Inserting the balance carried down together with date and details;**
- **Inserting the totals; and**
- **Inserting the balance brought down together with date and details.**

Zahra Zee

Date 20XX	Details	Amount £	Date 20XX	Details	Amount £
1 Oct	Balance b/f	14,264	22 Oct	Bank	1,525
11 Oct	Invoice 3225	977	29 Oct	Credit Note C112	3,714
🔽	🔽		🔽	🔽	
	Total			Total	
🔽	🔽		🔽	🔽	

Drop-down list:

1 Nov
31 Oct
Balance b/d
Balance c/d
Zahra Zee

Task 9 (12 marks)

Some balances have been entered in the partially prepared trial balance below.

(a) Insert the totals of the debit and credit columns of the partially prepared trial balance. (2 marks)

Account name	Debit £	Credit £
General expense	3,189	
Motor vehicles	19,250	
Bank loan		7,500
Rent and rates	1,950	
Commission received		1,200
Sales		29,184
Totals		

The remainder of the balances have now been extracted from the accounting records, as shown below.

Sales ledger	£
Sam South	3,187
Leo Waines	16,220

Purchases ledger	£
Bindi Bragg	14,212
Pierre White	376

General ledger	£
Equipment hire	993
Sales ledger control	19,407
Capital	9,816
Purchases ledger control	14,588
Legal fees	781
Discounts received	73
Drawings	3,250
Purchases	16,492

Other balances	£
Cash book - overdraft	3,126
Petty cash book	175

(b) **Complete the trial balance by transferring the relevant amounts to the debit or credit column.** **(10 marks)**

Do not enter figures with decimal places in the trial balance and do not enter a zero in unused cells.

Account name	Debit £	Credit £
General expense	3,189	
Motor vehicles	19,250	
Bank loan		7,500
Rent and rates	1,950	
Commission received		1,200
Sales		29,184
Purchases ledger control		
Equipment hire		
Legal fees		
Petty cash		
Drawings		
Discounts received		
Bank (overdraft)		
Purchases		
Capital		
Sales ledger control		

Task 10 (12 marks)

A new business has allocated a customer account code to each customer in the sales ledger, as shown below. The code is made up of the first four letters of the customer's name, followed by the number of the ledger page allocated to each customer in that alphabetical group.

Customer name	Customer account code
Aspen Ltd	ASPE01
Attwood Ltd	ATTW02
Dunston Designs	DUNS01
Genie Products	GENI01
Latham Ltd	LATH01
Pemberton Ltd	PEMB01
Penn Ltd	PENN02

The two new customer accounts shown below have been added to the sales ledger and need to be allocated a customer account code.

(a)   Insert the relevant account codes for each customer.   (2 marks)

Hartstone plc   Account code: [   ]   **Parker Printing**   Account code: [   ]

Date 20XX	Details	Amount £	Date 20XX	Details	Amount £
3 Dec	Invoice 115	628			

Date 20XX	Details	Amount £	Date 20XX	Details	Amount £
3 Dec	Invoice 116	943			

One customer has been offered a prompt payment discount for payment within 10 days.

(b)   Show what TWO actions should be taken if the customer takes the discount and pays within 10 days.   (2 marks)

Action	✓
Record the amount received in the cash book and ledgers.	
Change the amounts of the original invoice.	
Issue a new invoice for the amount paid.	
Issue a credit note for the discount taken plus VAT.	

The business has the following assets and liabilities.

Assets and liabilities	£
Premises	115,000
Loan from bank	45,000
Cash at bank	11,433
Furniture and fittings	12,392
Amounts owing to credit suppliers	22,396
Amounts owing from credit customers	14,224

(c)   Show the accounting equation by inserting the appropriate figures. Enter all figures as positive amounts.   **(3 marks)**

Assets £	Liabilities £	Capital £

The transactions below have taken place.

(d)   Show whether each transaction will be classified as capital expenditure, capital income, revenue expenditure or revenue income by placing the appropriate classification against each transaction in the table below. You can use each classification more than once.   **(5 marks)**

Transaction	Classification
Purchased motor van for delivery of goods.	
Purchased stationery for use in the office.	
Purchased train tickets for business travel.	
Received cash for the sale of goods.	
Received a cheque from the owner.	

Classification:

Capital expenditure

Capital income

Revenue expenditure

Revenue income

AAT AQ2016 ASSESSMENT 1
BOOKKEEPING TRANSACTIONS

ANSWERS

Bookkeeping Transactions (BTRN)
AAT practice assessment 1

Task 1 (12 marks)

(a) Calculate the amounts to be included in the invoice.   **(4 marks)**

	£
Net amount before discount	432.00
Net amount after discount	399.60
VAT	79.92
Total	479.52

(b) What will be the amounts entered in the sales daybook when the invoice in (a) has been prepared?   **(3 marks)**

Sales daybook

Date 20XX	Details	Invoice number	Total £	VAT £	Net £
12 Mar	JABC Ltd	1320	479.52	79.92	399.60

(c) Show which THREE transactions are still outstanding by circling the relevant transactions below.   **(3 marks)**

Transactions
Balance b/f   ⬭Invoice 1223   Invoice 1250   Invoice 1268   ⬭Invoice 1281⬭
Credit note 88   Bank   Credit note 91   ⬭Credit note 96⬭

A quotation to supply goods for £3,550.00 plus VAT has been sent to JABC Ltd offering a prompt payment discount of 2% for payment within 10 days.

(d) What will be the amount JABC Ltd will pay if they purchase the goods and pay within 10 days?   **(2 marks)**

£	4,174.80

Task 2 (9 marks)

(a) Identify any discrepancies on the invoice by drawing a line from each left hand box to the appropriate right hand box.

(4 marks)

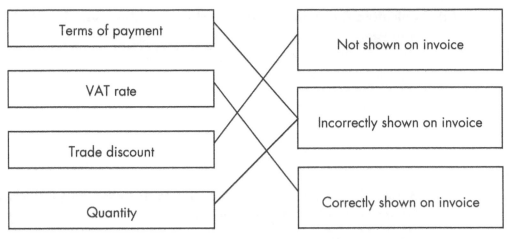

(b) Record the invoice in the appropriate daybook by:

- **Selecting the correct daybook title; and**
- **Making the necessary entries.** **(5 marks)**

Purchases daybook

Date 20XX	Details	Invoice number	Total £	VAT £	Net £
15 Apr	Benton plc	13985	256.50	42.75	213.75

Task 3 (9 marks)

(a) **Statement of account** **(3 marks)**

DBL Ltd
149 Field Road, Darton, DF12 8GH

STATEMENT OF ACCOUNT

To: Cross plc   30 June 20XX

Date 20XX	Invoice/credit note number	Details	Amount £	Not be ✓	to paid
1 Jun	C33	Goods returned	150	☐	
10 Jun	3921	Goods	462	☐	
15 Jun	4003	Goods	9,216	☐	
16 Jun	C37	Goods returned	129	✓	
17 Jun	4034	Goods	1,187	✓	
21 Jun	4079	Goods	1,543	☐	
29 Jun	4170	Goods	3,926	✓	

(b) **What will be the amount paid?** **(1 mark)**

£ | 11,071

(c) **What will be the amount to be paid to Stone plc once the credit note has been entered into their account?** **(1 mark)**

£ | 2,233

(d) **Calculate the amount to be paid to each supplier if the discount is taken and show the date by which the supplier should receive the payment.** **(4 marks)**

Supplier	£	Date by which payment should be received by supplier
Baker plc	1,323	15 July 20XX
Goodwin Ltd	3,100.50	19 July 20XX

Task 4 (15 marks)

(a) Make the necessary entries in the cash book and total each column. **(13 marks)**

Cash book – debit side

Details	Cash £	Bank £	VAT £	Trade receivables £	Cash sales £
Balance b/f	183	3,220			
Burgess Retail		474		474	
Alba plc	326	1,000	221		1,105
Totals	509	4,694	221	474	1,105

The credit side of the cash book shows total cash payments during the week were £342.

(b) Using your answer to (a), calculate the cash balance. **(1 mark)**

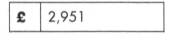

£	167

The credit side of the cash book shows total bank payments during the week were £1,743.

(c) Using your answer to (a), calculate the bank balance. Use a minus sign if your calculations indicate an overdrawn bank balance, eg –123. **(1 mark)**

£	2,951

Task 5 (15 marks)

An organisation restores the petty cash imprest level of £175.00 on the last day of each month.

The petty cash book below shows all of the petty cash payments in August.

Date 20XX	Details	Amount £	Date 20XX	Details	Amount £	VAT £	Office expenses £	Postage and carriage £	Miscellaneous expenses £
1 Aug	Bal/bf	175.00	10 Aug	Compton Craft	30.66	5.11	25.55		
			18 Aug	Hughes Ltd	46.50	7.75			
			29 Aug	Jay Jones	37.20	6.20		31.00	38.75
			29 Aug	D Holmes	15.92		15.92		

(a) **What will be the entry in the petty cash book to restore the imprest level on 31 August?** **(3 marks)**

Details £	Amount £	Debit	Credit
Cash from bank ▼	130.28	✓	☐

(b) **What will be the entry in the petty cash book to record the closing balance on 31 August after the imprest level has been restored?** **(3 marks)**

Details £	Amount £	Debit	Credit
Balance c/d ▼	175	☐	✓

(c) **What will be the total of the VAT coloumn in the petty cash book?** **(1 mark)**

£	19.06

On 2 September the petty cash vouchers below are ready to be recorded.

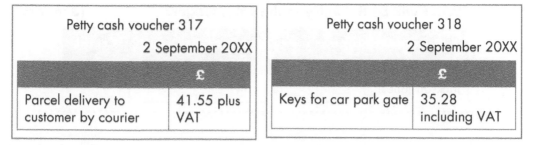

Petty cash voucher 317 2 September 20XX	
	£
Parcel delivery to customer by courier	41.55 plus VAT

Petty cash voucher 318 2 September 20XX	
	£
Keys for car park gate	35.28 including VAT

(d) What will be the total, VAT and net amounts to be entered in the petty cash book? **(6 marks)**

Petty cash voucher number	Total £	VAT £	Net £
317	49.86	8.31	41.55
318	35.28	5.88	29.40

(e) Which analysis columns in the petty cash book will be used to record the net amounts of the petty cash payments in (d)? **(2 marks)**

Petty cash voucher number	Analysis column
317	Postage and carriage ▼
318	Miscellaneous expenses ▼

···

Task 6 (12 marks)

(a) What will be the entries in the general ledger? **(9 marks)**

Account name	Amount £	Debit ✓	Credit ✓
Discounts allowed	425	✓	
VAT	85	✓	
Sales ledger control	510		✓

One of the entries in the discounts allowed daybook is for a credit note sent to Jackson Jones for £70 plus VAT.

(b) What will be the entry in the sales ledger? **(3 marks)**

Account name	Amount £	Debit ✓	Credit ✓
Jackson Jones	84		✓

···

Task 7 (12 marks)

What will be the entries in the general ledger? (12 marks)

Account name	Amount £	Debit ✓	Credit ✓
VAT	59	✓	
Purchases ledger control	9,942	✓	
Cash purchases	295	✓	
Sales ledger control	16,370		✓

Task 8 (12 marks)

(a) **What will be the balance brought down at 1 November on each account?** (4 marks)

Account	Balance b/d at 1 November	Debit	Credit
Loan from bank	35,455		✓
Office equipment	14,589	✓	

The following account is in the sales ledger at the close of day on 31 October.

(b) **Complete the account below by:** (8 marks)

- **Inserting the balance carried down together with date and details;**
- **Inserting the totals; and**
- **Inserting the balance brought down together with date and details.**

Zahra Zee

Date 20XX	Details	Amount £	Date 20XX	Details	Amount £
1 Oct	Balance b/f	14,264	22 Oct	Bank	1,525
11 Oct	Invoice 3225	977	29 Oct	Credit Note C112	3,714
			31 Oct	Balance c/d	10,002
	Total	15,241		Total	15,241
1 Nov	Balance b/d	10,002			

Task 9 (12 marks)

(a) **Insert the totals of the debit and credit columns of the partially prepared trial balance.** **(2 marks)**

Account name	Debit £	Credit £
General expense	3,189	
Motor vehicles	19,250	
Bank loan		7,500
Rent and rates	1,950	
Commission received		1,200
Sales		29,184
Totals	24,389	37,884

The remainder of the balances have now been extracted from the accounting records, as shown below.

Sales ledger	£
Sam South	3,187
Leo Waines	16,220

Purchases ledger	£
Bindi Bragg	14,212
Pierre White	376

General ledger	£
Equipment hire	993
Sales ledger control	19,407
Capital	9,816
Purchases ledger control	14,588
Legal fees	781

General ledger	£
Discounts received	73
Drawings	3,250
Purchases	16,492

Other balances	£
Cash book-overdraft	3,126
Petty cash book	175

(b) **Complete the trial balance by transferring the relevant amounts to the debit or credit column.** **(10 marks)**

Do not enter figures with decimal places in the trial balance and do not enter a zero in unused cells.

Account name	Debit £	Credit £
General expense	3,189	
Motor vehicles	19,250	
Bank loan		7,500
Rent and rates	1,950	
Commission received		1,200
Sales		29,184
Purchases ledger control		14,588
Equipment hire	993	
Legal fees	781	
Petty cash	175	
Drawings	3,250	
Discounts received		73
Bank (overdraft)		3,126
Purchases	16,492	
Capital		9,816
Sales ledger control	19,407	

Task 10 (12 marks)

(a) **Insert the relevant account codes for each customer.** **(2 marks)**

Hartstone plc   Account code: | HART01 | **Parker Printing**   Account code: | PARK03 |

Date 20XX	Details	Amount £	Date 20XX	Details	Amount £	Date 20XX	Details	Amount £	Date 20XX	Details	Amount £
3 Dec	Invoice 115	628				3 Dec	Invoice 116	943			

One customer has been offered a prompt payment discount for payment within 10 days.

(b) **Show what TWO actions should be taken if the customer takes the discount and pays within 10 days.** **(2 marks)**

Action	✓
Record the amount received in the cash book and ledgers.	✓
Change the amounts of the original invoice.	
Issue a new invoice for the amount paid.	
Issue a credit note for the discount taken plus VAT.	✓

(c) **Show the accounting equation by inserting the appropriate figures.** **(3 marks)**

Assets £	Liabilities £	Capital £
153,049	67,396	85,653

The transaction below has taken place.

(d) **Show whether each transaction will be classified as capital expenditure, capital income, revenue expenditure or revenue income by placing the appropriate classification against each transaction in the table below. You can use each classification more than once.** **(5 marks)**

Transaction	Classification
Purchased motor van for delivery of goods.	Capital expenditure
Purchased stationery for use in the office.	Revenue expenditure
Purchased train tickets for business travel.	Revenue expenditure
Received cash for the sale of goods.	Revenue income
Received a cheque from the owner.	Capital income

Classification:

Capital expenditure

Capital income

Revenue expenditure

Revenue income

AAT AQ2016 ASSESSMENT 2 BOOKKEEPING TRANSACTIONS

You are advised to attempt assessment 2 online from the AAT website. This will ensure you are prepared for how the assessment will be presented on the AAT's system when you attempt the real assessment. Please access the assessment using the address below:

https://www.aat.org.uk/training/study-support/search

AAT AQ2016 PRACTICE ASSESSMENT 2

BPP PRACTICE ASSESSMENT 1
BOOKKEEPING TRANSACTIONS

Time allowed: 1.5 hours

Bookkeeping Transactions (BTRN)
BPP practice assessment 1

Introduction

The tasks in this assessment are set in different business situations where the following apply:

All businesses use a manual bookkeeping system.

Double entry takes place in the general ledger. Individual accounts of trade receivables and trade payables are kept in the sales and purchases ledgers as subsidiary accounts.

The cash book and petty cash book should be treated as part of the double entry system unless the task instructions state otherwise.

The VAT rate is 20%.

Task 1 (12 marks)

A sales invoice is being prepared for goods supplied, as shown in the customer order below.

Customer order

Jules Ltd
Order number 1739
Please supply: 18 April 20XX
55 units of product C54
@ £13 each less 10% trade discount.

(a)   Calculate the amounts to be included in the invoice.   (4 marks)

	£
Net amount before discount	
Net amount after discount	
VAT	
Total	

(b) What will be the amounts entered in the sales daybook when the invoice in (a) has been prepared? **(3 marks)**

Sales daybook

Date 20XX	Details	Invoice number	Total £	VAT £	Net £
18 Apr	Jules Ltd	621			

A cheque for £1,287 has been received from Jules Ltd which they incorrectly state is in full settlement of the account at 31 May. The customer's account in the sales ledger is shown below.

Jules Ltd

Date 20XX	Details	Amount £	Date 20XX	Details	Amount £
1 May	Balance b/f	652	1 May	Credit note 7	120
8 May	Invoice 52	301	4 May	Bank	532
17 May	Invoice 63	1,001	13 May	Credit note 11	15
23 May	Invoice 65	251	25 May	Credit note 13	99
28 May	Invoice 66	2,639			

(c) Show which THREE transactions are still outstanding by circling the relevant transactions below. **(3 marks)**

Transactions
Balance b/f   Invoice 52   Invoice 63   Invoice 65   Invoice 66
Credit note 7   Bank   Credit note 11   Credit note 13

A quotation to supply goods for £11,390.00 plus VAT has been sent to Jules Ltd offering a prompt payment discount of 3% for payment within 14 days.

(d) What will be the amount Jules Ltd will pay if they purchase the goods and pay within 14 days? **(2 marks)**

£ [ ]

Task 2 (9 marks)

The invoice and purchase order below relate to goods received from XYZ Ltd.

Invoice

XYZ Ltd
VAT Registration number 963 5353 01
Invoice No. 8753
To: B Smith   19 May 20XX

	£
50 product code 5357 @ £5 each	250.00
Trade discount @10%	25.00
Total	225.00

Terms: 3% discount for payment within 10 days

Purchase order

B Smith
Order PO432

To: XYZ Ltd   13 May 20XX

Please supply:

100 product code 5357 @ £5 each less 10% trade discount

As agreed, terms of payment are 3% discount for payment within 10 days.

(a) **Identify any discrepancies on the invoice by drawing a line from each left hand box to the appropriate right hand box.**

(4 marks)

| Terms of payment |

| VAT rate |

| Trade discount |

| Quantity |

| Not shown on invoice |

| Incorrectly shown on invoice |

| Correctly shown on invoice |

The invoice below has been received from Clinton plc.

Invoice

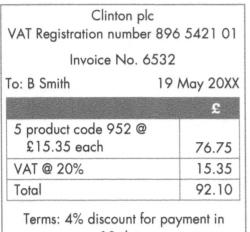

Clinton plc	
VAT Registration number 896 5421 01	
Invoice No. 6532	
To: B Smith 19 May 20XX	
	£
5 product code 952 @ £15.35 each	76.75
VAT @ 20%	15.35
Total	92.10

Terms: 4% discount for payment in 10 days

(b)   Record the invoice in the appropriate daybook by:

- **Selecting the correct daybook title; and**
- **Making the necessary entries.**   **(5 marks)**

▼

Picklist:

Discounts allowed daybook
Discounts received daybook
Purchases daybook
Purchases returns daybook
Sales daybook
Sales returns daybook

Date 20XX	Details	Invoice number	Total £	VAT £	Net £
19 May	▼	6532			

Picklist:

B Smith
Clinton plc

Task 3 (9 marks)

It is the policy of Rigley plc to check statements of account when they are received and pay only those transactions that are included in the supplier's account in the purchases ledger. This is the account of Rowley Ltd in the purchases ledger and the statement of account received from them.

(a) **Place a tick next to the three items in the statement of account that are not to be paid because they are missing from the supplier's account.** **(3 marks)**

Rowley Ltd

Date 20XX	Details	Amount £	Date 20XX	Details	Amount £
1 Sept	Credit note C25	75	1 Sept	Balance b/f	15,895
4 Sept	Bank	15,895	10 Sept	Invoice 321	501
			15 Sept	Invoice 333	1,365
			29 Sept	Invoice 378	2,300

Statement of account

Rowley Ltd
34 Allridge Way, Rigby DF12 8GH

STATEMENT OF ACCOUNT

To: Rigley plc   30 Sept 20XX

Date 20XX	Invoice/credit note number	Details	Amount £	Not to be paid ✓
1 Sept	C25	Goods returned	75	☐
10 Sept	321	Goods	501	☐
15 Sept	333	Goods	1,365	☐
16 Sept	C26	Goods returned	55	☐
17 Sept	334	Goods	894	☐
21 Sept	371	Goods	1,654	☐
29 Sept	378	Goods	2,300	☐

(b)   What will be the amount paid?   **(1 mark)**

£ ⎢   ⎥

This is the account of Pebble plc in the purchases ledger and a credit note that has been received from the supplier but not yet entered into their account.

Pebble plc

Date 20XX	Details	Amount £	Date 20XX	Details	Amount £
1 Oct	Bank	1,532	1 Oct	Balance b/f	4,527
1 Oct	Credit note C53	653	3 Oct	Invoice I592	891
			4 Oct	Invoice I699	998
			4 Oct	Invoice I703	1,452

Credit note

Pebble plc	
VAT Registration number 412 3297 00	
Credit note No. C65	
To: Rigley plc 5 Oct 20XX	

	£
To correct overcharge on Invoice I589	89.00
VAT @ 20%	17.80
Total	106.80

Terms: Net monthly account

(c)   What will be the amount to be paid to Pebble plc once the credit note has been entered into their account?   (1 mark)

£ ⎢   ⎥

The two invoices below were received on 6 October from credit suppliers who offer a prompt payment discount.

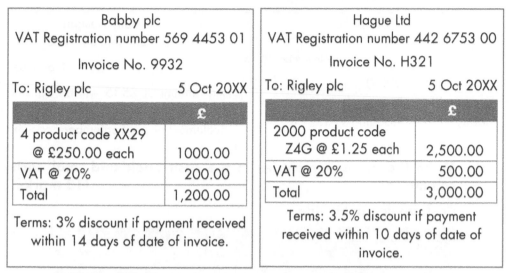

Invoice

Babby plc	
VAT Registration number 569 4453 01	
Invoice No. 9932	
To: Rigley plc	5 Oct 20XX
	£
4 product code XX29 @ £250.00 each	1000.00
VAT @ 20%	200.00
Total	1,200.00

Terms: 3% discount if payment received within 14 days of date of invoice.

Invoice

Hague Ltd	
VAT Registration number 442 6753 00	
Invoice No. H321	
To: Rigley plc	5 Oct 20XX
	£
2000 product code Z4G @ £1.25 each	2,500.00
VAT @ 20%	500.00
Total	3,000.00

Terms: 3.5% discount if payment received within 10 days of date of invoice.

(d) **Calculate the amount to be paid to each supplier if the discount is taken and show the date by which the supplier should receive the payment.** **(4 marks)**

Supplier	£	Date by which payment should be received by supplier	
Babby plc			▼
Hague Ltd			▼

Picklist:

5 October 20XX
6 October 20XX
15 October 20XX
16 October 20XX
19 October 20XX
20 October 20XX

Task 4 (15 marks)

The two amounts shown below have been received from customers and are ready to be entered in the cash book.

Receipt 56
1 November 20XX
Cheque for £500 and cash £124 received from Beta plc for goods supplied today – £624 including VAT.

Bally Designs Remittance advice
1 November 20XX
An amount of £535 will be transferred to your bank account today by BACS, in full settlement of our September account.

(a) **Make the necessary entries in the cash book and total each column.** **(13 marks)**

Cash book – debit side

Details	Cash £	Bank £	VAT £	Trade receivables £	Cash sales £
Balance b/f	183	3,220			
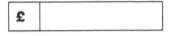					
▼					
Totals					

Picklist:

Bally Designs
Bank
Beta plc
Cash
Trade receivables
VAT

The credit side of the cash book shows total cash payments during the week were £256.

(b) **Using your answer to (a), calculate the cash balance.** **(1 mark)**

£ [   ]

The credit side of the cash book shows total bank payments during the week were £1,743.

(c) **Using your answer to (a), calculate the bank balance. Use a minus sign if your calculations indicate an overdrawn bank balance, eg –123.** **(1 mark)**

£	

Task 5 (15 marks)

The two petty cash vouchers below are ready to be entered into the partially completed petty cash book.

Petty cash voucher 255	
	31 October 20XX
	£
Motor repairs	42.50
VAT is not applicable.	

Petty cash voucher 256	
	31 October 20XX
	£
Printer paper	15.50
VAT @ 20%	3.10
Total	18.60

(a) **Complete the petty cash book by:** **(14 marks)**

- **Entering both transactions into the petty cash book below; and**

- **Totalling the petty cash book and inserting the balance carried down at 31 October.**

Petty cash book

Date 20XX	Details	Amount £	Date 20XX	Details	Amount £	VAT £	Motor expenses £	Office expense £
24 Oct	Balance b/f	37.60	27 Oct	Postage stamps	5.45			5.45
24 Oct	Cash from bank	72.40	31 Oct	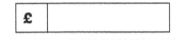				
			31 Oct	▼				
			31 Oct	▼				
	Total			Totals				

Picklist:

Balance b/f
Balance c/d
Motor expenses
Motor repairs
Office expenses
Stationery
VAT

(b) **What will be the amount of cash withdrawn from the bank to restore the imprest level of £110.00?** **(1mark)**

£

....

Task 6 (12 marks)

These are the totals of the discounts allowed daybook at the end of the month.

Discounts allowed daybook

Details	Total £	VAT £	Net £
Totals	378	63	315

(a) **What will be the entries in the general ledger?** **(9 marks)**

Account name	Amount £	Debit ✓	Credit ✓
▼			
▼			
▼			

Picklist:

Discounts allowed
Discounts received
Purchases
Purchases ledger control
Purchases returns
Sales
Sales ledger control
Sales returns
VAT

One of the entries in the discounts allowed daybook is for a credit note sent to Samuel Smith for £112 plus VAT.

(b) **What will be the entry in the sales ledger?** **(3 marks)**

Account name	Amount £	Debit ✓	Credit ✓
▼			

Picklist:

Discounts allowed
Discounts received
Purchases
Purchases ledger control
Purchases returns
Sales
Sales ledger control
Sales returns
Samuel Smith
VAT

Task 7 (12 marks)

These are totals of the cash book at the end of the month.

Cash book

Cash £	Bank £	VAT £	Trade receivables £	Cash sales £	Cash £	Bank £	VAT £	Trade payables £	Cash purcha £
657	8,255	–	8,255	–	657	8,255	63	5,450	295

What will be the entries in the general ledger?   **(12 marks)**

Account	name	Amount £	Debit ✓	Credit ✓
	▼			
	▼			
	▼			
	▼			

Picklist:

Bank
Cash
Cash purchases
Cash sales
Purchases ledger control
Sales ledger control
VAT

....

Task 8 (12 marks)

The following two accounts are in the general ledger at close of day on 31 January.

Loan from bank

Date 20XX	Details	Amount £	Date 20XX	Details	Amount £
15 Jan	Bank	3,050	1 Jan	Balance b/f	36,525
			31 Jan	Bank	20,000

Motor Vehicles

Date 20XX	Details	Amount £	Date 20XX	Details	Amount £
1 Jan	Balance b/f	32,900	30 Jan	Journal	500
8 Jan	Bank	2,500			

(a) **What will be the balance brought down at 1 February on each account?** **(4 marks)**

Account	Balance b/d at 1 February	Debit ✓	Credit ✓
Loan from bank			
Motor Vehicles			

The following account is in the sales ledger at the close of day on 31 January.

(b) **Complete the account below by:** **(8 marks)**

- **Inserting the balance carried down together with date and details.**

- **Inserting the totals.**

- **Inserting the balance brought down together with date and details.**

Trevor Tate

Date 20XX	Details	Amount £	Date 20XX	Details	Amount £
1 Jan	Balance b/f	9,899	22 Jan	Bank	5,780
11 Jan	Invoice 155	1,001	29 Jan	Credit Note C15	714
▼	▼		▼	▼	
	Total			Total	
▼	▼		▼	▼	

Picklist:

1 Feb
31 Jan
Balance b/d
Balance c/d
Trevor Tate

Task 9 (12 marks)

Below are two general ledger accounts and a partially completed trial balance.

Complete the trial balance by: (12 marks)

- **Transferring the balances of the two general ledger accounts to the debit or credit column of the trial balance;**

- **Entering the amounts shown against each of the other account names into the debit or credit column of the trial balance; and**

- **Totalling both columns of the trial balance.**

Do not enter figures with decimal places in this task and do not enter a zero in unused column cells.

Sales

Date 20XX	Details	Amount £	Date 20XX	Details	Amount £
31 Mar	Journal	350	1 Mar	Balance b/f	73,481
31 Mar	Balance c/d	91,500	31 Mar	Sales ledger control	18,369
		91,850			91,850

Purchases

Date 20XX	Details	Amount £	Date 20XX	Details	Amount £
1 Mar	Balance b/f	25,300	31 Mar	Balance c/d	34,156
31 Mar	Purchases ledger control	8,856			
		34,156			34,156

Trial balance as at 31 March

Account name	Amount £	Debit £	Credit £
Sales			
Purchases			
Administration expenses	8,965		
Bank (overdraft)	3,000		
Motor vehicle	35,505		
Motor expenses	1,392		
Sales ledger control	21,456		
Purchase ledger control	8,423		
Rent and rates	3,250		
Capital	1,801		
Totals			

Task 10 (12 marks)

A new business has allocated a customer account code to each customer in the sales ledger, as shown below. The code is made up of the first four letters of the customer's name, followed by the number of the ledger page allocated to each customer in that alphabetical group.

Customer name	Customer account code
Aspen Ltd	ASPE01
Attwood Ltd	ATTW02
Dunston Designs	DUNS01
Genie Products	GENI01
Latham Ltd	LATH01
Pemberton Ltd	PEMB01
Penn Ltd	PENN02

The two new customer accounts shown below have been added to the sales ledger and need to be allocated a customer account code.

(a) **Insert the relevant account codes for each customer.** **(2 marks)**

General plc   Account code: [   ]   **Multipack Ltd**   Account code: [   ]

Date 20XX	Details	Amount £	Date 20XX	Details	Amount £	Date 20XX	Details	Amount £	Date 20XX	Details	Amount £
3 Dec	Invoice 115	628				3 Dec	Invoice 116	943			

A supplier has offered the company a prompt payment discount for payment within 14 days.

(b) **Show what TWO events or actions would happen if the company chooses to take the discount and pays within 14 days.** **(2 marks)**

Action	✓
Record the amount paid in the cash book and ledgers.	
Change the amounts of the original invoice in the purchases ledger.	
Receive a credit note for the discount taken plus VAT.	
Request a new invoice for the amount actually paid.	

The business has the following assets and liabilities.

Assets and liabilities	£
Premises	111,000
Loan from bank	5,000
Cash at bank	11,433
Motor Vehicles	15,390
Amounts owing to credit suppliers	22,446
Amounts owing from credit customers	11,233

(c) **Show the accounting equation by inserting the appropriate figures.** **(3 marks)**

Assets £	Liabilities £	Capital £

The transactions below have taken place.

(d) **Show whether each transaction will be classified as capital expenditure, capital income, revenue expenditure or revenue income by placing the appropriate classification against each transaction in the table below. You can use each classification more than once.** **(5 marks)**

Transaction	Classification
Purchased computers for use in the office	
Purchased stationery for use in the office	
Purchased a car for the sales person to use for business trips	
Received cheque for the sale of goods	
Sold a van the company owned	

Classification:

Capital expenditure

Capital income

Revenue expenditure

Revenue income

BPP PRACTICE ASSESSMENT 1
BOOKKEEPING TRANSACTIONS

ANSWERS

Bookkeeping Transactions (BTRN)
BPP practice assessment 1

Task 1

(a)

	£
Net amount before discount	715.00
Net amount after discount	643.50
VAT	128.70
Total	772.20

Workings

Net before discount: $55 \times £13 = £715$, net after discount: $£715 \times 90\% = £643.50$, VAT: $£643.50 \times 20\% = £128.7$

(b) Sales daybook

Date 20XX	Details	Invoice number	Total £	VAT £	Net £
18 Apr	Jules Ltd	621	772.20	128.70	643.50

(c)

Transactions
Balance b/f   Invoice 52   Invoice 63   (Invoice 65)   (Invoice 66)
Credit note 7   Bank   Credit note 11   (Credit note 13)

Working

$£652 - £120 - £532 = 0$; $£301 + £1,001 - £15 = £1,287$

(d)

£	13,257.96

Working

Gross: $£11,390 + (£11,390 \times 20\%) = £13,668$

Amount paid: $£13,668 \times 97\% = £13,257.96$

Task 2

(a)

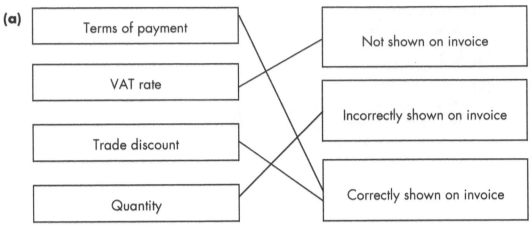

Terms of payment		Not shown on invoice
VAT rate		Incorrectly shown on invoice
Trade discount		Correctly shown on invoice
Quantity		

(b)

Purchases daybook

Date 20XX	Details	Invoice number	Total £	VAT £	Net £
19 May	Clinton plc	6532	92.10	15.35	76.75

Task 3

Statement of account

(a)

		Rowley Ltd 34 Allridge Way, Rigby DF12 8GH STATEMENT OF ACCOUNT			
To: Rigley plc				30 Sept 20XX	
Date 20XX	**Invoice/credit note number**	**Details**	**Amount £**	**Not to be paid** ✓	
1 Sept	C25	Goods returned	75	☐
10 Sept	321	Goods	501	☐
15 Sept	333	Goods	1,365	☐
16 Sept	C26	Goods returned	55	☑
17 Sept	334	Goods	894	☑
21 Sept	371	Goods	1,654	☑
29 Sept	378	Goods	2,300	☐

(b)

£	4,091

Working

£501 + £1,365 + £2,300 – £75 = £4,091

(c)

£	5,576.20

Working

£4,527 + £891 + £998 + £1,452 – £1,532 – £653 – £106.80 = £5,576.20

(d)

Supplier	£	Date by which payment should be received by supplier
Babby plc	1,164	19 October 20XX
Hague Ltd	2,895	15 October 20XX

Working

Babby plc £1,200 × 97% = £1,164
Hague Ltd £3,000 × 96.5% = £2,895

Task 4

(a) Cash book – debit side

Details	Cash £	Bank £	VAT £	Trade receivables £	Cash sales £
Balance b/f	183	3,220			
Bally Designs		535		535	
Beta plc	124	500	104		520
Totals	307	4,255	104	535	520

(b)

£	51

Working

£307 – £256 = £51

(c)

£	2,512

Working

£4,255 – £1,743 = £2,512

Task 5

(a)   Petty cash book

Date 20XX	Details	Amount £	Date 20XX	Details	Amount £	VAT £	Motor expenses £	Office expenses £
24 Oct	Balance b/f	37.60	27 Oct	Postage stamps	5.45			5.45
24 Oct	Cash from bank	72.40	31 Oct	Motor repairs	42.50		42.50	
			31 Oct	Stationery	18.60	3.10		15.50
			31 Oct	Balance c/d	43.45			
	Total	110.00		**Totals**	110.00	3.10	42.50	20.95

(b)

£	66.55

Working

£5.45 + £42.50 + £18.60 = £66.55

Task 6

(a)

Account name	Amount £	Debit ✓	Credit ✓
Discounts allowed	315	✓	
VAT	63	✓	
Sales ledger control	378		✓

(b)   What will be the entry in the sales ledger?

Account name	Amount £	Debit ✓	Credit ✓
Samuel Smith	134.4		✓

Working

£112 + (£112 × 20%) = £134.4

Task 7

Account name	Amount £	Debit ✓	Credit ✓
VAT	63	✓	
Purchases ledger control	5,450	✓	
Cash purchases	295	✓	
Sales ledger control	8,255		✓

Task 8

(a)

Account	Balance b/d at 1 February	Debit	Credit
Loan from bank	53,475		✓
Motor Vehicles	34,900	✓	

Workings

Loan from bank

Date 20XX	Details	Amount £	Date 20XX	Details	Amount £
15 Jan	Bank	3,050	1 Jan	Balance b/f	36,525
31 Jan	Balance c/d	53,475	31 Jan	Bank	20,000
	Total	56,525		Total	56,525

Motor vehicles

Date 20XX	Details	Amount £	Date 20XX	Details	Amount £
1 Jan	Balance b/f	32,900	30 Jan	Journal	500
8 Jan	Bank	2,500	31 Jan	Balance c/d	34,900
	Total	35,400		Total	35,400

(b) **Trevor Tate**

Date 20XX	Details	Amount £	Date 20XX	Details	Amount £
1 Jan	Balance b/f	9,899	22 Jan	Bank	5,780
11 Jan	Invoice 155	1,001	29 Jan	Credit Note C15	714
			31 Jan	Balance c/d	4,406
	Total	10,900		Total	10,900
1 Feb	Balance b/d	4,406			

Task 9

Trial balance as at 31 March

Account name	Amount £	Debit £	Credit £
Sales			91,500
Purchases		34,156	
Administration expenses	8,965	8,965	
Bank (overdraft)	3,000		3,000
Motor vehicle	35,505	35,505	
Motor expenses	1,392	1,392	
Sales ledger control	21,456	21,456	
Purchase ledger control	8,423		8,423
Rent and rates	3,250	3,250	
Capital	1,801		1,801
Totals		104,724	104,724

Task 10

(a)

General plc Account code: ┌─────────┐ GENE02 └─────────┘   Multipack Ltd   Account code: ┌─────────┐ MULT01 └─────────┘

(b)

Action	✓
Record the amount paid in the cash book and ledgers.	✓
Change the amounts of the original invoice in the purchases ledger.	
Receive a credit note for the discount taken plus VAT.	✓
Request a new invoice for the amount actually paid.	

(c)

Assets £	Liabilities £	Capital £
149,056	27,446	121,610

Workings

Assets = £111,000 + £11,433 + £15,390 + £11,233 = £149,056

Liabilities = £5,000 + £22,446 = £27,446

Capital = Assets − Liabilities = £149,056 − £27,446 = £121,610

(d)

Transaction	Classification
Purchased computers for use in the office	Capital expenditure
Purchased stationery for use in the office	Revenue expenditure
Purchased a car for the sales person to use for business trips	Capital expenditure
Received cheque for the sale of goods	Revenue income
Sold a van the company owned	Capital income

BPP PRACTICE ASSESSMENT 2
BOOKKEEPING TRANSACTIONS

Time allowed: 1.5 hours

Bookkeeping Transactions (BTRN)
BPP practice assessment 2

Task 1 (12 marks)

On 5 July Trappic Ltd delivered the following goods to a credit customer, Nemesis Ltd.

Trappic Ltd

8 Highview Road
Arbuckle
AR7 4LX

Nemesis Ltd
36 Ventnor Road
Arbuckle
AR7 9LC

Delivery note No. 8793   Customer account code: NEM893
05 July 20XX

200 polishing cloths, product code C420.

The list price of the goods was £0.50 per cloth plus VAT. Nemesis Ltd is to be given a 10% trade discount and a 4% bulk discount.

(a)   Complete the invoice below.

Trappic Ltd

8 Highview Road
Arbuckle
AR7 4LX

Nemesis Ltd
36 Ventnor Road
Arbuckle
AR7 9LC
Date: 6 July 20XX

Invoice No: 67282
Delivery note number: 8793

VAT Registration No. 782 8723 23

Customer account code: NEM893

Quantity of goods	Product code	Total list price £	Net amount after trade discount £	Net amount after all discounts £	VAT £	Gross £

(b) **What will be the amounts entered in the sales daybook when the invoice in (a) has been prepared?**

Sales daybook

Date 20XX	Details	Invoice number	Total £	VAT £	Net £
6 July	Nemesis Ltd	67282			

Trappic Ltd offers each customer a discount of 5% if any order amounts to £1,000 or over.

(c) **What is the name of this type of discount?**

[▼]

Picklist:

Bulk discount
Prompt payment discount
Trade discount

The account shown below is in the sales ledger of Trappic Ltd. A cheque for £2,311 has now been received from this customer.

Sibley & Co

Date 20XX	Details	Amount £	Date 20XX	Details	Amount £
1 May	Balance b/d	2,897	2 June	Credit note 5530	173
3 June	Invoice 66100	2,556	25 June	Bank	2,724
28 June	Invoice 66800	2,453	26 June	Credit note 5570	245

(d) **Which outstanding item has not been included in the payment of £2,311?**

[▼]

Picklist:

Balance b/d
Bank
Sales invoice 66100
Sales invoice 66800
Sales returns credit note 5530
Sales returns credit note 5570

Invoice 66801 for £4,866.00 including VAT has been sent to Sibley & Co offering a prompt payment discount of 3% for payment within 14 days.

(e) What will be the amount Sibley & Co will pay if they pay within 14 days?

£ [   ]

Task 2 (9 marks)

A supply of cleaning fluid has been delivered to Trappic Ltd by OMKG Chemicals. The purchase order sent from Trappic Ltd, and the invoice from OMKG Chemicals, are shown below.

Trappic Ltd
8 Highview Road
Arbuckle
AR7 4LX

Purchase Order No. 637821

To: OMKG Chemicals

Date: 15 July 20XX

Please supply 1000 litres cleaning fluid product code 7638XX
Purchase price: £8.00 per 10 litres, plus VAT
Discount: less 15% trade discount, as agreed

OMKG Chemicals 76 Grange Road, Arbuckle AR1 0HJ VAT Registration No. 653 9922 33

Invoice No. 76383

Trappic Ltd
8 Highview Road
Arbuckle
AR7 4LX

22 July 20XX

	£
1,000 litres cleaning fluid product code 7638XX @ £0.80 per litre	800.00
Less trade discount at 12.5%	100.00
	700.00
VAT @ 20%	140.00
Total	840.00

Terms: 30 days net

(a) **Check the invoice against the purchase order and answer the following questions.**

	Yes ✓	No ✓
Has the correct purchase price of the cleaning fluid been charged?		
Has the correct discount been applied?		

	Amount £
What would be the VAT amount charged if the invoice was correct?	
What would be the total amount charged if the invoice was correct?	

The credit note below has been received from Bingley & Co in relation to some faulty goods.

Credit note

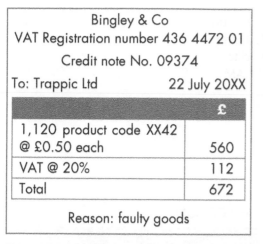

Bingley & Co
VAT Registration number 436 4472 01
Credit note No. 09374

To: Trappic Ltd   22 July 20XX

	£
1,120 product code XX42 @ £0.50 each	560
VAT @ 20%	112
Total	672

Reason: faulty goods

(b)   Record the credit note in the appropriate daybook by:

- **Selecting the correct daybook title; and**
- **Making the necessary entries.**

▼

Picklist:

Discounts allowed daybook
Discounts received daybook
Purchases daybook
Purchases returns daybook
Sales daybook
Sales returns daybook

Date 20XX	Details	Credit note number	Total £	VAT £	Net £
22 Jul	▼	09374			

Picklist:

Bingley & Co
Trappic Ltd

Task 3 (9 marks)

Shown below is a statement of account received from a credit supplier, and the supplier's account as shown in the purchases ledger of Trappic Ltd.

<table>
<tr><td colspan="6" align="center">Lemonfresh Ltd
90 West Street
Arbuckle
AR4 8AM</td></tr>
<tr><td colspan="6">To: Trappic Ltd
8 Highview Road
Arbuckle
AR7 4LX</td></tr>
</table>

STATEMENT OF ACCOUNT

Date 20XX	Invoice Number	Details	Invoice amount £	Cheque amount £	Balance £
1 May	1267	Goods	180		180
3 June	1387	Goods	230		410
7 June	1422	Goods	290		700
10 June	1498	Goods	800		1,500
16 June		Cheque		510	990

Lemonfresh Ltd

Date 20XX	Details	Amount £	Date 20XX	Details	Amount £
16 June	Bank	510	1 May	Invoice 1267	180
16 June	Credit note 535	10	3 June	Invoice 1387	230
			7 June	Invoice 1422	290

(a) **Which item is missing from the statement of account from Lemonfresh Ltd?**

	▼

Picklist:

Cheque for £510
Credit note 535
Invoice 1267
Invoice 1387
Invoice 1422
Invoice 1498

(b) **Which item is missing from the supplier's account in Trappic Ltd's purchases ledger?**

	▼

Picklist:

Cheque for £510
Credit note 535
Invoice 1267
Invoice 1387
Invoice 1422
Invoice 1498

(c) **Assuming any differences between the statement of account from Lemonfresh Ltd and the supplier's account in Trappic Ltd's purchases ledger are simply due to omission errors, what is the amount owing to Lemonfresh Ltd?**

£	

Trappic Ltd prepares a remittance advice note in respect of Lemonfresh Ltd.

(d) **Which of the following statements is true?**

	✓
The remittance advice note will be sent to the customer to advise them of the amount being paid.	
The remittance advice note will be sent to the supplier's bank to advise them of the amount being paid.	
The remittance advice note will be sent to the supplier to advise them of the amount being paid.	
The remittance advice note will be sent to the accounts department at Lemonfresh Ltd to request that a cheque is raised.	

An invoice dated 18 June 20XX has been received from Lemonfresh Ltd for £760.00 plus VAT. A prompt payment discount of 5% is offered for payment within 10 days.

(e) **Calculate the amount to be paid to Lemonfresh Ltd if the discount is taken and show the date by which Lemonfresh Ltd should receive the payment.**

Supplier	Amount £	Date by which payment should be received by supplier
Lemonfresh Ltd		▼

Picklist:

18 June 20XX
27 June 20XX
28 June 20XX
29 June 20XX
30 June 20XX

Task 4 (20 marks)

Russell Hardware has made three payments which are to be entered in its cash book.

Receipts for payments

Received cash with thanks for goods bought.	Received cash with thanks for stationery bought.
From Russell Hardware, a customer without a credit account.	From Russell Hardware, a customer without a credit account.

	£
Net	240
VAT	48
Total	288

Gesteor & Co

Net   £167
(No VAT)

Stationery Shop

Cheque book stubs

Weston Ltd
(Purchase ledger account WES001)

£1,452

In settlement of outstanding balance
109923

(a) Enter the details from the payments into the credit side of the cash book shown below and total each column.

Cash book – credit side

Details	Cash £	Bank £	VAT £	Trade payables £	Cash purchases £	Stationery £
Balance b/f		135				
▼						
▼						
▼						
Totals						

Picklist:

Bank
Cash
Gesteor & Co
Stationery
Stationery Shop
Trade payables
VAT
Weston Ltd

There are also two cheques from credit customers to be entered in Russell Hardware's cash book:

Middle Firth Ltd   £673
High Tops plc   £1,092

(b) **Enter the above details into the debit side of the cash book and total each column.**

Cash book – debit side

Details	Cash £	Bank £	Trade receivables £
Balance b/f	629		
Middle Firth Ltd			
High Tops plc			
Total			

(c) **Using your answers to (a) and (b) above, calculate the cash balance.**

£

(d) **Using your answers to (a) and (b) above, calculate the bank balance. Use a minus sign if your calculations indicate an overdrawn bank balance, eg –123.**

£

(e) **Will the bank balance calculated in (d) above be a debit or credit balance?**

	✓
Debit	
Credit	

Task 5 (15 marks)

This is a summary of petty cash payments made by Russell Hardware.

Office Supplies Ltd paid	£26.00 (plus VAT)
Post Office paid	£12.00 (no VAT)
RN Travel paid	£33.00 (no VAT)
Speedy Taxis paid	£15.00 (no VAT)
Corner Shop paid (coffee etc)	£5.50 (plus VAT)

(a) **Complete the petty cash book by:**

- **Entering the five transactions into the petty cash book below; and**

- **Totalling the petty cash book and inserting the balance carried down.**

Petty cash book

Debit side		Credit side					
Details	Amount £	Details	Amount £	VAT £	Postage £	Travel £	Office expenses £
Balance b/f	250.00	▼					
		▼					
		▼					
		▼					
		▼					
		▼					
		▼					
		▼					
Total		Totals					

Picklist:

Amount
Balance b/d
Balance c/d
Corner Shop
Details
Office expenses
Office Supplies Ltd
Post Office
Postage
RN Travel
Speedy Taxis
Travel
VAT

At the end of the month the cash in the petty cash box was £11.95.

(b) **Complete the petty cash reimbursement document below to restore the imprest amount of £250.**

Petty cash reimbursement		
Date: 31.07.20XX		
Amount required to restore the cash in the petty cash box	£	

Task 6 (12 marks)

These are the totals of the discounts received daybook at the end of the month.

Discounts received daybook

Details	Total £	VAT £	Net £
Totals	444	74	370

(a) **What will be the entries in the general ledger?**

Account name		Amount £	Debit ✓	Credit ✓
	▼			
	▼			
	▼			

Picklist:

Discounts allowed
Discounts received
Purchases
Purchases ledger control
Purchases returns
Sales
Sales ledger control
Sales returns
VAT

One of the entries in the discounts received daybook is for a credit note received from Roger Ras for £224 plus VAT.

(b) **What will be the entry in the purchases ledger?**

Account name	Amount £	Debit ✓	Credit ✓
▼			

Picklist:

Discounts allowed
Discounts received
Purchases
Purchases ledger control
Purchases returns
Roger Ras
Sales
Sales ledger control
Sales returns
VAT

Task 7 (10 marks)

The following transactions all took place on 30 June and have been entered into the sales day book as shown below. No entries have yet been made into the ledger system.

Sales day book

Date 20XX	Details	Invoice number	Total £	VAT £	Net £
30 Jun	Trilby & Co	5264	3,936	656	3,280
30 Jun	R Strang Ltd	5265	1,776	296	1,480
	Totals		5,712	952	4,760

(a) What will be the entries in the sales ledger?

Sales ledger

Account name		Amount £	Debit ✓	Credit ✓
	▼			
	▼			

Picklist:

Purchases
Purchases ledger control
Purchases returns
R Strang Ltd
Sales
Sales ledger control
Sales returns
Trilby & Co
VAT

(b) What will be the entries in the general ledger?

General ledger

Account name		Amount £	Debit ✓	Credit ✓
	▼			
	▼			
	▼			

Picklist:

Purchases
Purchases ledger control
Purchases returns
R Strang Ltd
Sales
Sales ledger control
Sales returns
Trilby & Co
VAT

Task 8 (10 marks)

The following two accounts are in the general ledger at the close of day on 30 June.

(a) **Complete the accounts below by:**

- **Inserting the balance carried down together with date and details;**

- **Inserting the totals; and**

- **Inserting the balance brought down together with date and details.**

Heat and light

Date 20XX	Details	Amount £	Date 20XX	Details	Amount £
01 Jun	Balance b/d	2,039	▼	▼	
26 Jun	Purchases ledger control	348	▼	▼	
▼	▼		▼	▼	
	Total			Total	
▼	▼		▼	▼	

Picklist:

1 Jul
30 Jun
Balance b/d
Balance c/d
Bank
Purchases ledger control

Sales

Date 20XX	Details	Amount £	Date 20XX	Details	Amount £
		▼	01 Jun	Balance b/d	32,986
		▼	22 Jun	Bank	750
▼		▼	▼	▼	
	Total			Total	
▼		▼	▼	▼	

Picklist:

1 Jul
30 Jun
Balance b/d
Balance c/d
Bank
Sales ledger control

The following account is in the sales ledger at the close of day on 30 June.

Tango Ltd

Date 20XX	Details	Amount £	Date 20XX	Details	Amount £
1 Jun	Balance b/f	899	22 Jun	Bank	780
11 Jun	Invoice 158	201	29 Jun	Credit Note 18	71

(b) What will be the balance brought down at 1 July on Tango Ltd's account?

Account	Balance b/d at 1 July	Debit ✓	Credit ✓
Tango Ltd			

Task 9 (12 marks)

Below are two general ledger accounts and a partially completed trial balance.

Complete the trial balance by:

- **Transferring the balances of the two general ledger accounts to the debit or credit column of the trial balance;**

- **Entering the amounts shown against each of the other account names into the debit or credit column of the trial balance; and**

- **Totalling both columns of the trial balance.**

Do not enter figures with decimal places in this task and do not enter a zero in unused column cells.

Discounts received

Date 20XX	Details	Amount £	Date 20XX	Details	Amount £
31 Mar			1 Mar	Balance b/f	150
31 Mar	Balance c/d	987	31 Mar	Sales ledger control	837
		987			987

Machinery

Date 20XX	Details	Amount £	Date 20XX	Details	Amount £
1 Mar	Balance b/f	5,300	31 Mar	Balance c/d	15,000
31 Mar	Bank	9,700			
		15,000			15,000

Account name	Amount £	Debit £	Credit £
Discounts received			
Machinery			
Cash at bank	1,342		
Sales ledger control	9,486		
Purchases ledger control	4,003		
VAT (owing to HM Revenue & Customs)	1,880		
Capital	4,708		
Loan from bank	2,500		
Sales	56,262		
Purchases	43,278		
Administration expenses	1,234		
Totals			

Task 10 (11 marks)

Trappic Ltd codes all purchase invoices with a supplier code **and** a general ledger code.

A selection of the codes used is given below.

Supplier	Supplier Code
Bridgend plc	BRI12
Distinct Ltd	DIS53
Finish Clear & Co	FIN09
Hepplewhite Clean Ltd	HEP76
Mirrors and Glass Ltd	MIR22

Item	General Ledger Code
Cleaning fluids	GL234
Mops and buckets	GL237
Brushes	GL240
Cloths	GL244
Protective clothing	GL248

This is an invoice received from a supplier.

Distinct Ltd
89 Northcourt Road, Arbuckle AR5 3VB
VAT Registration No. 837 4777 33

Trappic Ltd
8 Highview Road
Arbuckle
AR7 4LX

22 July 20XX

	£
10 mops with buckets @ £12.60 each	126.00
VAT @ 20%	25.20
Total	151.20

(a) **Select which codes would be used to code this invoice.**

Supplier code	▼
General ledger code	▼

Picklist:

BRI12
DIS53
FIN09
HEP76
MIR22
GL234
GL237
GL240
GL244
GL248

(b) Why is it necessary to use a supplier code?

▼

Picklist:

To help find the total amount of purchases
To help trace relevant information quickly and easily
To help when ordering an item
To help when storing an item of inventory

The transactions below have taken place.

(c) Select one option in each instance below to show whether, in relation to Trappic Ltd, the item will be capital expenditure, revenue expenditure, capital income or revenue income.

Item	Capital expenditure ✓	Revenue expenditure ✓	Capital income ✓	Revenue income ✓
Purchase of mops and buckets for resale				
Receipt from sale of an item of Trappic Ltd's machinery				
Purchase of delivery vehicle				
Cash purchases of stationery				
Payments to credit suppliers				
Sale of goods for cash				

Financial accounting is based upon the accounting equation.

(d) Show whether the following statements are true or false.

	True ✓	False ✓
Income less expenditure is equal to assets		
Capital plus liabilities are equal to assets		
Liabilities equal assets plus capital		

(e) **Classify each of the following items as an asset, a liability or capital.**

Item	Asset, liability or capital?	
Money contributed by the owners		▼
Bank overdraft		▼
Petty cash		▼

Picklist:

Asset
Capital
Liability

BPP PRACTICE ASSESSMENT 2
BOOKKEEPING TRANSACTIONS

ANSWERS

Bookkeeping Transactions (BTRN)
BPP practice assessment 2

Task 1

(a)

Trappic Ltd	
8 Highview Road, Arbuckle AR7 4LX	
VAT Registration No. 782 8723 23	

Nemesis Ltd	Customer account code: NEM893
36 Ventnor Road	
Arbuckle	
AR7 9LC	
	Date: 6 July 20XX
Invoice No: 67282	
Delivery note number: 8793	

Quantity of goods	Product code	Total list price £	Net amount after trade discount £	Net amount after all discounts £	VAT £	Gross £
200	C420	100.00	90.00	86.40	17.28	103.68

Tutorial note. The trade discount is deducted first, followed by the bulk discount.

Workings

List price £200 × 0.50 = £100.00, Net after trade discount = £100 × 90% = £90.00, Net after trade and bulk discounts = £90 × 96% = £86.40 VAT = £86.40 × 20% = £17.28

(b) Sales daybook

Date 20XX	Details	Invoice number	Total £	VAT £	Net £
6 July	Nemesis Ltd	67282	103.68	17.28	86.40

(c) The correct answer is: Bulk discount

(d) The correct answer is: Sales invoice 66800

(e) The correct answer is: | £ | 4,720.02 |

Workings

£4,866.00 × 97% = £4,720.02

Task 2

(a)

	Yes ✓	No ✓
Has the correct purchase price of the cleaning fluid been charged?	✓	
Has the correct discount been applied?		✓

	Amount £
What would be the VAT amount charged if the invoice was correct?	136
What would be the total amount charged if the invoice was correct?	816

Workings

VAT: (£800 – (£800 × 15%)) × 20/100 = £136

Total: (£800 – (£800 × 15%)) + £136 = £816

(b) | Purchases returns daybook |

Date 20XX	Details	Credit note number	Total £	VAT £	Net £
22 July	Bingley & Co	09374	672	112	560

Task 3

(a)

Credit note 535

(b)

Invoice 1498

(c)

£	980

Workings

£990 – £10 = £980

(d)

	✓
The remittance advice note will be sent to the customer to advise them of the amount being paid	
The remittance advice note will be sent to the supplier's bank to advise them of the amount being paid	
The remittance advice note will be sent to the supplier to advise them of the amount being paid	✓
The remittance advice note will be sent to the accounts department at Lemonfresh Ltd to request that a cheque is raised	

(e)

Supplier	Amount £	Date by which payment should be received by supplier
Lemonfresh Ltd	866.40	28 June 20XX

Working

VAT = £760 × 20% = £152, Gross amount = £760 + £152 = £912,

Gross less discount = £912 × 95% = £866.40

Task 4

(a) **Cash book – credit side**

Details	Cash £	Bank £	VAT £	Trade payables £	Cash purchases £	Stationery £
Balance b/f		135				
Gesteor & Co	288		48		240	
Stationery Shop	167					167
Weston Ltd		1,452		1,452		
Totals	455	1,587	48	1,452	240	167

(b) **Cash book – debit side**

Details	Cash £	Bank £	Trade receivables £
Balance b/f	629		
Middle Firth Ltd		673	673
High Tops plc		1,092	1,092
Total	629	1,765	1,765

(c)

£	174

Workings

£629 – £455 = £174

(d)

£	178

Workings

£1,765 – £1,587 = £178

(e)

	✓
Debit	✓
Credit	

Task 5

(a) Petty cash book

Debit side		Credit side					
Details	Amount £	Details	Amount £	VAT £	Postage £	Travel £	Office expenses £
Balance b/f	250.00	Office Supplies Ltd	31.20	5.20			26.00
		Post Office	12.00		12.00		
		RN Travel	33.00			33.00	
		Speedy Taxis	15.00			15.00	
		Corner Shop	6.60	1.10			5.50
		Balance c/d	152.20				
	250.00		250.00	6.30	12.00	48.00	31.50

(b)

Petty cash reimbursement		
Date: 31.07.20XX		
Amount required to restore the cash in the petty cash box	£	238.05

Workings

£250 – £11.95 = £238.05

Task 6

(a)

Account name	Amount £	Debit ✓	Credit ✓
Discounts received	370		✓
VAT	74		✓
Purchases ledger control	444	✓	

(b)

Account name	Amount £	Debit ✓	Credit ✓
Roger Ras	268.80	✓	

Workings

Working VAT: £224 × 20% = £44.80, Gross = £224 + £44.80 = £268.80

Task 7

(a) Sales ledger

Account name	Amount £	Debit ✓	Credit ✓
Trilby & Co	3,936	✓	
R Strang Ltd	1,776	✓	

(b) General ledger

Account name	Amount £	Debit ✓	Credit ✓
Sales	4,760		✓
VAT	952		✓
Sales ledger control	5,712	✓	

Task 8

(a)

Heat and light

Date 20XX	Details	Amount £	Date 20XX	Details	Amount £
01 Jun	Balance b/d	2,039			
26 Jun	Purchases ledger control	348	30 Jun	Balance c/d	2,387
	Total	2,387		Total	2,387
1 Jul	Balance b/d	2,387			

Sales

Date 20XX	Details	Amount £	Date 20XX	Details	Amount £
			01 Jun	Balance b/d	32,986
30 Jun	Balance c/d	33,736	22 Jun	Bank	750
	Total	33,736		Total	33,736
			1 Jul	Balance b/d	33,736

(b)

Account	Balance b/d at 1 July	Debit ✓	Credit ✓
Tango Ltd	249	✓	

Tutorial note. Tango Ltd's ledger account is balanced off as follows:

Tango Ltd

Date 20XX	Details	Amount £	Date 20XX	Details	Amount £
1 Jun	Balance b/f	899	22 Jun	Bank	780
11 Jun	Invoice 158	201	29 Jun	Credit Note 18	71
			30 Jun	Balance c/d	249
	Total	1,100		Total	1,100
1 Jul	Balance b/d	249			

Task 9

Account name	Amount £	Debit £	Credit £
Discounts received			987
Machinery		15,000	
Cash at bank	1,342	1,342	
Sales ledger control	9,486	9,486	
Purchases ledger control	4,003		4,003
VAT (owing to HM Revenue & Customs)	1,880		1,880
Capital	4,708		4,708
Loan from bank	2,500		2,500
Sales	56,262		56,262
Purchases	43,278	43,278	
Administration expenses	1,234	1,234	
Totals		70,340	70,340

Task 10

(a)

Supplier code	DIS53
General ledger code	GL237

(b)

To help trace relevant information quickly and easily

(c)

Item	Capital expenditure ✓	Revenue expenditure ✓	Capital income ✓	Revenue income ✓
Purchase of mops and buckets for resale		✓		
Receipt from sale of an item of Trappic Ltd's machinery			✓	
Purchase of delivery vehicle	✓			
Cash purchases of stationery		✓		
Payments to credit suppliers		✓		
Sale of goods for cash				✓

(d)

	True ✓	False ✓
Income less expenditure is equal to assets		✓
Capital plus liabilities are equal to assets	✓	
Liabilities equal assets plus capital		✓

(e)

Item	Asset, liability or capital?
Money contributed by the owners	Capital
Bank overdraft	Liability
Petty cash	Asset

BPP PRACTICE ASSESSMENT 3
BOOKKEEPING TRANSACTIONS

Time allowed: 1.5 hours

PRACTICE ASSESSMENT 3

Bookkeeping Transactions (BTRN)
BPP practice assessment 3

Task 1 (12 marks)

On 10 July Hazelcombe & Co delivered the following goods to a credit customer, Warriner plc.

Hazelcombe & Co
42 Turnstile Trading Estate
Luscombe
LU9 0FG

Delivery note No. 90230
10 July 20XX

Warriner plc   Customer account code: W981
45 Printer Lane
Luscombe
LU3 9LA

500 fixings, product code FX827

The list price of the goods was £20.00 per box of 10 fixings plus VAT. Warriner plc is to be given a 20% trade discount.

(a)   Calculate the amounts to be included in the invoice.

	£
Net amount before discount	
Net amount after discount	
VAT	
Total	

(b)   What will be the amounts entered in the sales daybook when the invoice in (a) has been prepared?

Sales daybook

Date 20XX	Details	Invoice number	Total £	VAT £	Net £
11 Jul	Warriner plc	21026			

The account shown below is in the sales ledger of Hazelcombe & Co. A remittance advice for an automated payment of £3,376 has now been received from this customer.

Oster Ltd

Date 20XX	Details	Amount £	Date 20XX	Details	Amount £
15 May	Invoice 19011	1,920	28 May	Credit note 801	84
16 June	Invoice 20332	1,743	15 June	Bank	1,836
17 June	Invoice 21276	1,633	15 June	Credit note D76	56
22 June	Invoice 21280	650	23 June	Credit note 893	209

(c) **Show which THREE transactions are still outstanding by circling the relevant transactions below.**

Transactions			
Invoice 19011	Invoice 20332	Invoice 21276	Invoice 21280
Credit note 801	Bank	Credit note D76	Credit note 893

An invoice is being prepared to be sent to Oster Ltd for £1,180.00 plus VAT. A prompt payment discount of 2% will be offered for payment within 10 days.

(d) **What is the amount Hazelcombe & Co should receive if payment is NOT made within 10 days?**

£

(e) **What is the amount Hazelcombe & Co should receive if payment is made within 10 days?**

£

Task 2 (9 marks)

A supply of parts has been delivered to Hazelcombe & Co by Handiparts Ltd. The purchase order sent from Hazelcombe & Co, and the invoice from Handiparts Ltd, are shown below.

Hazelcombe & Co
42 Turnstile Trading Estate
Luscombe
LU9 0FG

Purchase Order No. 89374

To: Handiparts Ltd

Date: 10 July 20XX

Please supply 5000 facings, product code 76253AA
Purchase price: £22.00 per 50, plus VAT
Discount: less 20% trade discount, as agreed

Handiparts Ltd
87 Radley Road, Luscombe LU8 4AZ
VAT Registration No. 874 2309 93

Invoice No. 8749

Hazelcombe & Co
42 Turnstile Trading Estate
Luscombe
LU9 0FG

12 July 20XX

	£
5000 facings product code 7253AA @ £0.50 each	2,500.00
Less trade discount at 20%	500.00
Net amount	2,000.00
VAT @ 20%	400.00
Total	2,400.00
Terms: 30 days net	

(a) Check the invoice against the purchase order and answer the following questions.

	Yes ✓	No ✓
Has the correct purchase price of the facings been charged?		
Has the correct discount rate been applied?		

	£
What would be the VAT amount charged if the invoice was correct?	
What would be the total amount charged if the invoice was correct?	

The credit note below has been received from a credit supplier, Corona Ltd, in respect of a prompt payment discount taken.

Credit note

Corona Ltd
VAT Registration number 436 4472 01

Credit note No. 89

To: Hazelcombe & Co   13 July 20XX

	£
Prompt payment discount taken	66.50
VAT @ 20%	13.30
Total	79.80

Reason: prompt payment discount taken

(b) Record the credit note in the appropriate daybook by:

- **Selecting the correct daybook title; and**
- **Making the necessary entries.**

[▼]

Picklist:

Discounts allowed daybook
Discounts received daybook
Purchases daybook
Purchases returns daybook
Sales daybook
Sales returns daybook

Date 20XX	Details	Credit note number	Total £	VAT £	Net £
13 Jul	▼	89			

Picklist:

Corona Ltd

Hazelcombe & Co

Task 3 (9 marks)

Shown below is a statement of account received from a credit supplier, SpareParts plc, and the supplier's account as shown in the purchases ledger of Hazelcombe & Co.

SpareParts plc Unit 50 Hunston Park Trading Estate Luscombe LU3 6XC

To: Hazelcombe & Co
42 Turnstile Trading Estate
Luscombe
LU9 0FG

STATEMENT OF ACCOUNT

Date 20XX	Number	Details	Amount £	Balance £
15 May	1893	Invoice	2,395	2,395
6 June	C043	Credit note	−456	1,939
11 June	1999	Invoice	7,832	9,771
17 June	1034	Invoice	2,347	12,118
30 June		Payment	−2,395	9,723

SpareParts plc

Date 20XX	Details	Amount £	Date 20XX	Details	Amount £
29 June	Bank – cheque	2,395	15 May	Invoice 1893	2,395
29 June	Credit note D91	27	11 June	Invoice 1999	7,832
			17 June	Invoice 1034	2,347

(a) Which item is missing from the statement of account from SpareParts plc?

	▼

Picklist:

Cheque for £2,395
Credit note C043
Credit note D91
Invoice I034
Invoice I893
Invoice I999

(b) Which item is missing from the supplier account in Hazelcombe & Co's purchases ledger?

	▼

Picklist:

Cheque for £2,395
Credit note C043
Credit note D91
Invoice I034
Invoice I893
Invoice I999

(c) Assuming any differences between the statement of account from SpareParts plc and the supplier account in Hazelcombe & Co's purchases ledger are simply due to omission errors, what is the amount owing to SpareParts plc?

£	

This is the account of Cooper Foundry Ltd in the purchases ledger of Hazelcombe & Co, and an invoice that has been received from the supplier but not yet entered into their account.

Cooper Foundry Ltd

Date 20XX	Details	Amount £	Date 20XX	Details	Amount £
1 July	Bank	2,450	1 July	Balance b/f	3,235
1 July	Credit note D11	80	1 July	Invoice 09364	982
6 July	Credit note 039	45	15 July	Invoice 09528	2,386

Invoice

Cooper Foundry Ltd	
VAT Registration number 896 5421 01	
Invoice No. 6532	
To: Hazelcombe & Co 20 July 20XX	
	£
Goods supplied 100 product C456	275
VAT @ 20%	55
Total	330

Terms: net monthly account

(d) **What will be the amount to be paid to Cooper Foundry Ltd once the invoice has been entered into their account?**

£ [   ]

The two invoices below were received on 20 July from credit suppliers who offer a prompt payment discount.

Invoice

Brixton Ltd	
VAT Registration number 569 4453 01	
Invoice No. 9932	
To: Hazelcombe & Co 20 July 20XX	
	£
Goods supplied	2,500
VAT @ 20%	500
Total	3,000

Terms: 4% discount if payment received within 10 days of date of invoice.

Invoice

Harrier Ltd	
VAT Registration number 442 6753 00	
Invoice No. H321	
To: Hazelcombe & Co 20 July 20XX	
	£
Goods supplied	595
VAT @ 20%	191
Total	714

Terms: 2% discount if payment received within 14 days of date of invoice.

(e) Calculate the amount to be paid to each supplier if the discount is taken and show the date by which the supplier should receive the payment.

Supplier	Amount £	Date by which payment should be received by supplier
Brixton Ltd		▼
Harrier Ltd		▼

Picklist:

20 July
30 July
31 July
3 August
4 August

Task 4 (15 marks)

Finn Clothing has made two payments which are to be entered in its cash book.

Receipt for payment

Received cash with thanks for goods bought.

From Finn Clothing, a customer without a credit account.

Net   £920
VAT   £184
Total   £1,104

Wisper & Co

Cheque book stub

Lampetus Ltd
(Purchases ledger account LAM001)

£2,135
In settlement of outstanding account

003456

(a) **Make the necessary entries in the cash book and total each column.**

Cash book – credit side

Details		Cash £	Bank £	VAT £	Trade payables £	Cash purchases £
Balance b/f			1,902			
	▼					
	▼					
Totals						

Picklist:

Bank
Cash purchases
Lampetus Ltd
Trade payables
VAT
Wisper & Co

There are also two cheques from credit customers to be entered in Finn Clothing's cash book:

Prickles & Co £2,837
Dreston Proops £3,299

(b) **Enter the above details into the debit side of the cash book and total each column.**

Cash book – debit side

Details	Cash £	Bank £	Trade receivables £
Balance b/f	1,593		
Prickles & Co			
Dreston Proops			
Total			

(c) **Using your answers to (a) and (b) above, calculate the cash balance.**

£	

(d) Using your answers to (a) and (b) above, calculate the bank balance. Use a minus sign if your calculations indicate an overdrawn bank balance, eg –123.

£ [ ]

(e) Will the bank balance calculated in (d) above be a debit or credit balance?

	✓
Debit	.
Credit	

....

Task 5 (15 marks)

This is a summary of petty cash payments made by Finn Clothing.

Quick Bus Company paid	£12.50 (no VAT) on 27 September
Star's Stationery paid	£18.00 (plus VAT) on 30 September
Post Office paid	£8.00 (no VAT) on 30 September

(a) Complete the petty cash book by:

- Entering all the transactions into the petty cash book below; and

- Totalling the petty cash book and inserting the balance carried down at 30 September.

Petty cash book

Date	Details	Amount £	Date	Details	Amount £	VAT £	Stationery £	Travel £	Postage £
23 Sept	Balance b/f	120.00	27 Sept	▼					
			30 Sept	▼					
			30 Sept	▼					
			30 Sept	▼					
	Total			Totals					

332

Picklist:

Amount
Balance b/d
Balance c/d
Details
Postage
Post Office
Stationery
Star's Stationery
Quick Bus Company
Travel
VAT

(b) **What will be the amount of cash withdrawn from the bank to restore the imprest level of £120.00?**

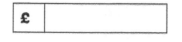

···

Task 6 (12 marks)

These are the totals of Hazelcombe & Co's discounts allowed daybook at the end of the month.

Discounts allowed daybook

Details	Total £	VAT £	Net £
Totals	90	15	75

(a) **Post the amounts from the daybook to the general ledger accounts below. You do NOT need to balance off the accounts.**

Discounts allowed

Details	Amount £	Details	Amount £
▼		▼	
▼		▼	

Picklist:

Discounts allowed
Discounts received
Purchases
Purchases ledger control
Purchases returns
Sales
Sales ledger control
Sales returns
VAT

VAT

Details	Amount £	Details	Amount £
▼		▼	
▼		▼	

Picklist:

Discounts allowed
Discounts received
Purchases
Purchases ledger control
Purchases returns
Sales
Sales ledger control
Sales returns
VAT

Sales ledger control

Details		Amount £	Details		Amount £
	▼			▼	
	▼			▼	

Picklist:

Discounts allowed
Discounts received
Purchases
Purchases ledger control
Purchases returns
Sales
Sales ledger control
Sales returns
VAT

One of the entries in the discounts allowed daybook is for credit note D86 sent to Susan Smith for £66 plus VAT.

(b) **Record the credit note in the appropriate sales ledger account by:**

- **Selecting the correct sales ledger account; and**
- **Making the necessary entries.**

	▼

Picklist:

Credit note D86
Discounts allowed
Discounts received
Hazelcombe & Co
Sales
Sales ledger control
Susan Smith

Details	Amount £	Details	Amount £
▼		▼	
▼		▼	

Picklist:

Credit note D86
Discount allowed
Hazelcombe & Co
Sale
Susan Smith
VAT

Task 7 (12 marks)

Hazelcombe & Co maintains a petty cash book as a book of prime entry only. The following transactions all took place on 30 June and have been entered in the petty cash book as shown below. No entries have yet been made in the general ledger.

Petty cash book – credit side

Date 20XX	Details	Amount £	VAT £	Distribution expenses £	Travel £	Office expenses £
30 Jun	Envelopes	18.24	3.04			15.20
30 Jun	Postage	13.40				13.40
30 Jun	De-icer	6.72	1.12	5.60		
30 Jun	Bus fares	17.65			17.65	
		56.01	4.16	5.60	17.65	28.60

What will be the five entries in the general ledger?

General ledger

Account name		Amount £	Debit ✓	Credit ✓
	▼			
	▼			
	▼			
	▼			
	▼			

Picklist:

Bank
Bus fares
De-icer
Distribution expenses
Envelopes
Office expenses
Petty cash control
Postage
Travel
VAT

Task 8 (12 marks)

The following account is in the general ledger at close of day on 30 June.

Purchases

Date 20XX	Details	Amount £	Date 20XX	Details	Amount £
1 Jun	Balance b/f	3,920	30 Jun	Journal	200
8 Jun	Purchases ledger control	2,357			

(a) What will be the balance brought down at 1 July?

Account	Balance b/d at 1 July	Debit ✓	Credit ✓
Purchases			

The following two accounts are in the general ledger and the purchases ledger respectively at the close of day on 30 June.

(b) Complete the accounts below by:

- **Inserting the balance carried down together with date and details;**

- **Inserting the totals; and**

- **Inserting the balance brought down together with date and details.**

GENERAL LEDGER

Office expenses

Date 20XX	Details	Amount £	Date 20XX	Details	Amount £
01 Jun	Balance b/d	12,945		▼	
30 Jun	Petty cash	42		▼	
30 Jun	Purchases ledger control	523		▼	
▼	▼		▼	▼	
	Total			Total	
▼	▼		▼	▼	

Picklist:

1 Jul
30 Jun
Balance b/d
Balance c/d
Bank
Petty cash
Purchases ledger control

PURCHASES LEDGER

Knowsley & Sons

Date 20XX	Details	Amount £	Date 20XX	Details	Amount £
27 June	Bank	1,009	01 Jun	Balance b/d	1,276
27 June	Credit note D56	65	16 Jun	Invoice 567	565
▼	▼		▼	▼	
	Total			Total	
▼	▼		▼	▼	

Picklist:

1 Jul
30 Jun
Balance b/d
Balance c/d
Knowsley & Sons

Task 9 (12 marks)

Below are two general ledger accounts and a partially completed trial balance.

Complete the trial balance by:

- **Transferring the balances of the two general ledger accounts to the debit or credit column of the trial balance.**

- **Entering the amounts shown against each of the other account names into the debit or credit column of the trial balance.**

- **Totalling both columns of the trial balance.**

Do not enter figures with decimal places in this task and do not enter a zero in unused column cells.

Bank

Date 20XX	Details	Amount £	Date 20XX	Details	Amount £
15 May	Sales ledger control	19,502	1 May	Balance b/f	1,200
31 May	Balance c/d	2,137	25 May	Purchases ledger control	20,439
		21,639			21,639

Purchases

Date 20XX	Details	Amount £	Date 20XX	Details	Amount £
1 May	Balance b/f	58,950	31 May	Balance c/d	81,744
30 May	Purchases ledger control	22,794			
		81,744			81,744

Account name	Amount £	Debit £	Credit £
Bank			
Purchases			
Administrative expenses	52,165		
Capital	4,870		
Discounts allowed	1,986		
Discounts received	2,543		
Inventory	12,354		
Petty cash	250		
Purchases ledger control	6,297		
Sales	152,242		
Sales ledger control	24,910		
VAT (owing to HM Revenue & Customs)	5,320		
Totals			

Task 10 (12 marks)

Hazelcombe & Co codes all purchase invoices with a supplier code AND a general ledger code. A selection of the codes used is given below.

Supplier	Supplier Code
Curran Mews Ltd	C783
Findlay & Co	F920
Gosling Ltd	G224
Meston plc	M029
Postlethwaite Brothers	P673

Item	General Ledger Code
Facings	GL956
Fixings	GL962
Leads	GL967
Lights	GL971
Pumps	GL975

This is an invoice received from a supplier.

Findlay & Co **98 Green Road, Luscombe LU9 0CV** **VAT Registration No. 987 3666 237**	
Hazelcombe & Co 42 Turnstile Trading Estate Luscombe LU9 0FG 17 July 20XX	
	£
20 lights (product code 72836) @ £6.80 each	136.00
VAT @ 20%	27.20
Total	163.20

(a) **Select which codes would be used to code this invoice.**

Supplier code	▼
General ledger code	▼

Picklist:

C783
F920
G224
GL956
GL962
GL967
GL971
GL975
M029
P673

(b) **Why is it necessary to use a general ledger code for different types of purchases?**

	▼

Picklist:

To help find the total amount of purchases
To help identify how much is owed to a supplier
To help identify the amount spent on a particular category of inventory
To help identify when to re-order an item of inventory

(c) **Select one option in each instance below to show whether the item will be capital expenditure, revenue expenditure, capital income or revenue income.**

Item	Capital expenditure ✓	Revenue expenditure ✓	Capital income ✓	Revenue income ✓
Cash sales				
Purchase on credit of lights for resale				
Sale of goods on credit				
Purchase of office computer				
Payments to credit suppliers				
Receipt from sale of an item of Hazelcombe & Co's furniture and fittings				

(d) **Show whether the following statements are true or false.**

	True ✓	False ✓
An increase in an asset is shown as a credit entry in the general ledger.		
A decrease in liabilities is shown as a credit entry in the general ledger.		
An increase in capital is shown as a credit entry in the general ledger.		

(e) **Identify from the picklist an example of an asset, a liability and a capital transaction.**

Item	Example	
Asset		▼
Liability		▼
Capital transaction		▼

Picklist:

Bank overdraft
Drawings
Trade receivables

BPP PRACTICE ASSESSMENT 3
BOOKKEEPING TRANSACTIONS

ANSWERS

Bookkeeping Transactions (BTRN)
BPP practice assessment 3

Task 1

(a)

	£
Net amount before discount	1,000.00
Net amount after discount	800.00
VAT	160.00
Total	960.00

Working

List price £20 × 500/10 = £1,000, Net after trade discount = £1,000 × 80% = £800, VAT £800 × 20% = £160

(b) Sales daybook

Date 20XX	Details	Invoice number	Total £	VAT £	Net £
11 Jul	Warriner plc	21026	960.00	160.00	800.00

(c)

Transactions
Invoice 19011   Invoice 20332   Invoice 21276   ⟨Invoice 21280⟩
Credit note 801   Bank   ⟨Credit note D76⟩   ⟨Credit note 893⟩

(d)

£	1,416

Working

VAT £1,180 × 20% = £236, Gross £1,180 + £236 = £1,416

(e)

£	1,387.68

Working

£1,416 × 98% = £1,387.68

....

Task 2

(a)

	Yes ✓	No ✓
Has the correct purchase price of the facings been charged?		✓
Has the correct discount rate been applied?	✓	

	£
What would be the VAT amount charged if the invoice was correct?	352
What would be the total amount charged if the invoice was correct?	2,112

Tutorial note.

VAT: ((5,000 × £22/50) – (5,000 × £22/50 × 20/100)) × 20/100 = £352

Total: (5,000 × £22/50) × 0.80 × 1.2 = £2,112

(b) | Discounts received daybook |

Date 20XX	Details	Credit note number	Total £	VAT £	Net £
13 Jul	Corona Ltd	89	79.80	13.30	66.50

....

Task 3

(a)

Credit note D91

(b)

Credit note C043

(c)

£	9,696

Working

£9,723 – £27 = £9,696

(d)

£	4,358

Working

£3,235 + £982 + £2,386 – £2,450 – £80 – £45 + £330 = £4,358

(e)

Supplier	Amount £	Date by which payment should be received by supplier
Brixton Ltd	2,880.00	30 July
Harrier Ltd	699.72	3 August

Workings

Brixton Ltd £3,000 × 96% = £2,880
Harrier Ltd £714 × 98% = £699.72

Task 4

(a) Cash book – credit side

Details	Cash £	Bank £	VAT £	Trade payables £	Cash purchases £
Balance b/f		1,902			
Wisper & Co	1,104		184		920
Lampetus Ltd		2,135		2,135	
Totals	1,104	4,037	184	2,135	920

(b) Cash book – debit side

Details	Cash £	Bank £	Trade receivables £
Balance b/f	1,593		
Prickles & Co		2,837	2,837
Dreston Proops		3,299	3,299
Totals	1,593	6,136	6,136

(c)

£	489

Workings

£1,593 – £1,104 = £489

(d)

£	2,099

Workings

£6,136 – £4,037 = £2,099

(e)

	✓
Debit	✓
Credit	

Task 5

(a) Petty cash book

Date	Details	Amount £	Date	Details	Amount £	VAT £	Stationery £	Travel £	Postage £
23 Sept	Balance b/f	120.00	27 Sept	Quick Bus Company	12.50			12.50	
			30 Sept	Star's Stationery	21.60	3.60	18.00		
			30 Sept	Post Office	8.00				8.00
			30 Sept	Balance c/d	77.90				
	Total	120.00		Totals	120.00	3.60	18.00	12.50	8.00

(b)

£	42.10

Working

£12.50 + £21.60 + £8.00 = £42.10

....

Task 6

(a)

Discounts allowed

Details	Amount £	Details	Amount £
Sales ledger control	75		

VAT

Details	Amount £	Details	Amount £
Sales ledger control	15		

Sales ledger control

Details	Amount £	Details	Amount £
		Discounts allowed	75
		VAT	15

(b) Susan Smith

Details	Amount £	Details	Amount £
		Credit note D86	79.20

Working

VAT = £66 × 20% = £13.20, gross amount = £66 + 13.20 = £79.20

Task 7

General ledger

Account name	Amount £	Debit ✓	Credit ✓
Petty cash control	56.01		✓
Distribution expenses	5.60	✓	
Office expenses	28.60	✓	
Travel	17.65	✓	
VAT	4.16	✓	

Task 8

(a)

Account	Balance b/d at 1 July	Debit ✓	Credit ✓
Purchases	6,077	✓	

Tutorial note. The balanced off purchases ledger account looks like this:

Purchases

Date 20XX	Details	Amount £	Date 20XX	Details	Amount £
1 Jun	Balance b/f	3,920	30 Jun	Journal	200
8 Jun	Purchases ledger control	2,357	30 Jun	Balance c/d	6,077
	Total	6,277		Total	6,277

(b) **GENERAL LEDGER**

Office expenses

Date 20XX	Details	Amount £	Date 20XX	Details	Amount £
01 Jun	Balance b/d	12,945			
30 Jun	Petty cash	42			
30 Jun	Purchases ledger control	523	30 Jun	Balance c/d	13,510
	Total	13,510		Total	13,510
1 Jul	Balance b/d	13,510			

PURCHASES LEDGER

Knowsley & Sons

Date 20XX	Details	Amount £	Date 20XX	Details	Amount £
27 June	Bank	1,009	01 Jun	Balance b/d	1,276
27 June	Credit note D56	65	16 Jun	Invoice 567	565
30 Jun	Balance c/d	767			
	Total	1,841		Total	1,841
			1 Jul	Balance b/d	767

Task 9

Account name	Amount £	Debit £	Credit £
Bank			2,137
Purchases		81,744	
Administrative expenses	52,165	52,165	
Capital	4,870		4,870
Discounts allowed	1,986	1,986	
Discounts received	2,543		2,543
Inventory	12,354	12,354	
Petty cash	250	250	
Purchases ledger control	6,297		6,297
Sales	152,242		152,242
Sales ledger control	24,910	24,910	
VAT (owing to HM Revenue & Customs)	5,320		5,320
Totals		173,409	173,409

Task 10

(a)

Supplier code	F920
General ledger code	GL971

(b)

To help identify the amount spent on a particular category of inventory

(c)

Item	Capital expenditure ✓	Revenue expenditure ✓	Capital income ✓	Revenue income ✓
Cash sales				✓
Purchase on credit of lights for resale		✓		
Sale of goods on credit				✓
Purchase of office computer	✓			
Payments to credit suppliers		✓		
Receipt from sale of an item of Hazelcombe & Co's furniture and fittings			✓	

(d)

	True ✓	False ✓
An increase in an asset is shown as a credit entry in the general ledger.		✓
A decrease in liabilities is shown as a credit entry in the general ledger.		✓
An increase in capital is shown as a credit entry in the general ledger.	✓	

(e)

Item	Example
Asset	Trade receivables
Liability	Bank overdraft
Capital transaction	Drawings

355

BPP PRACTICE ASSESSMENT 4
BOOKKEEPING TRANSACTIONS

Time allowed: 1.5 hours

Bookkeeping Transactions (BTRN)
BPP practice assessment 4

Task 1 (12 marks)

On 21 July, Mandarin Ltd received the following goods returned note from a credit customer, Jessop Brothers.

Jessop Brothers
Unit 10 Eastern Trading Estate
Cinnadon
CN1 1PP

GOODS RETURNED NOTE

GRN no: 567

To: Mandarin Ltd
    Mandarin House   21 July 20XX
    25 Jedward Street   Delivery note No. 452634
    Cinnadon
    CN6 6LW   Order No. 876238

20 womens decorative tops, product code WT555.

Reason for return: faulty

The list price of the goods was £30 per box of five tops plus VAT. Jessop Brothers was given a 10% trade discount.

(a) **Complete the credit note below.**

Mandarin Ltd Mandarin House, 25 Jedward Street Cinnadon CN6 6LW	Jessop Brothers Unit 10 Eastern Trading Estate Cinnadon CN1 1PP Customer account code: SL930

VAT Registration No. 928 2781 110

CREDIT NOTE

Credit note number no: CN01256 Delivery note number: 452634 Order number: 876238	Date: 22 July 20XX

Quantity of goods	Product code	Total list price £	Net amount after discount £	VAT £	Gross £

(b) **Record the credit note in the appropriate daybook by:**

- **Selecting the correct daybook title; and**
- **Making the necessary entries.**

[▼]

Picklist:

Discounts allowed daybook
Discounts received daybook
Purchases daybook
Purchases returns daybook
Sales daybook
Sales returns daybook

Date 20XX	Details	Credit note number	Total £	VAT £	Net £
22 Jul	▼	CN01256			

Picklist:

Jessop Brothers
Mandarin Ltd

The account shown below is in the sales ledger of Mandarin Ltd. A remittance advice for an automated payment of £5,426 has now been received from this customer which they incorrectly state is in full settlement of their account at 31 May.

Plews & Co

Date 20XX	Details	Amount £	Date 20XX	Details	Amount £
1 May	Balance b/f	551	2 May	Bank	551
12 May	Invoice 0024	2,910	5 May	Credit note C1	16
23 May	Invoice 0095	1,663	15 May	Credit note 009	125
28 May	Invoice 0102	2,739	25 May	Credit note 017	98
30 May	Invoice 0110	1,337			

(c)   Show which THREE transactions are still outstanding by circling the relevant transactions below.

Transactions
Balance b/f   Invoice 0024   Invoice 0095   Invoice 0102   Invoice 0110
Bank   Credit note C1   Credit note 009   Credit note 017

An invoice is being prepared to be sent to Plews & Co for £2,560.00 plus VAT. A prompt payment discount of 5% will be offered for payment within 10 days.

(d)   What is the amount Mandarin Ltd should receive if payment is NOT made within 10 days?

£

(e)   What is the amount Mandarin Ltd should receive if payment is made within 10 days?

£

Task 2 (9 marks)

A supply of clothing has been delivered to Mandarin Ltd by Rainbow Fashions Ltd. The purchase order sent from Mandarin Ltd, and the invoice from Rainbow Fashions Ltd, are shown below.

Mandarin Ltd
Mandarin House, 25 Jedward Street
Cinnadon
CN6 6LW

Purchase Order No. 093247

To: Rainbow Fashions Ltd

Date: 17 July 20XX

Please supply 40 mens polo shirts, product code MPS45
Purchase price: £36.00 per pack of 5, plus VAT
Discount: less 10% trade discount, as agreed

Terms: 2% discount for payment within 14 days

Rainbow Fashions Ltd
92 Norman Street, Cinnadon CN4 2KJ
VAT Registration No. 903 2838 39

Invoice No. 83792

Mandarin Ltd
Mandarin House, 25 Jedward Street
Cinnadon
CN6 6LW

22 July 20XX

40 mens polo shirts product code MPS45 @ £7.60 each	£304.00
Less trade discount at 10%	£30.40
Net amount	£273.60

Terms: 30 days net

(a) **Identify any discrepancies on the invoice by drawing a line from each left hand box to the appropriate right hand box.**

Terms of payment	Not shown on invoice
VAT rate	Incorrectly shown on invoice
Trade discount	
Purchase price	Correctly shown on invoice

(b)

	Amount £
What would be the VAT amount charged if the invoice was correct?	
What would be the total amount charged if the invoice was correct?	

Invoices from suppliers have been checked and partially entered in the purchases day book, as shown below.

(c) **Complete the purchases day book by:**

- **Inserting the appropriate figures for each invoice in the relevant columns;**

- **Totalling the last five columns of the purchases day book.**

Purchases day book

Date 20XX	Details	Invoice number	Total £	VAT £	Net £	Women's clothing £	Men's clothing £
30 Jun	Forfar Textiles plc	C9230	1,872				1,560
30 Jun	Jessamy Fashion Inc	0024567	3,216		2,680	2,680	
30 Jun	Lindstrom Ltd	726		648		3,240	
	Totals						

Task 3 (9 marks)

Shown below is a statement of account received from a credit supplier, and the supplier's account as shown in the purchases ledger of Mandarin Ltd.

Bella Designs
34-36 Bath Street
Cinnadon
CN3 1GH

To: Mandarin Ltd
Mandarin House
25 Jedward Street
Cinnadon
CN6 6LW

STATEMENT OF ACCOUNT

Date 20XX	Number	Details	Amount £	Balance £
26 May	6723	Invoice	1,092	1,092
3 June	6801	Invoice	894	1,986
15 June		Payment	−1,986	0
15 June	7013	Invoice	3,267	3,267
18 June	C67	Credit note	−62	3,205
27 Jun	7226	Invoice	2,674	5,879
30 June	C98	Credit note	−89	5,790

Bella Designs

Date 20XX	Details	Amount £	Date 20XX	Details	Amount £
15 June	Bank – cheque	1,986	26 May	Invoice 6723	1,092
18 June	Credit note C67	62	3 June	Invoice 6801	894
30 June	Bank – cheque	3,205	15 June	Invoice 7013	3,267
			27 June	Invoice 7226	2,674

(a) **Which item is missing from the statement of account from Bella Designs?**

▼

Picklist:

Credit note C67
Credit note C98
Invoice 6723
Invoice 6801
Invoice 7013
Invoice 7226
Payment for £1,986
Payment for £3,205

(b) **Which item is missing from the supplier account in Mandarin Ltd's purchases ledger?**

▼

Picklist:

Credit note C67
Credit note C98
Invoice 6723
Invoice 6801
Invoice 7013
Invoice 7226
Payment for £1,986
Payment for £3,205

(c) **Assuming any differences between the statement of account from Bella Designs and the supplier account in Mandarin Ltd's purchases ledger are simply due to omission errors, what is the amount owing to Bella Designs?**

£	

365

The two invoices below were received on 30 June from credit suppliers who offer a prompt payment discount.

Invoice

Bumble plc	
VAT Registration number 445 5693 01	
Invoice No. F196	
To: Mandarin Ltd	29 June 20XX
	£
150 Leather jackets	3,750.00
VAT @ 20%	750.00
Total	4,500.00

Terms: 1% discount if payment received within 14 days of date of invoice.

Invoice

Hallidays Ltd	
VAT Registration number 675 4423 00	
Invoice No. 658	
To: Mandarin Ltd	29 June 20XX
	£
500 Leather trousers	2,500.00
VAT @ 20%	500.00
Total	3,000.00

Terms: 5% discount if payment received within 10 days of date of invoice.

(d) **Calculate the amount to be paid to each supplier if the discount is taken and show the date by which the supplier should receive the payment.**

Supplier	£	Date by which payment should be received by supplier
Bumble plc		▼
Hallidays Ltd		▼

Picklist:

29 June 20XX
8 July 20XX
9 July 20XX
10 July 20XX
13 July 20XX
14 July 20XX

Task 4 (15 marks)

The two amounts shown below have been received from customers and are ready to be entered in the cash book.

Vampeter Ltd
Remittance advice note
15 July 20XX
Please find enclosed a cheque for £1,256 in settlement of invoice number 4876.

Sales receipt
15 July 20XX
£900 including VAT cash received from Propos Co for goods purchased.

(a) **Enter the above details into the debit side of the cash book and total each column.**

Cash book – debit side

Details	Cash £	Bank £	VAT £	Trade receivables £	Cash sales £
Balance b/f	1,869				
Vampeter Ltd					
Propos Co					
Total					

There were also two payments to enter in to the Cash book – credit side.

Cheque book stubs

Diston Ltd
(Purchases ledger account DIS057)
£4,295
In settlement of outstanding balance
209345

Opra Office Supplies
(We have no credit account with this supplier)
£336 including VAT
209346

(b) Enter the details from the payments into the credit side of the cash book shown below and total each column.

Cash book – credit side

Details	Cash £	Bank £	VAT £	Trade payables £	Cash purchases £	Office expenses £
Balance b/f		1,249				
Diston Ltd						
Opra Office Supplies						
Total						

(c) Using your answers to (a) and (b) above, calculate the cash balance.

£ [   ]

(d) Using your answers to (a) and (b) above, calculate the bank balance. Use a minus sign if your calculations indicate an overdrawn bank balance, eg –123.

£ [   ]

(e) Will the bank balance calculated in (d) above be a debit or credit balance?

	✓
Debit	
Credit	

Task 5 (15 marks)

This is a summary of petty cash payments made by Scriven Trading.

Harry's Café paid	£26.30 (no VAT)
Tune Travel paid	£32.40 (plus VAT)
Robby's Taxis paid	£15.20 (plus VAT)

(a)   Complete the petty cash book by:

- **Entering the transactions into the petty cash book below; and**

- **Totalling the petty cash book and inserting the balance carried down.**

Petty cash book

Details	Amount £	Details	Amount £	VAT £	Entertainment £	Travel £
Balance b/f	100.00	▼				
		▼				
		▼				
		▼				
		▼				
Total		Totals				

Picklist:

Amount
Balance b/d
Balance c/d
Details
Entertainment
Harry's Café
Robby's Taxis
Travel
Tune Travel
VAT

Mandarin Ltd maintains a petty cash book as a book of prime entry only. The following transactions all took place on 30 June and have been entered in the petty cash book (credit side) as shown below. No entries have yet been made in the general ledger.

Petty cash book – credit side

Date 20XX	Details	Amount £	VAT £	Motor expenses £	Postage £	Sundry expenses £
30 Jun	Taxi fares	15.98				15.98
30 Jun	Printer paper	8.16	1.36			6.80
30 Jun	Petrol	51.36	8.56	42.80		
30 Jun	Postage stamps	17.26			17.26	
		92.76	9.92	42.80	17.26	22.78

(b) **What will be the five entries in the general ledger?**

General ledger

Account name		Amount £	Debit ✓	Credit ✓
	▼			
	▼			
	▼			
	▼			
	▼			

Picklist:

Bank
Motor expenses
Petrol
Petty cash control
Postage
Postage stamps
Printer paper
Sundry expenses
Taxi fares
VAT

Task 6 (12 marks)

One of the entries in Mandarin Ltd's discounts allowed daybook is for credit note D34 sent to Rupert Reynolds for £33 including VAT.

(a) **Record the invoice in the appropriate sales ledger account by:**
- **Selecting the correct sales ledger account; and**
- **Making the necessary entries.**

	▼

Picklist:

Credit note D34
Discounts received
Mandarin Ltd
Rupert Reynolds
Sales
Sales ledger control

Details		Amount £	Details		Amount £
	▼			▼	
	▼			▼	

Picklist:

Credit note D34
Discount allowed
Mandarin Ltd
Rupert Reynolds
Sale
VAT

These are the totals of Mandarin Ltd's discounts received daybook at the end of the month.

Discounts received daybook

Details	Total £	VAT £	Net £
Totals	762	127	635

(b) **Post the amounts from the daybook to the general ledger accounts below. You do not need to balance off the accounts.**

Discounts received

Details		Amount £	Details		Amount £
	▼			▼	
	▼			▼	

Picklist:

Discounts allowed
Discounts received
Purchases
Purchases ledger control
Purchases returns
Sales
Sales ledger control
Sales returns
VAT

VAT

Details		Amount £	Details		Amount £
	▼			▼	
	▼			▼	

Picklist:

Discounts allowed
Discounts received
Purchases
Purchases ledger control
Purchases returns
Sales
Sales ledger control
Sales returns
VAT

Purchases ledger control

Details		Amount £	Details		Amount £
	▼			▼	
	▼			▼	

Picklist:

Discounts allowed
Discounts received
Purchases
Purchases ledger control
Purchases returns
Sales
Sales ledger control
Sales returns
VAT

Task 7 (12 marks)

The following transactions all took place on 30 June and have been entered in the debit side of the cash book as shown below. No entries have yet been made in the ledgers.

Cash book – debit side

Date 20XX	Details	Cash £	Bank £	VAT £	Trade receivables £	Cash sales £
30 Jun	Singer & Co		1,934		1,934	
30 Jun	Cash sale	756		126		630

(a) **What will be the entry in the sales ledger?**

Sales ledger

Account name	Amount £	Debit ✓	Credit ✓
▼			

Picklist:

Bank
Cash
Cash sales
Discounts allowed
Discounts received
Purchases
Purchases ledger control
Sales
Sales ledger control
Singer & Co
VAT

(b) **What will be the THREE entries in the general ledger?**

General ledger

Account name	Amount £	Debit ✓	Credit ✓
▼			
▼			
▼			

Picklist:

Bank
Cash
Cash sales
Discounts allowed
Discounts received
Purchases
Purchases ledger control
Sales
Sales ledger control
Singer & Co
VAT

Task 8 (12 marks)

The following two accounts are in the general ledger at the close of day on 30 June.

Complete the accounts below by:

- **Inserting the balance carried down together with date and details;**

- **Inserting the totals; and**

- **Inserting the balance brought down together with date and details.**

Motor expenses

Date 20XX	Details	Amount £	Date 20XX	Details	Amount £
01 Jun	Balance b/d	2,904			
15 Jun	Purchases ledger control	276			
30 Jun	Purchases ledger control	184			
▼		▼	▼		▼
	Total			Total	
▼		▼	▼		▼

Picklist:

1 Jul
30 Jun
Balance b/d
Balance c/d
Bank
Purchases ledger control
Sales ledger control

Discounts received

Date 20XX	Details	Amount £	Date 20XX	Details	Amount £
			01 Jun	Balance b/d	926
			15 Jun	Purchases ledger control	64
			30 Jun	Purchases ledger control	25
▼		▼	▼		▼
	Total			Total	
▼		▼	▼		▼

Picklist:

1 Jul
30 Jun
Balance b/d
Balance c/d
Bank
Purchases ledger control
Sales ledger control

Task 9 (12 marks)

Below are two general ledger accounts and a partially completed trial balance.

Complete the trial balance by:

- **Transferring the balances of the two general ledger accounts to the debit or credit column of the trial balance;**

- **Entering the amounts shown against each of the other account names into the debit or credit column of the trial balance; and**

- **Totalling both columns of the trial balance.**

Do not enter figures with decimal places in this task and do not enter a zero in unused column cells.

Salaries

Date 20XX	Details	Amount £	Date 20XX	Details	Amount £
30 Jun	Balance b/f	4,537			
30 Jun	Bank	2,901	30 Jun	Balance c/d	7,438
		7,438			7,438

Purchases ledger control account

Date 20XX	Details	Amount £	Date 20XX	Details	Amount £
			1 Jun	Balance b/f	29,389
30 Jun	Balance c/d	35,267	30 Jun	Purchases	5,878
		35,267			35,267

Account name	Amount £	Debit £	Credit £
Salaries			
Purchases ledger control			
Bank	9,267		
Capital	1,000		
Discounts allowed	1,004		
Discounts received	2,940		
Motor vehicles	15,000		
Administration expenses	5,903		
Purchases	89,262		
Sales	90,326		
Bank loan	11,892		
Inventory	16,006		
VAT (owing to HM Revenue & Customs)	2,455		
Totals			

Task 10 (12 marks)

Mandarin Ltd allocates a customer account code to each customer in the sales ledger, as shown below. The code is made up of the first two letters of the customer's name, followed by a number allocated to each customer in that alphabetical group.

Customer name	Customer account code
Dapple Ltd	DA01
Gadabout UK plc	GA01
Grundy Ltd	GR02
Indigo & Co	IN01
Ibber Ltd	IB02
New Aim Ltd	NE01
Roughtrap Ltd	RO01

The two new customer accounts shown below have been added to the sales ledger and need to be allocated a customer account code.

(a)   Insert the relevant account codes for each customer.

Doddle plc Account code: [   ]   Marrion Ltd   Account code: [   ]

Date 20XX	Details	Amount £	Date 20XX	Details	Amount £	Date 20XX	Details	Amount £	Date 20XX	Details	Amount £
3 Aug	Inv 83	532				3 Aug	Inv 91	876			

Mandarin Ltd codes all purchase invoices with a general ledger code. A selection of the codes used is given below.

Item	General Ledger Code
Men's shirts	GL001
Men's trousers	GL002
Women's tops	GL003
Women's trousers	GL004
Sundry clothing	GL005

This is an invoice received from a supplier.

New Aim Ltd 35 Didcot Road, Cinnadon CN7 3DD VAT Registration No. 356 2368 302
Mandarin Ltd Mandarin House 25 Jedward Street Cinnadon CN6 6LW 23 July 20XX 30 womens trousers (product code WT673) @ £16 each   £480.00 VAT @ 20% £96.00 Total   £576.00

(b)   **Select which code would be used to code this invoice.**

General ledger code	▼

Picklist:

GL001
GL002
GL003
GL004
GL005

(c) Show whether each transaction will be classified as capital expenditure, capital income, revenue expenditure or revenue income by placing the appropriate classification against each transaction in the table below. You can use each classification more than once.

Transaction	Classification
Receipt from sale of a motor vehicle	
Purchase on credit of clothing for resale	
Sale of clothing with one month to pay	
Purchase of shop fittings	
Sale in the factory shop with payment by debit card	
Payment to supplier with one month credit taken	

Classification:

Capital expenditure

Capital income

Revenue expenditure

Revenue income

The business has the following assets and liabilities.

Assets and liabilities	£
Property	35,000
Cash at bank (overdraft)	2,005
Motor Vehicles	15,435
Inventories	3,780
VAT owed to HMRC	22,446
Amounts owing from credit customers	11,223

(d) Show the accounting equation by inserting the appropriate figures.

Assets £	Liabilities £	Capital £

(e) **For each of the items below, identify an example from the picklist provided.**

Item	Example
Asset	▼
Liability	▼
Capital transaction	▼

Picklist:

Contribution from owners
Petty cash
Trade payables

BPP PRACTICE ASSESSMENT 4
BOOKKEEPING TRANSACTIONS

ANSWERS

Bookkeeping Transactions (BTRN)
BPP practice assessment 4

Task 1

(a)

Mandarin Ltd	
Mandarin House, 25 Jedward Street	
Cinnadon	
CN6 6LW	

VAT Registration No. 928 2781 110

CREDIT NOTE

Jessop Brothers	Customer account code: SL930
Unit 10 Eastern Trading Estate	
Cinnadon	
CN1 1PP	

Credit note number no: CN01256	Date: 22 July 20XX
Delivery note number: 452634	
Order number: 876238	

Quantity of goods	Product code	Total list price £	Net amount after discount £	VAT £	Gross £
20	WT555	120.00	108.00	21.60	129.60

Workings

List price 20 × £30/5 = £120, net after trade discount = £120 × 90% = £108, VAT = £108 × 20% = £21.60

(b)

Sales returns daybook

Date 20XX	Details	Credit note number	Total £	VAT £	Net £
22 Jul	Jessop Brothers	CN01256	129.60	21.60	108.00

(c)

Transactions				
Balance b/f	Invoice 0024	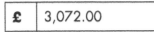 Invoice 0095	Invoice 0102	Invoice 0110
Bank	Credit note C 	Credit note 009	Credit note 017	

(d)

£	3,072.00

Working

Gross amount before discount: £2,560.00 + (£2,560.00 × 20%) = £3,072.00

After discount: £3,072.00 × 95% = £2,918.40

(e)

£	2,918.40

Working

Gross amount before discount: £2,560.00 + (£2,560.00 × 20%) = £3,072.00

After discount: £3,072.00 × 95% = £2,918.40

Task 2

(a)

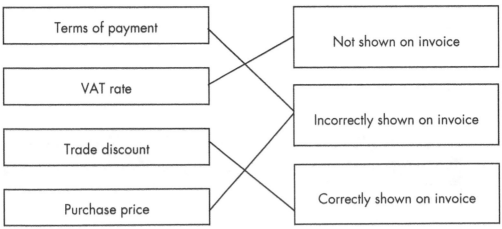

(b)

	Amount £
What would be the VAT amount charged if the invoice was correct?	51.84
What would be the total amount charged if the invoice was correct?	311.04

Workings

Purchase price: 40 × £36/5 = £288
Price after discount: £288 × 90% = £259.20
VAT: £259.20 × 20% = £51.84
Total: £259.20 + £51.84 = £311.04

(c) **Purchases day book**

Date 20XX	Details	Invoice number	Total £	VAT £	Net £	Women's clothing £	Men's clothing £
30 Jun	Forfar Textiles plc	C9230	1,872	312	1,560		1,560
30 Jun	Jessamy Fashion Inc	0024567	3,216	536	2,680	2,680	
30 Jun	Lindstrom Ltd	726	3,888	648	3,240	3,240	
	Totals		8,976	1,496	7,480	5,920	1,560

Task 3

(a)
Payment for £3,205

(b)
Credit note C98

(c)
2,585

Workings

£5,790 – £3,205 = £2,585

(d)

Supplier	£	Date by which payment should be received by supplier
Bumble plc	4,455	13 July 20XX
Hallidays Ltd	2,850	9 July 20XX

Workings

Bumble plc: £4,500 × 99% = £4,455
Hallidays Ltd: £3,000 × 95% = £2,850

Task 4

(a) Cash book – debit side

Details	Cash £	Bank £	VAT £	Trade receivables £	Cash sales £
Balance b/f	1,869				
Vampeter Ltd		1,256		1,256	
Propos Co	900		150		750
Total	2,769	1,256	150	1,256	750

(b) Cash book – credit side

Details	Cash £	Bank £	VAT £	Trade payables £	Cash purchases £	Office expenses £
Balance b/f		1,249				
Diston Ltd		4,295		4,295		
Opra Office Supplies		336	56			280
Total		5,880	56	4,295		280

(c)

£	2,769

(d)

£	– 4,624

Workings

£1,256 – £5,880 = – £4,624

(e)

	✓
Debit	
Credit	✓

Task 5

(a) Petty cash book

Details	Amount £	Details	Amount £	VAT £	Entertainment £	Travel £
Balance b/f	100.00	Harry's Café	26.30		26.30	
		Tune Travel	38.88	6.48		32.40
		Robby's Taxis	18.24	3.04		15.20
		Balance c/d	16.58			
Total	100.00	Totals	100.00	9.52	26.30	47.60

(b) General ledger

Account name	Amount £	Debit ✓	Credit ✓
Motor expenses	42.80	✓	
Sundry expenses	22.78	✓	
Postage	17.26	✓	
VAT	9.92	✓	
Petty cash control	92.76		✓

Task 6

(a) Rupert Reynolds

Details	Amount £	Details	Amount £
		Credit note D34	33

(b) Discounts received

Details	Amount £	Details	Amount £
		Purchases ledger control	635

VAT

Details	Amount £	Details	Amount £
		Purchases ledger control	127

Purchases ledger control

Details	Amount £	Details	Amount £
Discounts received	635		
VAT	127		

Task 7

(a) Sales ledger

Account name	Amount £	Debit ✓	Credit ✓
Singer & Co	1,934		✓

(b) General ledger

Account name	Amount £	Debit ✓	Credit ✓
Sales ledger control	1,934		✓
Cash sales	630		✓
VAT	126		✓

Task 8

Motor expenses

Date 20XX	Details	Amount £	Date 20XX	Details	Amount £
01 Jun	Balance b/d	2,904			
15 Jun	Purchases ledger control	276			
30 Jun	Purchases ledger control	184			
			30 Jun	Balance c/d	3,364
	Total	3,364		Total	3,364
1 Jul	Balance b/d	3,364			

Discounts received

Date 20XX	Details	Amount £	Date 20XX	Details	Amount £
			01 Jun	Balance b/d	926
			15 Jun	Purchases ledger control	64
			30 Jun	Purchases ledger control	25
30 Jun	Balance c/d	1,015			
	Total	1,015		Total	1,015
			1 Jul	Balance b/d	1,015

Task 9

Account name	Amount £	Debit £	Credit £
Salaries		7,438	
Purchases ledger control			35,267
Bank	9,267	9,267	
Capital	1,000		1,000
Discounts allowed	1,004	1,004	
Discounts received	2,940		2,940
Motor vehicles	15,000	15,000	
Administration expenses	5,903	5,903	
Purchases	89,262	89,262	
Sales	90,326		90,326
Bank loan	11,892		11,892
Inventory	16,006	16,006	
VAT (owing to HM Revenue & Customs)	2,455		2,455
Totals		143,880	143,880

Task 10

(a) **Doddle plc Account code:** DO02

Marrion Ltd Account code: MA01

(b)

General ledger code	GL004

(c)

Transaction	Classification
Receipt from sale of a motor vehicle	Capital income
Purchase on credit of clothing for resale	Revenue expenditure
Sale of clothing with one month to pay	Revenue income
Purchase of shop fittings	Capital expenditure
Sale in the factory shop with payment by debit card	Revenue income
Payment to supplier with one month credit taken	Revenue expenditure

(d)

Assets £	Liabilities £	Capital £
65,438	24,451	40,987

Working

Assets = £35,000 + £15,435 + £3,780 + £11,223 = £65,438

Liabilities = £2,005 + £22,446 = £24,451

Capital = Assets − Liabilities = £65,438 − £24,451 = £40,987

(e)

Item	Example
Asset	Petty cash
Liability	Trade payables
Capital transaction	Contribution from owners